# THE REPUBLIC OF PLATO

*Translated, with an Introduction, by*
A. D. LINDSAY

*A Dutton* **dep** *Paperback*

NEW YORK
E. P. DUTTON

*This paperback edition of The Republic of Plato
Published 1957 by E. P. Dutton & Co., Inc.
All rights reserved. Printed in the U.S.A.*

SBN 0-525-47004-2

# THE REPUBLIC OF PLATO

Great works: assign only
1-62; 70-92, 139-167,
256-265,
243-252, 393-406
(10/83).

=m { 1-59,
67-80,
counted 119-143,
211-220,
227-235,
346-359.

PLATO was born in 427 B.C., the son of noble parents. In 407 B.C. he became the friend and pupil of Socrates. In 388 B.C. he lived for a time at the court of Dionysius the Elder, tyrant of Syracuse in Sicily. On his return to Athens, Plato founded his Academy in 386 B.C. He died in 347 B.C.

# CONTENTS

# INTRODUCTION

WHAT is the subject of the *Republic*? That seems a simple question, but it is hard to answer. The dialogue opens by Socrates telling us how he went down to the Peiraeus to see a festival, and how Polemarchus and some friends met him and induced him to stay with them for the evening to see the torch race and the night festival. He goes home with them, and finds a circle of his friends there, with one or two sophists, and begins to talk to Polemarchus' father, Cephalus, and to question him about old age. Cephalus tells his experience simply, saying that he has found that happiness depends mainly on men's dispositions, not on their riches, and that the consciousness of approaching death makes a man thoughtful about his life and careful to pay all his debts to God and man. Then Socrates, partly as though he wished to understand Cephalus' secret, partly as though the words had raised again a question over which he had long puzzled, asks: "But as to this justice, can we quite, without qualification, define it as truthfulness and repayment of anything that we have received? or are these very actions sometimes just and sometimes unjust?" The discussion does not interest Cephalus. He goes off to pay one of his debts of sacrifice to God, and leaves the young men to frame a satisfactory definition of his conduct. So the subject of the conversation becomes, What is justice? But as various answers are being discussed, the sophist Thrasymachus sweeps aside the attempt to define justice by declaring that injustice is a far wiser and stronger and better thing. Then from the attempt to define justice Socrates turns to meet the assertion that the unjust life is the better life. "I attach much greater importance," he says (347), "to Thrasymachus' present position that the life of the unjust man is superior to that of the just man."

Though Thrasymachus is easily silenced, his defeat is not the end of the discussion. Socrates reviewing the argument at the end of Book I says that until we know what justice and injustice are, we cannot really tell whether the just or the unjust is the better. The two subjects are therefore united. The conversation is now directed towards the aim of so defining justice and injustice, and describing their necessary results on society and the soul of man, that an answer may be given to the question between the just and the unjust life based on such universal and ultimate facts of human experience that it must win the agreement of every man who will consent to use his reason. With this the rest of the dialogue is concerned, and at the end of Book IX the results are gathered together. The superiority of the just life is established by three proofs—one based on what we have learnt about justice and injustice from their effects on society, the second on what we now know of the constitution of the human soul, and the third on the account of the nature of reality and truth which has been discussed in Books VI and VII. Finally, in Book X the Myth of Er reaffirms this superiority from the standpoint of eternity.

This is perhaps a fair statement of what may be called the formal subject of the *Republic,* but it is not the answer we should give if we were asked what the *Republic* is about. For justice is discovered and defined at the end of the fourth book, and then follow three books in which it is hardly mentioned. The means which Socrates uses to bring the conversation to the desired conclusion become at times all-important, and are discussed for their own sakes: the very name *Republic,* which in its Greek form goes back to Aristotle, proves this. That name implies that the description of how justice does or would embody itself in social life, which Socrates at one time (472) expressly declares to be only a way of proving the superiority of the just life, has become the real subject of the dialogue. Most people would probably describe the *Republic* as Plato's account of the ideal state.

But if we are not content with the formal subject we shall hardly be satisfied with the clue furnished by the traditional title. Can it stand against the rival claims that the *Republic* is an exposition of Plato's metaphysical teaching, or even that it is a treatise on education or psychology? In Books II—IV the ideal state, the proper education of the young, and the psychology of the moral self seem all equally prominent subjects. In Books V—VII the outline of the state becomes shadowy and vague, and the dialogue busies itself with the small class of true philosophers, describes how they will live together, how they will be introduced to philosophy by means of the sciences, and what it will be their aim as philosophers to understand. Books VIII and IX are political and psychological, obviously connected with the question between the just and the unjust life. Then we again leave politics, and are warned of the evil effects which poetry may have on philosophers, and are told of the life after death in that curious last book which begins with an attack on poetry and ends with a poem.

Each of these subjects comes on in turn, and for a little while assumes the chief place. Socrates himself compares them to players going on and off the stage (451). How are we to choose between them and select one as the real subject of the dialogue?

But there is a further strangeness about this conversation. As Socrates sits in the court with Polemarchus and his friends and goes on with his wonderful talk, forgetting all temporal affairs, the torch race on horseback and the all-night festival apparently included, a change comes over him.

The Socrates who questions Cephalus and argues with Polemarchus and Thrasymachus is the Socrates represented in the early dialogues of Plato, very like, probably, to the historical Socrates. In Books II—IV he carries on the argument in quite a different way, and is much more constructive and systematic than he is ever represented in the really dramatic dialogues. In Books V—VII he changes still more, and teaches elaborate doctrines which it is unlikely that the real Socrates ever held.

At first he is the eager questioner, the examiner and tester of other persons' knowledge, professing no knowledge himself. Thrasymachus at the beginning of their argument refers to "Socrates' usual game of refusing to answer himself, listening to another's answer and then refuting it," and Socrates replies in true Socratic style, "My good sir, how can a man answer when, in the first place, he is ignorant and confesses his ignorance, and when, secondly, even if he has any opinion on the subject, he has been forbidden to say what he thinks by a man of no mean authority? It is much better that you should speak, for you say that you know" (337). This is indeed "our ironical Socrates whom we all know so well" as he has been described by Plato in the purely dramatic dialogues. If we examine this first conversation we find that the arguments in it are all arguments which we have good reason to believe Socrates actually used; that therefore this first book represents not only the way in which Socrates talked, but the things he said. If we know the earlier dialogues, we are not surprised when his conversation with Thrasymachus ends with a confession of ignorance. All that has been discovered is that the opinions so confidently held by the others are wrong. Socrates has silenced them, charmed them like a snake, as Glaucon says, but they are not satisfied, because they have been convinced of nothing but their own inability to furnish an answer which will stand the test of his dialectic.

But this, as Socrates says in the beginning of Book II, was only a prelude. The conversation is renewed at the request of Glaucon and Adeimantus, and the search after justice begun in a different way. Here we mark the first change. The arguments are still those which the historical Socrates might possibly have used. They seem to be the results of a searching examination of Greek life. Their aim is to preserve those elements in it which were good, or, as Socrates prefers to say, natural, to reject all that is unnecessary or merely conventional, and to build together the accepted elements into a society in which each man will be made to do that for which he is best fitted, and which is therefore his natural work. We know that the historical Socrates preached insistently that knowledge ought to be applied to conduct in the same way as it was already applied with such success to carpentry, or shoe-making, or medicine; that the first thing needful was to find out what you want to do or the end of your action, and the second to select those means which have been observed to lead to that end. The conversation which results in the discovery of justice in Book IV might be described as beginning with an analysis of what men want in their relations with one another, the natural ends of society. It goes on to select from the contemporary Greek life the means best calculated to further these ends. There is nothing here that is not at least an obvious working out of what Socrates taught. At the same time these books are never described as Socratic. For in them Socrates is no longer examining the opinions of others. He is leading the conversation to an end already apprehended by himself. He is no longer an inquirer but a teacher. His companions cease to argue as Thrasymachus had argued. Glaucon and Adeimantus still take some real share in the conversation, but after their first long statements they play the part, not of rival disputants, but of slow-witted pupils for whom the master sometimes goes too fast.

In the next three books the change is complete. The form of conversation is still kept up, but there is no longer much reality in it. Glaucon and Adeimantus say little but "Yes" or "No" or "I don't understand, Socrates"; there is less pretence that the conversation is "following wherever the wind of the argument may take it." These books are an exposition of systematic authoritative teaching. The dialogue form is not of their essence. It is used only to emphasize and draw attention to special difficulties in the subject-matter. It is significant that in one passage where we have opposing views compared (in the account of the Form of the Good), the rejected views are only referred to and described by Socrates. In a real dialogue they would not have been described but represented by persons taking part in the dialogue; as they are, for instance, in the *Philebus.* We have now left the house of Polemarchus in the Peiraeus, and are at the Academy listening to Plato lecturing. Further, these books deal with subjects in which we know that Socrates had no interest. The seventh book, for example, is largely taken up with an account of the education of the guardians in science, and the historical Socrates seems to have turned away from such scientific inquiry. The political outlook too has changed. Books II—IV have some of the hopefulness which is apparent in Socrates' political views as described in Xenophon's *Memorabilia.* These later books still maintain the possibility of the ideal state, but they discourage the philosopher from taking part in practical politics. He is sadly advised to "hold his peace and do his work, like a man in a storm sheltering behind a wall from the driving storm of dust and hail." This is assuredly Plato speaking of the experience of the one true philosopher he had known. The realization of the ideal state depends upon the people's recognition of the philosophers right to rule, and Athens had put Socrates to death.

Books VIII and IX return to what may be called Socratic subjects, but they are the application of Plato's teaching to the question which Socrates had not been able to answer. And when the dialogue ends the companions who had become pupils have ceased to interrupt, for Socrates has passed from Plato the teacher into Plato the poet.

This development in form needs explanation. The *Republic* represents neither of the two ways in which we might expect dialogue to be written. A dialogue may be mainly dramatic. Plato might have aimed merely to showing what Socrates was like, what he thought and how he talked. He has done that in dialogues like the *Laches* or the *Protagoras,* which throughout are like Book I of the *Republic.* Or he might have wished to express certain views of his own in contrast with other views, and put them into the mouth of Socrates and his companions. That would give a dialogue something like those of Berkeley or Hume. Plato has done that in the *Philebus,* for example. In the *Republic* he does neither one nor the other. When it begins it is dramatic, a representation of the historical Socrates. It becomes a dialogue which conveys Plato's teaching.

These difficulties of subject and form have led certain critics to assert that the *Republic* was written by Plato at different times, and was never properly put together. But this is to ignore the real unity of the dialogue. It expresses different levels of philosophic thought and uses the dramatic form in different ways. Yet all the parts fit wonderfully together and need each other. The more the *Republic* is read the more apparent does that become. Book I shows that Socrates' question cannot be answered by Socratic methods. Books II—IV bring us nearer an answer. They show us that justice can only be understood in society, but they also are incomplete and in themselves unintelligible. Society cannot be understood properly unless we know the principles on which it is constructed, and for that we must have the knowledge of the Form of the Good and philosophy as expounded in Books V—VII. The questions propounded in Book I are answered in Book IX with the help of the politics and psychology of Books II—IV and the metaphysics of Books V—VII, and they could not have been answered in any other way.

Book X perhaps seems to have the least real connection with the rest of the work. But we were warned by Cephalus in the beginning of Book I that questions of conduct and behaviour in this world are closely connected with imaginings of the life after death. Plato is dealing with the deepest and most important question of life. He has determined that the intrinsic superiority of justice to injustice shall be proved by logical argument and rational inquiry, not by appeals to sentiment or hope. By the end of Book IX that has been done. Plato begins the last book by explaining and emphasizing the importance of this procedure. Poetry cannot do the work of philosophy or science. It may seem to offer us an easy road to knowledge which will save us the trouble of thinking; that fatal delusion must be dispelled. But when the warning has been given against the wrong use of poetry, and the desired conclusion has been reached by consistent hard thinking, then Plato can leave that behind him, knowing that there are no difficulties and no adverse arguments which he has not honestly faced and beaten on their own ground, and can go on to describe in the language of poetic imagination the feelings and attitude towards life and death which the long logical inquiry has shown to be warranted. Where knowledge, or at least our knowledge, must stop, there poetry has its place; and if founded on the results of knowledge and rational inquiry it can help us to look at life "both here and in the journey of a thousand years."

Further, the question as to the nature of justice was one which it was natural for Socrates to ask, and impossible for him to answer. All that Socrates could do was to show that the answers ordinarily given were inadequate. In Book I we have a dramatic representation of his doing this. Socrates had also left some hints as to how questions of that kind ought to be answered. These are worked out in Books II—IV, which are less dramatic than Book I, because, as has been noted above, we have in these books Plato's development of Socratic teaching. But this method in turn proves inadequate. Recourse is now had to Plato's metaphysics, and Socrates becomes merely the mouthpiece of his teaching. The dialogue has this curious form because that form is demanded by Plato's attempt to answer a question which Socrates had suggested, and which only Plato helped by Socrates could answer. It is difficult to say precisely what is the subject of the *Republic,* because in Plato's belief it is impossible to answer satisfactorily the question between the just and the unjust life without at the same time answering other questions of almost equal interest.

And so Plato has given the *Republic* this curious form, because he believed that Socrates in his person and his life offered the real answer to the questions he propounded, and which his teaching never solved. For we shall give a fairly comprehensive description of what the *Republic* is about if we say that it is an attempt to show the superiority of justice to injustice by a description of the philosophic life. That description of course includes an account of how the philosopher would affect society if he had the power as he has the knowledge, what society ought to be if it is to be worthy of him, and what it will become, or indeed has become, as a result of rejecting his advice. But the manifestation of what the philosopher really is, is the vital part of the work. In Books V—VII Plato has almost forgotten the ordinary problems of society, while in Book IX the only real proof of the superiority of the philosopher is based on the knowledge of the philosophic life. Now for Plato the true philosopher is Socrates. He is pre-eminently the godlike and divine man whom the legislator is to copy when he is constructing the ideal state (501).

Thus in a sense the whole dialogue is a representation of Socrates, of how he talked, of his teaching, but above all of the value and meaning of his life. The real Socrates could not define justice, but he manifested it in his conduct, and, unlike Cephalus in the dialogue, he felt that a definition was necessary. This Plato is prepared to give, thanks to the development of the Socratic method into his own metaphysics.

If, then, the difficulties in the form and subject of the *Republic* are to be explained by the relation in which Plato conceived himself to stand to Socrates, it may be well to give a brief account of that relation and of some of the tendencies of thought, as Plato conceived them, existing in the society by which Socrates was surrounded, and which explain the significance of his work.

The *Republic* has been called an indictment of Greek civilization. It is certainly written with a full consciousness of the failure of Athens and of the deterioration of the Greek city state which had happened in Plato's lifetime. Plato was born in 427, in the fifth year of the Peloponnesian war. It was the year of the massacres at Corcyra, which led Thucydides to reflect on the fearful change in men's conduct and passions which the war brought about. "In peace and prosperity," he says, "cities and individuals follow higher counsels. They have not fallen into straits which make them act against their will. But war, which takes away the margin of daily life, is a hard master, and makes men's passions alike in the face of their circumstances.[1]When civil strife began in the cities, the knowledge of what had been done already made the strife that came later worse and worse. Men tried to outdo all inventions in the ingenuity of their enterprises and the extraordinary character of their revenges." Greek morality broke down under the strain of the long, bitter war. The noble aspirations of the age of Pericles came to be regarded as merely fine sentiments, and gave place to the hard, clever cynicism which Thucydides reproduces in the Melian dialogue or in the speech of the Athenian envoy at Camarina. Every city was rent asunder by the merciless strife between oligarch and democrat. Athens fell in 404. The victorious Sparta showed herself as cruel and rapacious as ever Athens had been, without any of the brilliance and genius which redeemed the Athenian empire. In the fourth century the history of Greece is a record of petty struggles, constant intrigue, and universal faction.

Plato grew up in Athens during the Peloponnesian war, and saw this process of degeneration going on around him. He belonged by birth to a class of rich aristocrats who hated the democracy and scorned the assumptions on which it was based. Critias, his cousin, a poet like himself, was one of the Thirty tyrants. But in Athens Plato met Socrates, and became his disciple. That did not make him a democrat; intercourse with Socrates had not that effect. But it enabled him to accept the new learning and the new spirit of criticism and inquiry, and yet believe in goodness and moral obligation and patriotism. In the *Gorgias* Plato makes Socrates assert that he is the only statesman of the time. He was for Plato the only man who could save Athens or, indeed, Greek civilization. He alone attacked the cynicism and moral scepticism of the day, not by appealing to convictions and beliefs that were now

[1] Mr. Gilbert Murray's translation. Cf. his introduction to his translation of Euripides' *Bacchae*.

worn out, but by using the weapons of free criticism and inquiry to support and not to destroy morality. It was because of this that he was so misunderstood—attacked by Aristophanes as a scientific enthusiast and a religious sceptic, and finally put to death by the restored democracy in 399 on a charge of corrupting the youth and blaspheming the gods. Athens had been unable to distinguish between Socrates and Thrasymachus.

In the characters of Book I Plato has represented this conflict of the old and new and the part played in it by Socrates. Curiously enough, none of the other characters in this book were Athenians. Cephalus and Polemarchus were originally from Syracuse, and were settled in Athens as resident aliens, and Thrasymarchus came from Chalcedon. But they stand for Athenian types. We are first introduced to Cephalus, the good, simple old man. He asserts, indeed, that he enjoys philosophic conversation, but we feel sure that it must be such as tends to edification, and that he is much more concerned with being good than with talking about it. He has that simplicity which Thucydides describes as "so large an element in a noble nature," and which he says was laughed out of existence in the war. Cephalus shows us what men were like before the war had taken away the margin of everyday life, when it was easier to be good. He represents the old generation which had almost passed away.

His son Polemarchus has a harder time before him. Does his goodness rest on foundations which are proof against the evil force of public opinion at the end of the war? Polemarchus has had the ordinary education of a well-to-do young Athenian. He has been brought up on the poets, and is confident that he can answer any question by a quotation. His confidence is rudely shaken by Socrates. He soon learns that he had never understood what the quotation meant, and that his rough and ready morality, that a man should help his friends and harm his enemies, will not stand the test of criticism. What chance had he against the clever half-truths of Thrasymachus and his school? When Thrasymachus breaks in upon the conversation with his impatient and contemptuous remarks, Polemarchus leaves Socrates to answer, and we hear no more of him.

Cephalus will not defend the old morality, and Polemarchus cannot. We are now confronted with the new. Thrasymachus of Chalcedon was a sophist, and, like most sophists, a teacher of rhetoric, one of those professor journalists who were educating the younger generation. The place of the sophists in Greek philosophy need not be discussed here. An adequate account of them will be found in Gomperz's *Greek Thinkers,* vol. ii. Plato's attitude towards their teaching is invariably hostile, though he speaks of some individual sophists—Gorgias and Protagoras, for example—with great respect. It is enough for our present purpose to remember that they supplied the demand for a systematic and professional education. They taught mainly rhetoric and the elements of success in public life. Socrates in the *Meno* is represented as asking Anytus, an old-fashioned Athenian democrat, whether a boy should be sent to the sophists in order to learn virtue, and Anytus exclaims against the idea, saying that any Athenian gentleman taken at random would do the boy more good. The argument of the *Meno* makes it clear that these were the only alternative methods of education. If a man wanted his son seriously trained for public life, he had to send him to a sophist. Now the *Republic* is not only an account of the philosophic life; it is a treatise on education. For Plato believed that only a very few persons would ever have ability to lead the philosophic life. The others were to be brought up on a system of education devised and managed by the philosophers. The philosopher is described as the saviour of society, and his main work in saving society is to turn all the powerful educative forces of public opinion and environment to the aid of virtue. The *Republic* in this way is the last of a series of dialogues in which Plato has been asking how virtue can be taught and who there are to teach it. The anti-moral doctrines are put into the mouth of a sophist that we may realize that these are not only the opinions of an individual; they will be taught to the younger generation. The other side to this is seen in Book VI, 492, where Plato's complaint against the sophists is not that they are subversive of ordinary opinions, but that they are not revolutionary enough. The sophists tell people what they wish to hear. They give public and emphatic expression to opinions already in the air. Thrasymachus appears in this capacity. He says what a large number of people in Athens thought already. The same brutal and cynical sentiments are in the *Gorgias* put into the mouth of a well-to-do Athenian gentleman, Callicles; they are the sentiments of the hard, successful man who is clever enough to see through the conventions and hypocrisies which are common in any society in a stage of transition, and is not clever or good enough to see any further. The doctrine that might is right had long been applied to politics. It was the professed justification of the Athenian empire in its later stages. When the Melians in Thucydides (V, 150) claim that the gods will help them and defend them against the unwarranted aggression of Athens, the Athenian envoys reply that in their action they are doing nothing to which the gods are likely to object. "For we believe, as regards the gods, and as regards men we are perfectly certain, that it is a necessary and universal law of nature that the stronger rules. We did not make the law, and we were not the first to use it. But there it is." "We know, and you know," they had already said, "that men dispute about justice when their forces are equal, but the stronger do what they can, and the weaker give in" (c. 89). Whether the cold-blooded brutality of the Melian dialogue was actually spoken or not matters little. No one can read Thucydides without seeing that the gospel of the strong and the successful, which some people now unfairly attribute to Nietzsche, was very much in the air in Athens at the end of the fifth century B.C.

In the first of these two passages from the Melian dialogue there is a significant word—nature. Brutality and violence are described as laws of nature. Justice is a fine sentiment, very useful in a speech if your listeners are fools, but with no reality behind it. We find the same thing in Plato's dramatic representation of the doctrine. Thrasymachus indeed says nothing about it, but his counterpart, Callicles, in the *Gorgias* makes a great deal of the opposition between nature and law or convention, and enforces his argument with references to the wild beasts and international politics, quite in the manner of Hobbes or a modern writer who talks about the struggle for existence. Glaucon in the beginning of Book II develops the argument at length with an account of the social contract. It is a forcible doctrine, especially when many men are practising it. It enables the successful bad man to deprive the unsuccessful but virtuous man of his claim to moral superiority, and it has just enough truth in it to make it hard of refutation.

It was this doctrine or the attitude towards life expressed by it which in Plato's opinion was ruining Greece. Strong enough in its appeal to the lower elements of man's nature, it acquired an additional force by enlisting much of the new learning and enlightenment on its side. The distinction between law and nature of which the sophists made so much offered it a scientific basis. Unscrupulous politicians might thus with a fine show of philosophy maintain that the stars in their courses, not to mention the universal practice of animals and cities, were witnesses on their side. In such a case appeals to sentiment and to beliefs which were outworn could be of little use. Religion itself, as Adeimantus shows in the beginning of Book II, was impregnated with the same ideas. If science and learning were against morality, there was little hope for the issue. It was at such a crisis that Socrates came to the rescue. His weapons were a passionate conviction of the difference between good and evil and of the intrinsic worth and beauty of goodness, a conviction which he practised as well as preached, and a keen critical mind which exposed the pretensions of the new morality to be scientific. Socrates had a greater belief in logical argument and more skill in using it than any of his contemporaries. He was convinced that justice was a reality, and he could show the worthlessness of all previous attemps to explain it, especially of all attempts to explain it away in the name of science. His actual teaching was mainly negative. There is good ground for believing that he was influenced by the successes of the new school of medicine which had attacked the cosmological speculations of the Ionian philosophers. He had no belief in the scientific inquiry of the day, but he had a great belief in the application of what we should call the scientific method to all branches of men's actions. Every successful craftsman, he considered, showed the value and the worth of knowledge. Even the Athenian assembly took only expert advice in questions which concerned particular trades, but in matters of conduct and in questions regarding the origin and nature of the world there were no such recognized authorities. All the ingenious speculations of previous philosophers had brought them to no certain conclusions and added no value to life. Therefore Socrates turned away from speculations about the outside world, and devoted himself to an attempt to apply the scientific method to conduct as thoroughly as it was every day applied to technical processes of manufacture. He repudiated all attempts to know the world without as useless labour. Its changes are in the hands of the gods, and they have hidden knowledge of them from men. Conduct, on the other hand, is our affair. Moreover, our conduct is determined by what we think about it, by what we make the end of our actions. Its sources are, therefore, within ourselves, and we must be capable of knowing them. Moral questions, then, are both the only ones worth knowing and the only ones that can be known; and yet it is just of these matters that men are most ignorant. Socrates is always comparing the successful way in which men applied knowledge and scientific method to the arts and crafts with their disregard of it in conduct. No man could make a shoe if he did not first know what he wanted to make, i.e. did not know what a shoe was. How can he any more do justice if he does not know what justice is?

The negative side of this examination of the assumption on which we act and the ends we set before ourselves is seen in the argument with Thrasymachus. For Thrasymachus is merely contending that the absence of law or restraint is in itself good, and Socrates very easily shows that all successful action implies law, measure, and also cooperation. The new-fashioned morality has no more claim to be regarded as scientific or reasonable than the old. But merely negative arguments are not enough. The theories of Thrasymachus and his school can only be answered by an alternative definition of justice. Whether Socrates himself was taking quite the right way towards that is doubtful. It is probable that he never saw the inadequacy of his favourite analogy between the arts and conduct; but he helped towards a real solution of the question. The arguments with Thrasymachus are not only negative. They assume that successful and clever conduct involves a rule or principle which can be stated; that competitive action is weak and co-operative action is strong; and lastly, and most important, that everything in

the world has its specific function or purpose by which it
can best be understood and in the performance of which
lies happiness. These assumptions imply that if we are
to understand the true principles of man's conduct, we
must try to discover what man's specific function or purpose is, what he is meant by nature to do, and we must
look for this, not in his selfish and individualistic actions,
but in the actions in which he co-operates with other men.
It is on these lines that Plato develops Socrates' teaching
into his own philosophy. The doctrine that might is right
depended on a theory of nature. It is answered by an
alternative theory which argues that justice, not injustice,
is according to nature.

This point is explained by Plato in a passage in the
*Laws* (X, 889), where he connects the moral theories of
the sophists with their metaphysical views, and shows how
they are to be answered. "There are some persons," he
says, "who hold that fire and water and earth and air exist
by nature and by chance, that all things have been compounded out of a mixture of opposites according to
chance and necessity." This curious phrase means that
nature is the result of necessary law, but that that law
has no purpose working behind it, or, as we should say,
is not to be interpreted teleologically. No *mind* has co-
operated in producing the world. "These persons," he
says, "insist that politics and legislation are not natural
but artificial, and rest on assumptions which are not true,
and they say that what is just has nothing to do with
nature at all, because it is created by art and law, and gets
its validity from the convictions which creates it." This
doctrine obviously springs from the contrast between the
universal and unchanging laws of material nature, and
the changing diverse laws of cities and nations. What is
just and lawful in one place is unjust and unlawful in
another, and therefore men who assume that material
laws are primary and natural will insist that human law,

just because it is variable, is unnatural, and will try to find the natural law of man's actions in some simple material or physical principle which really inspires all his conduct—such as the principle that the strongest rules. The moral theory of Thrasymachus then assumes materialism, and can only be properly answered by a refutation of materialism. "The exponent of this doctrine thinks that fire and water and earth and air are first of all things, and calls these things nature, and says that soul is produced later out of them." This "well of nonsensical opinions" can only be done away with by a more satisfying metaphysic. "Almost all these persons seem to be ignorant of the nature and power of mind, that it comes into being before bodies, and rules all the changes and determinations of bodies, and therefore what they wrongly call natural, is really secondary," and they ought to apply the words "natural" and "nature" to mind and what mind does. Plato then goes on to a metaphysical argument for the priority of mind in the universe. The purport of this passage may be stated thus. Both Plato and his opponents wish to explain man and the material world as parts of a single system. His opponents began with the material world, which they regarded as determined by necessary and blind law. They tried to explain man's conduct in the same way, and argued that his actions were really determined by a necessary physical principle of this sort. Morality and political law could not be regarded in this way, and therefore they asserted that morality and political law were unnatural, and ought to be disregarded. Socrates protested against this denial of morality, and argued that man's conduct could only be understood by the conception of end or purpose—that from any other point of view it was unintelligible. But Socrates did not attempt to apply this to the material world. He only insisted that because it could not be so applied, the material world could

not be known. Plato argues that the materialistic theory
will not explain even the material world, but that that
can be known and understood if things are interpreted,
in the same way as human actions, by reference to what
they are meant to be. And such an interpretation is offered in Plato's theory of "forms" or "ideas." So that the
laws of conduct as expressed in morality are not an exception to the laws of material things. These laws can
be properly understood only in the light of the principles
expressed in conduct, or, as Plato says, in the light of the
good.

This is the explanation of the presence of Books V, VI,
and VII in the *Republic*. The doctrines brought forward
by Thrasymachus, Glaucon, and Adeimantus depend upon a mistaken view of nature—an attempt to apply an
inadequate conception of the material universe to man's
actions. They looked on laws and institutions as Perdita
in the *Winter's Tale* looked on "streak'd gillyvors, which
some call nature's bastards." She, like them, despises an
art "which shares with great creating nature." The teaching of Plato's metaphysics is to show that right conduct
is not only, in the words of Polixenes,

> An art
> Which does mend nature, change it rather, but
> The art itself is nature,

but rather that, as being more akin to the real laws of the
universe, it is more natural than what we call natural law.
Plato in Books II-IV gives an empirical answer to this
inadequate conception by an examination of society, and
shows, firstly, that the very existence of society implies
another conception of nature; and, secondly, that the
most efficient and enduring, and therefore the most natural society, will be that which is organized throughout
according to this conception.

In Book V Plato goes deeper. Book IV is only concerned with justice—the relations of men to one another; but for successful conduct, and for the proper understanding of conduct, we must know not only how the laws of different people's conduct are to be mutually adjusted, but how their conduct will agree with the laws of the universe. Therefore we must understand how to discover the principle which will explain man in his relation to the world. Only if we are in possession of that can we know how to construct society as it ought to be. The realization of this ideal society will be difficult, and may never come about in this present evil world. But in the meantime the life of the philosopher is a perpetual witness that it is no vain ideal (it is at least a pattern laid up in heaven), and that a life lived according to its laws gives a happiness the like of which no other life can possibly enjoy.

The attempt to discover the relation of man to the universe involves science, and the beginning of science for Plato is found in the theory of εἴδη. Science comes into being because of the contradictions and difficulties of ordinary sense experience.

The philosopher, as described in the end of Book V, is the man who will not rest content with these contradictions, but tries to discover the unity which makes that experience intelligible. The theory of ideas comes from a simple logical analysis of the ordinary judgments we make about experience, and in its simple form is irrefutable. In any judgment we call different things by the same name, and in saying that the judgment is true, we imply that we do this not just because we so please, but because there is something in the different individual things which justifies or, indeed, compels our judgment. As we say, with less exactness than Plato, we call leaves and grass green, because they have the same quality of greenness. What we call a quality or a relation, Plato calls an εἶδος or ἰδέα. The words come from a root meaning to see. The first is used of "group," "element," and even "bodily shape," and means that by which we visually or, in the developed use, intellectually grasp anything; ἰδέα is less common, and has more reference to vision. It is used in the more imaginative passages. Perhaps the best word for εἶδος is "form." It does not mean idea. Plato uses more often the expression αὐτὸ ὃ ἔστιν ἕκαστον, just what each is. αὐτὸ is a word which in this use of it defies translation. It means "actual," "mere," "very," or "real." Plato's expression for what we call beauty, or the abstract quality of beauty, is αὐτὸ τὸ καλόν, "the actual *beautiful.*" Now whenever we call things by the same name, they must be expressions of a common "form"; otherwise we have no right to call them by the same name. An animal, e.g., is a horse, because, and in so far as, it participates in a certain sameness with other animals which are also horses. Therefore these samenesses make things what they are, and therefore, according to Plato, they are more real than the individual things which manifest them. The difficulty is that horseness is not a thing which can be touched or even seen; it can only be thought. But that does not mean that it is unreal. We cannot make a single judgment about things we see, or touch, or taste without implying the reality of what we can only think and not perceive. The more we know the world, the more we use what we see or touch as a stepping-stone to what we can only think. For the philosopher or the scientist therefore the real world is the world of the "forms," which unite particulars, or, as we should say, of the laws which govern particular things.

It is very hard to say what is the relation between the "forms" and the individual things in which they find expression, just as it is hard to say what is the relation between laws which are valid and things which exist. But that is a question with which Plato is little concerned in the *Republic.* He is content to insist that we can only understand the world by means of the "forms," and that they are therefore the proper objects of knowledge. Another and almost more difficult question is discussed in Books VI and VII, viz. the relation of the forms to one another. The account of the Form of the Good is concerned with this. We understand the relation of different experiences to one another by means of the forms under which we think them. For perfect knowledge we ought to be able to understand the relation of the forms to one another by means of some single and ultimate form. This ideal of knowledge Plato calls the Form of the Good. We must remember that he says he cannot explain it to us. We could only understand it when we had perfect knowledge. What he is doing is to show us the kind of way in which we ought to be able to understand the world, the ideal which all knowing implies. Now in questions of action when we can explain conduct as accomplishing what we simply recognize as good, we need go no further. We ought to be able to do the same in science. Otherwise we should only have an endless succession of phenomena, coming we know not whence, leading we know not whither. We can never hope to get back to the beginning or on to the end; but it would be enough if we understood this changing world as the manifestation of a principle we regarded as good, not good *for* anything, least of all good for man, but as good in itself. If we could do that, then the laws of conduct and of things would be seen as manifestations of the same principle, and science and morality be completely united. This is the goal of philosophy, and the effort to reach this goal is the perfect life for man, a life which we cannot limit to this world, but which we must regard as continuing after death.

"But if you will listen to me and believe that the soul is immortal, and able to endure all evil and all good, we shall always hold to the upper road, and in every way follow justice and wisdom, and here and in the journey of a thousand years, which I have described to you, we shall fare well."

So Plato has made Socrates answer Thrasymachus. His dialectic destroys Thrasymachus' arguments. His conviction of the primary importance of morality is the basis for a rival theory of society. But in his life, devoted to a single-hearted search after truth, he had done even more to refute Thrasymachus, and therefore Plato devotes the most important part of the *Republic* to a description of the philosophic life, of the ideal of truth which it implies, the methods which it must use, and the services it would render to society if society would only understand how much it needed them. How much of the intellectual part of this had been worked out by Socrates it is hard to say; certainly, if we are to believe Aristotle, not all of it. But he had shown what the philosophic life might be, and Plato had developed his own philosophic theories by expanding the principles of the Socratic method. He has represented this development as taking place in the limits of a single conversation, first setting before us Socrates as he actually talked, and then, without any abrupt transition, using the conversational form to express his conception of the value and importance of Socrates' life.

This account may seem to do less than justice to the *Republic* as a storehouse of political theory. The purport of Plato's political teaching is that no laws or institutions are of any avail unless the people who administer them or live under them are imbued with the right spirit. If men will lead the life of philosophy or reverence it in others, states will reform themselves, and there is no other hope for them. At the same time much of what he says in the *Republic* is affected by his attitude towards the politics and reflects the history of his time, the beginning of the fourth century, after the conservative reactionary Sparta had conquered Athens, "the school of Hellas."

There is a passage in that great appreciation of the Athenian democracy, the funeral oration of Pericles (Thucydides, II, 39), on which much in the *Republic* is a pathetic commentary. Pericles there contrasts the liberty and joyousness of Athenian life with the hard discipline and rigour of Sparta, and claims that the Athenians are as brave and powerful and as likely to conquer as the Spartans, without paying for their pre-eminence the price of hard, soul-destroying discipline and a rigid, narrow constitution. "We love beauty, yet preserve economy; we love wisdom, without being effeminate." If Pericles had lived, that splendid confidence might have been justified. But after his death Athens had failed, and in the end had been beaten. The individualism and freedom of which Athenians were so proud had been preserved. They lacked discipline of mind. They failed to distinguish between practical politics and mad adventures. They would not recognize their own limitations, and so they were beaten by the Spartans, who were "brought up to be too stupid to despise their laws."

Plato's comments on Athenian democracy will be found in Book IV, 426, in the simile of the ship in Book VI, 488, and above all in the account of the democratic state and the democratic man in Book VIII, 557-62.

Sparta had the discipline and organization and respect for law which Athens lacked. But Sparta had failed as badly as Athens. The Spartan discipline was directed towards the wrong end—towards the holding down of a conquered people by sheer force—and when the Spartans had won they could not use their victory. The old Spartan discipline succumbed to prosperity, and their governors became mere robbers and tyrants. Plato admired Sparta because she had so much that Athens lacked, but he recognized her shortcomings. The lesson of this double failure is first pointed out in Book II, 375. The guardians of the city must be professional soldiers, and possess above all things courage, the conspicuous Spartan virtue. But they must also be gentle and lovers of learning, or they will only use their skill for purposes of tyranny and plunder. The purpose of the legislator therefore is to produce in the citizens of his state a character which has the good qualities of both Athenian and Spartan. That involves a thorough organization of all the forces of the state, so thorough that the rulers—the most important element in the state— must submit to state organization of their most private interests, their property, their marriage, and the upbringing of their children. For that is the meaning of Plato's communism. The state is to become a vast educational instrument, which shall use all the forces of society to produce the end it desires. That lesson Plato had learned from Sparta. But the end shall not be success in war, but the production of a character brave and yet gentle, steady and reliable and yet quick and intelligent, a state-organized imitation of Socrates.

Something must be said in conclusion of the language of the *Republic*. Like the matter, it bears the impress of the dialogue form. As Plato uses the form of a conversation for the purposes of metaphysical instruction, so he uses almost throughout the *Republic* the language of ordinary conversation instead of the technical terms to which we are accustomed in philosophic writing. The conversational form is as natural to English as it is to Greek. It is hard, if it is not impossible, to reproduce in English the conjunction of simple language and profound thought which is characteristic of Plato's prose. We cannot write philosophy in English without using technical terms, and no translation using such can give the effect of Plato's Greek. For example, the words εἶδος and ἰδέα referred to above are ordinarily treated by the word "idea," which has no other virtue except that it is a transliteration of one of the Greek words. Yet "idea" either means nothing as a translation of εἶδος or ἰδέα, or it means what is wrong. If we treat it as an ordinary English word, then, thanks to the abuse of the word by Locke and Hume, it suggests what is unreal and subjective, whereas Plato meant by it exactly the opposite. If we try to show that the words mean the Platonic idea by printing Idea, then we entirely neglect the fact that Plato all through the *Republic* uses the same words in connections where they have simple unphilosophic meanings, such as class, shape, or form, and so we use a dead and technical word where Plato uses a word that was alive and meant something. Similarly it is almost impossible to express at all the philosophical use which Plato makes of such pronouns as αὐτός, τοιοῦτος, or ἕκαστος.   For such reasons I have used the word "form" instead of "idea" in this translation, and have avoided as carefully as I could words like "correlative," "essence," "absolute," or "thing in itself." Such words have in most cases been so affected by later philosophical usage that they suggest wrong meanings in Plato, and in any case they give an appearance of technicality which is alien to the conversational form of the *Republic*.

An analysis of the argument will help to explain these general observations.

The dialogue begins with a picture of the aged Cepha- Book I lus, the old man who has led a just and pious life without troubling himself about what justice and piety mean. When Socrates asks him what justice is, or whether the few remarks he has let fall can serve as a satisfactory explanation of it, he begs to be excused from further talk and goes off to sacrifice, leaving the argument in the hands of Polemarchus. He thinks that he can answer the question by quoting a tag from Simonides to the effect that to render to every man what is owing is just. Socrates shows in the first place that such a definition is too vague to be of any use, and, secondly, that if we substitute for the words of Simonides what Polemarchus really meant, namely, that justice is to do good to one's friends and harm to one's enemies, this definition is partial and one-sided, and inconsistent with what we really mean by good and justice.

Here the sophist Thrasymachus comes upon the scene. He is the representative of the most modern school of thought. He has seen through the conventions of life, and considers the ordinary conventional notions of justice and goodness as the merest nonsense. He bids Socrates quit fooling and come to the facts. When pressed, he himself confidently offers the definition that justice is the advantage of the stronger. After a little examination he is discovered to mean that right and wrong are made by law, and that law is made by the few strong men who rule in a state and is for their advantage. A man does right because the law compels him, and the law has become what it is to suit the advantage of those who make it. The people obey because they are forced to. Socrates' first objection to this definition is that the ruler may make mistakes as to what is to his advantage, and that in that case the law commands the citizen to do what is according to Thrasymachus' theory unjust. Thrasymachus changes his ground and says that a ruler can't make mistakes, any more than a doctor as a doctor can make mistakes. If he does, that shows that he is not really a ruler. Thrasymachus, that is to say, bases his claim of obedience to the law not on force, but on the skill or knowledge of the ruler. Socrates then asks, Why should the ruler's skill, if directed towards his own advantage, be a motive for our obeying him? In all other cases where skill claims obedience, as, for example, in the case of a doctor, it is because the skill is exercised to the advantage of those who obey. We never appraise skill by the selfishness of the man who exercises it, but by the advantage it confers on those upon or among whom it is exercised. Thrasymachus' theory won't explain the fact of political obedience.

Here Thrasymachus gives up the argument and all serious attempts at defining justice. The people obey because they are weak, silly fools. Justice is not worth defining, because just people are either dupes or cowards. The ruler rules because he is unjust, and injustice is virtue and wisdom, strength and happiness. All men admit that this is the case with the successful villain, who is not hampered in his pursuit of happiness by being the dupe of moral conventions, and who is strong and clever enough to use other people for his own ends.

This raises a much more serious question, which becomes the main subject of the *Republic*. Does injustice, the freedom from all restraint and law, really lead to greater happiness than justice? In the rest of Book I Socrates shows that, according to our ordinary use of words, injustice, the freedom from all restraint, cannot possibly be wise or virtuous or strong, and therefore cannot lead to happiness. Thrasymachus is silenced, but Socrates is unsatisfied because he has not yet found a definition of justice. The arguments in this book rest upon our ordinary moral judgments of men and actions. Thrasymachus is refuted because his position is inconsistent with those judgments, and does not explain the facts of political obedience.

But in the beginning of Book II Glaucon and Adeimantus bring forward a theory which professes to explain the facts of political obedience and the general tenor of men's moral judgments in such a way as still to leave injustice intrinsically superior to justice. What all men would like is to do injustice and not to suffer it. But few men are strong enough to manage that, and therefore society and laws are founded in the interests of the great mass of the people, who can't get what they really want, and are determined at least to prevent other people from inflicting injustice on them. That is why they themselves obey the law and why they enforce it on other people, and they are so afraid of injustice that they pretend to each other, and carefully teach their children, that justice is really the thing most worth having. Our moral judgments represent, therefore, not the real values we set on things, but our fear of suffering injustice. Society makes laws and punishes because it is afraid. Every man would be unjust if he dared, or if he had the chance of being so with impunity. Socrates is therefore exhorted to rest his argument not on the awards given to justice by society, or on the conventional compliments which men pay to it, but on the actual and natural effects of justice and injustice in the soul of the individual.

Their argument rests on a distinction between what man is in himself and what he is in society. Socrates' answer asserts that this distinction is invalid and unreal. Justice exists in a state as well as in an individual, because a state is simply the lives of its citizens; and if we find that society is a natural expression of men's natures, we may conclude that social justice is the natural expression of the justice in men's souls. He therefore proposes to examine the origin of justice and injustice in society—first find what part they play in the state, and then by the help of analogy find what part they play in the soul of the individual. A city originates because by nature no man is self-sufficient. Men have common needs and different capacities to supply these needs. Therefore a society resting on the division of labour is the expression of men's nature, not the result of a convention. Dissatisfaction with simple bodily comforts and a demand for luxury necessitates an increase in the city's territory, and such an increase involves war. If we are to be faithful to the natural and economical principle of the division of labour, war will be entrusted to a soldier class. But how are we to procure professional soldiers who will not abuse their strength by opposing the other citizens? Here the account of the natural growth of any city passes insensibly into the construction of the ideal city. The soldiers or guardians must be brave and yet gentle. Such a result can only be produced by making them lovers of wisdom, and for that education is necessary.

Education should consist, as it has always done in Greece, of music and gymnastic. Music is considered first. The early education is of most importance, and that must be imparted at first by means of tales which are untrue. For the aim of early education is not to impart information, but to produce a certain type of character. But if the historical truth of stories told to children is unimportant, the moral effect which such stories are likely to produce is of the utmost consequence. Plato therefore proceeds to lay down canons to which poetry must conform, and by their help to critize Homer and the poets, who then formed the universal medium of Greek education. The stories which the children are to hear must convey such beliefs concerning gods and men as will produce III honest, brave, and steadfast characters. The general purpose of this education is summed up in a notable passage in Book III, 401—3. Not only the contents but also the form and style of poetry must conform to the same ethical purpose, because beauty and harmony and rhythm in nature correspond to and produce grace and harmony in the soul, and by constant association with beautiful objects the souls of the children will be unconsciously conformed to the beauty of reason, and they will be made ready to receive and understand reason when they come to a proper age.

Gymnastic is next discussed. It must be of the same simple character as music, producing a sound and healthy constitution, so that the citizens will need doctors as little as they ought to need lawyers. For Socrates asserts that a love of litigation and a desire for elaborated medical remedies are equally signs of a wrongly educated character. Gymnastic has already been described as attending to the body, but here it is pointed out that equally with music it is directed to the education of the soul. Education if exclusively musical tends to produce softness and effeminacy; if exclusively gymnastic, hardness and brutality. The two combined alone produce the desired harmony of the soul, and make it both brave and gentle. Such an education will produce guardians combining the qualities desired. The best of them are to be made rulers, the others will be their auxiliaries. The people are to be induced to obey them by being taught a myth. God has made the guardians of gold, the auxiliaries of silver, and themselves of copper, and they must loyally recognize the rule of the best element. The rulers and auxiliaries will have a camp within the city, have all their houses and property in common, and be supported by the other citizens. They will not be allowed to touch gold or silver.

**IV** Adeimantus here objects that this is treating the rulers very hardly. They will be in a position of power, and yet have none of the advantages enjoyed by other rulers. Socrates replies that he expects that the guardians will be found to be extremely happy, but in any case he is trying to secure the happiness not of one class, but of the whole state, and that can only be done by looking to the interests of the whole. This objection is an indication of the very great difference which must exist between the character of the ordinary ruler and of the ruler in the ideal state. Socrates goes on to explain how the guardians will have to guard against extreme wealth or extreme poverty. Adeimantus objects that if the city is not rich it will fall an easy prey to cities which are richer and therefore more powerful, but Socrates answers that this city is strong, first, because it is one as no other cities are, and, secondly, because it wants nothing. The ordinary details of legislation may be passed over. If the spirit inculcated by music is right, everything else will follow naturally; if it is not, no legislation will be of any use.

The city being founded, we have now to discover in it justice. There are four, and only four, important virtues which we may expect to find in the city—wisdom, courage, temperance, and justice. If we discover wherein the other three consist, we shall more easily find justice. The virtues of the state are the virtues of its citizens, in so far as these are exercised in the interests of the whole. Therefore the wisdom of the state resides in the guardians, who take thought for the whole community; the courage in the auxiliaries, who resist attack from without and sedition within. The real part played by courage is that it preserves the principles on which the state rests from all forces that would disturb them. Temperance resides in all three classes. It is the recognition on the part of the artisan and the soldier classes that the guardians deserve to rule, and the willingness on the part of the guardians to exercise their rule. There is still left unaccounted for the important principle on which the city was founded, the principle of the division of labour, that each man, and more especially each class, should do that work for which he or it is fitted, and no other. This, then, must be justice.

The discovery of justice in the state is then applied to the individual. The fact of struggle or dissension in the soul proves logically that there must be different parts or elements in it. These are distinguished as three —the reasoning, the spirited or assertive, and the desiring elements. The wisdom of the individual resides in his reason, courage in the spirited or assertive part, and temperance in the harmony of the three. So the justice of the soul will consist in each part doing that work for which it is fitted by nature, and no other. Social justice is simply the social expression of this condition of the soul. This account is found to be consistent with our ordinary notions of justice. Now that justice is discovered, it can easily be seen that it is the health of the soul, and injustice the disease, and it might readily be inferred that justice is better than injustice; but Socrates proposes that they should first of all examine injustice in four types of unjust cities. He is proceeding to do this when Adeimantus interrupts and says that he wants to hear more about the common property of the guardians. Socrates has only stated that like friends they will have things in common, but he wants to hear how this will work out in detail, especially how they can have wives and children in common. This is the beginning of the digression which lasts through Books V, VI, and VII, and of the transition to the most advanced thought of the *Republic*. The occasion for this transition is the recognition that this ideal and natural city will involve a far deeper and more thoroughgoing revolution in the ordinary ways of political life than was recognized at first sight. But it is also necessitated by the fact that almost nothing has been said about the wisdom of the guardians. The state of Books II-IV is pictured as receiving its principles of legislation from without, but if the state is to be really self-sufficient, its guardians must be capable of understanding for themselves the philosophical principles on which that legislation is based. For that metaphysics is necessary.

Socrates begins by declaring that women must share equally in the education and occupations of men, on the ground that there is no such fundamental difference between the sexes as would justify their present division of occupations. Only by such an arrangement can we use all the capabilities of the citizens for the good of the whole state. Next, he says that the guardians must have wives and children in common. No one is to know his father and mother. Marriage relations and the begetting and bringing up of children are far too important to be left to individuals and to chance. Therefore the marriages of the guardians must be regulated entirely by the state. The whole state will then be one family. There will be community of pleasure and pain throughout, and so we shall avoid the dissensions incident to private families and private property, and achieve the great aim of a state's existence, which is that it should have as much unity as possible. Socrates is explaining some further details regarding the behaviour of the citizens in war and their training, when Glaucon interrupts and says that he quite agrees with all that Socrates has said concerning the advantages of such a communistic scheme if it could be realized, but he insists on hearing what possibility there is of such realization. Socrates answers that this is much the most difficult point, and that it is not of vital importance that the scheme should be realizable. They only wanted to see how a perfectly just state would be organized in order that they might contrast it with the unjust and obtain an answer to their original question. But one way there is in which such a state could be realized, and one only; that is, by the philosophers becoming kings, or the kings or rulers of any city becoming philosophers. Glaucon objects that this is a preposterous statement, which will meet with a most unfavourable reception. Socrates answers that that is because the nature of a philosopher is not properly understood. A philosopher is a lover of learning or knowledge. But so are many strange people, it is objected. Yes, but the philosopher is distinguished by his love of truth. A man who seeks truth must recognize that where there are many things called by the same name, there must be some reason, some relation, some form, as Plato says, in virtue of which all those different things are the same. The particular things change and become different, but the forms are always the same. They alone are permanent, and are therefore the only objects of knowledge, and it is with them that truth is concerned. The philosopher is the man who recognizes this distinction, and he alone attains to knowledge of reality. Other people who recognize only particular things which they can see or touch have no knowledge, but only belief or opinion, and their belief has for its object what is half real and half unreal, the changing, unstable world of sense.

**VI**    The philosophers, then, are distinguished as the only men who know truth and reality, and they alone, therefore, will be capable of understanding the real principles underlying the legislation of the city. Obviously if their character corresponds to their knowledge, they must be made rulers. But a love of truth implies all other virtues. The true philosopher will be inevitably lofty-minded and gracious, a lover and a kinsman of truth, justice, courage, and temperance. Adeimantus objects that although the conclusion seems theoretically justified, actual philosophers are very different from this, and are usually either useless fools or rascals. Socrates admits the truth of this accusation, but says that this is the fault of society and of the thoroughly wrong conception of what a ruler ought to be, on which society is based. So long as men think that government is the art of obtaining office, and that it is the business of the ruler to follow the whims and ignorant opinions of the multitude, so long will society have no use for the philosopher. Rather it will want to use for its own wicked ends, and therefore to corrupt and turn from philosophy, all who have the rudiments of a philosophic nature. Noble qualities, rich endowments, even the ordinary virtues and a sound education, may thus become merely potent instruments of wickedness. The consequence is that there are only a very few genuine philosophers, men saved by some miracle of divine grace from the evil influences of their upbringing, and they realizing their powerlessness are content to lead their own life and leave the state alone. Because they are so few, the name of philosopher is usurped by those unworthy of it, and so philosophy is brought into disrepute. When the multitude recognize their mistake—and there is no reason why they should not—and philosophy is put in its proper place at the head of the state, then the ideal city will be realized. For the ideal city will be the only one worthy of the philosopher. This objection therefore, although founded on the facts of society as it now exists, has no force against the demand that philosophers should be kings. The philosopher is the only possible draughtsman of a constitution, for he alone knows the reality of justice and beauty and temperance which should find their expressions in the state. Socrates therefore returns to the consideration of this knowledge of reality and what it implies. The philosopher must have all ordinary intellectual accomplishments, but he must have a greater knowledge than this, the knowledge of that which gives value and meaning to everything else in the world. Just as there is no purpose in actions except in so far as they are good, so there is no value in knowing everything in the world unless that helps us to know the good. And as the philosopher has already gone beyond the appearances of things to their form or reality, so he must go beyond individual experiences of good to the Form of the Good. What, then, is this Form of the Good? Two previous answers, one that it is thought, and the other that it is pleasure, are examined and rejected. But when Socrates is pressed to give his own answer, he tells Glaucon that he can only describe it to him in an image. The Form of the Good bears the same relation to the intelligible world and to the mind as the sun does to the visible world and to the eye. The Form of the Good is the source of existence to all other objects of knowledge, and is that which enables the mind to know them and at the same time is itself the highest object of knowledge. Its nature is also typified in the simile of the divided line, where it is stated that mathematics stands to dialectic which comes to know the good as seeing images stands to seeing their objects. The progress of the mind towards this goal is described in the allegory of the Cave in the beginning of Book VII, where Plato represents knowledge as a kind of conversion of the soul from darkness to light. Most men live all their lives underground, seeing nothing but shadows, hearing nothing but echoes. The philosopher alone has made his way to the light of day above, and is therefore the only man who can compare the shadows over which men quarrel in law courts and assemblies with the realities. He must therefore be sent down into the cave to instruct the prisoners, and made to take part in politics and government instead of enjoying uninterrupted contemplation. The state will then have rulers who regard office as a duty forced upon them, not as a prize to quarrel about or an opportunity for plunder.

Now that Socrates has shown the necessity of this highest knowledge to the statesman, he turns to consider how it can be taught to young men possessing the proper natural gifts. The old combination of music and gymnastic is of no use now, for that only inculcated habit and disposition, not knowledge. Socrates therefore goes on to describe a further system of education, the object of which is gradually to draw the soul away from the variable, changing, and fleeting aspects of the world to the permanent and unchanging realities. But this is in other words a turning from sensation to thought. The required purpose, then, will be fulfilled by studies where thought is brought in to solve the puzzles and contradictions of the senses. Arithmetic is an obvious example of such. It will be followed by the other mathematical sciences—geometry, plane and solid, astronomy, regarded strictly as the science of solids in motion, and harmonics. Great care is to be taken to ensure that these sciences are studied in the right way. Their value consists in their power of training the mind to think and rise above the senses, not in any practical advantages which they may have for various professions. They are the prelude to the real philosophy which is called dialectic. But when Glaucon asks Socrates to explain this, its forms and its methods, Socrates answers that that is impossible. To fully understand dialectic is to have knowledge. All that can be said about it is, that it is the completion and the goal of the sciences which have been described. Unlike them it is wholly independent of the sensible world, and does not rest upon hypotheses. It moves entirely in the sphere of the intelligible. This, then, will be the completion of the guardians' education. Socrates adds certain details as to the selection of the guardians and the ages at which they must begin the various stages of their education, explains how they will begin their reforms, and so completes the account of how the ideal city is to be realized.

The ideal city having been fully described, Socrates **VIII** reverts to the point at which occurred the digression occupying Books V-VII, and proposes to give an account of unjust states. There are four prominent types of such, and as the character of a state is the result of the character of its inhabitants, there will be four corresponding types of individual men. They may be described as stages in the gradual degeneration of the just state and the just man. The just city will degenerate because decay is the lot of all mortal things, but the particular reasons of such decay cannot be explained; they can only be mythically expressed in a geometric number. The first stage of degeneracy is the timocratic state, of which Sparta is a conspicuous example, the

second is oligarchy, the third democracy, and the fourth
tyranny. Corresponding to these are the timocratic, the
oligarchical, the democratic, and the tyrannical man.
These are described in order, first city and then corresponding individual, with an account of the psychological and ethical causes which give rise to them. The
result of the whole description is, that the tyrannical man
ruling as a tyrant is seen to be the extreme of wickedness. Now this is the man whom Thrasymachus in the
first book declared to be the happiest of men, because
he is the most perfectly unjust, so that if he is compared
to the just man or the philosopher, a final and satisfactory answer may be obtained to the question whether
the just or the unjust life is the happier. Three proofs
are offered of the superior happiness of the philosopher.
The first is political. It has been shown that states are
really the counterparts of individuals, so that we may
argue that the misery which has been seen to be rife
in a tyranny has its counterpart in the misery of a tyrant's soul. The other proofs are concerned with the
nature of pleasure. The three men, philosopher, timo-
crat, and oligarch, are men who give pre-eminence in
their lives to different kinds of pleasure, the pleasures
of knowledge, of ambition, and the bodily pleasures
which can be got by money. Each if questioned will declare that his own life is the most pleasant. But the
philosopher must be declared to be right. Firstly, because he possesses reason, the instrument of comparison,
and has alone experienced all three kinds of pleasure.
Secondly, because a metaphysical examination of the
nature of pleasure and happiness shows that the pleasures of the philosopher are alone real and alone give
satisfaction. The demands made by Glaucon and Adeimantus in the beginning of Book II have now been
satisfied, and the just life is proved to be the happiest,
whatever may be the external consequences of justice

IX

or injustice. The philosopher will find perfect happiness if he can realize his just city; but even if that be impossible, he will rule his life as though he were a citizen of that city whose pattern is laid up in heaven.

The last book is taken up with a criticism of art and an account of the life after death. Art is reviewed in the light of the metaphysical doctrines expounded in Books V-VII, and it is shown that it deals with the most fleeting, unstable, and therefore most unreal aspects of the world. Its effect on the soul is precisely opposite to that of the education which is to be given to the guardians. It encourages the rule of the senses and the passions, and makes the soul incapable of ascending from the unreal and the unchanging to the permanent and the true. There is an ancient quarrel between art and philosophy, and until art can show that these charges are unjust, philosophy must exclude her from the ideal city.

Lastly, the account of the happiness of the just man is completed by a consideration of the life after death. Socrates first offers a proof of the immortality of the soul, and then describes a vision of the life after death in the story of Er, the son of Armenius, by which we are assured that the just life is not only the happiest in this world, but in the fortunes of the soul after death finds its continuation and its more complete vindication.

# THE REPUBLIC OF PLATO

# BOOK I

I WENT down to the Peiraeus yesterday with Glaucon, the son of Ariston. As this was the first celebration of the festival, I wished to make my prayers to the goddess and see the ceremony. I liked the procession of the residents, but I thought that the Thracians ordered theirs quite as successfully. We had offered our prayers and finished our sight-seeing, and were leaving for the city, when from some way off, Polemarchus, the son of Cephalus, saw that we were starting homewards, and sent his slave to run after us and bid us wait. The lad caught my cloak from behind and said:

"Polemarchus bids you wait."

I turned round and asked him where his master was.

"He is coming behind," he said; "but will you please wait?"

"Surely we will," said Glaucon.

Very soon up came Polemarchus, and with him Adeimantus, Glaucon's brother, and Niceratus the son of Nicias, and some others, evidently from the procession.

"Socrates," said Polemarchus, "you seem to be leaving, and to be on your way to the city."

"You are not far wrong," I said.

"Well," he said, " do you see our numbers?"

"Surely."

"Then either show yourselves the stronger or remain here."

"But there is still an alternative," I said. "What if we persuade you that you ought to let us go?"

"Do you mean to say," he said, "that you can persuade those who won't listen?"

"No, indeed," said Glaucon.

"Well, you may make up your minds that we won't."

"But you do not know," Adeimantus put in, "that in the evening there is to be a torch race on horseback in honour of the goddess?"

"On horseback?" I said. "That is certainly a novelty. Will it be a horse-race with the riders carrying torches and handing them to one another, or how will it be done?"

"As you say," said Polemarchus; "and there will be a night festival besides, which will be worth seeing. We can go out and watch it after dinner, and many of the young men here will join our party, and we shall talk. So, please, stay, and don't refuse."

"It seems that we had better," said Glaucon.

"Well, if you think so," I said, "let us stay."

We went home, therefore, with Polemarchus, and found there his brothers Lysias and Euthydemus, and with them also Thrasymachus of Chalcedon, Charmantides of Paeania and Cleitophon, the son of Aristomenes; within was Polemarchus' father, Cephalus. I thought him looking very old. It was indeed some time since I had seen him. He was sitting upon a cushioned chair, a garland on his head, for he had just been sacrificing in the court. There were seats round the room, and we sat down beside him. Cephalus, as soon as he saw me, greeted me, and said:

"You don't very often visit us in the Peiraeus, Socrates. But you ought to. If I were still able to walk to town easily, there would be no need for you to come here; we could come to you. But, as things are, you ought to come here oftener; for I find that as I lose my taste for bodily pleasures, I grow more eager than ever for discussion, and enjoy it more. So do not refuse me. Spend your time with these young men, and visit us here where you know you are with old friends."

"Indeed, Cephalus," I said, "I enjoy talking with very old men. I consider that they have gone before us along a road which we must all travel in our turn, and it is good that we should ask them of the nature of that road, whether it be rough and difficult, or easy and smooth. You, Cephalus, are now at that time of life which the poets call "old age the threshold," and I should particularly like to ask your thoughts on this question. Is it a painful period of life, or what is your news of it?"

"I will give you my own opinion gladly, Socrates," he said. "You know some of us old men are often together, true to the old proverb. Now most of the company whenever they meet lament their wretched lot. They long for the pleasures of youth, and call to mind the delights of love, and drink and feasting, and so on. They complain that they are as men who have lost a great treasure, who once lived well, and now don't live at all; and some of them bewail the insults which their kinsfolk heap upon their years, and therefore they decry old age for all the evils it has brought upon them. But in my opinion, Socrates, they don't really see what is wrong. If they were right, then I too, and all who have come to my time of life, would by reason of old age have suffered as they have; but, as a matter of fact, I have met many whose experience is different. Take the poet Sophocles, for example. I was with him once, when someone asked him: "How do you stand, Sophocles, in respect to the pleasures of sex? Are you still capable of intercourse?" "Hush, sir," he said. "It gives me the greatest joy to have escaped the clutches of that savage and fierce master." I thought then that he spoke wisely, and I think so still, for certainly old age brings great peace and freedom from passions such as these. When the desires grow less intense and slacken, most certainly it is as Sophocles says: it means release from masters many and ravening. But all these troubles, their complaints against their kinsfolk among them, have but one cause, and that is not old age, Socrates, but men's dispositions; for old age lays but a moderate burden on men who have order and peace within themselves, but ill-governed natures find youth and old age alike irksome."

I was delighted with him for what he said, and, wishing to hear more, I tried to draw him out by saying: "I fancy, Cephalus, that most people don't admit what you say, but consider that you find old age pleasant, not because of your disposition, but because of your great wealth; for the rich, they say, have many consolations."

"True," he said, "they do not admit it, and in a sense they are right; but not so right as they think. There is great force in that retort of Themistocles to a Seriphian who said sneeringly that his fame was due not to himself but to his city. "Certainly," said Themistocles, "I should not have become famous were I a Seriphian, but neither would you were you an Athenian." The same applies to men who are not rich and cannot endure old age. A good man even would not easily endure old age and poverty conjoined, nor would the bad man, though he got riches, ever attain peace with himself."

"Did you inherit the greater part of your wealth, Cephalus," I said, "or have you made it?"

"What have I made myself, Socrates?" he said. "In the matter of money-making, I might be called the mean between my grandfather and my father. My grandfather, Cephalus, inherited about as much wealth as I now possess, and increased it many times, while Lysanias, my father, reduced it to even less than it is now. But I am content if I leave these young men not less, but perhaps a little more than I inherited."

"I asked," I said, "because you seemed to me not excessively fond of money; and that is usually the case with men who have not made it. But those who have made their money are twice as much attached to it as others; for as poets love their poems and fathers their children, just so money-makers value their money, not only for its uses, as other people do, but because it is their own production. They are disagreeable people to meet for that reason: they have no praise for anything but riches."

"You are right," he said.

"Yes," I said, "but tell me this: What do you consider the greatest good in the possession of ample means?"

"Something that perhaps few men will credit," he said. "But you know, Socrates, when a man faces the thought that he must die, there come upon him fear and foreboding about things that have not troubled him before. Once he laughed at the tales about those in Hades, of punishment to be suffered there by him who here has done injustice. But now his soul is tormented by the thought that these may be true, and whether from the bodily weakness of old age, or because he is now nearer that other world, he himself sees those things more clearly. He becomes full of fear and suspicion. He begins to reckon up and consider if he has done any injustice to any man. And finding in his life many such acts, often, like a child, he awakes out of sleep in terror, and lives in expectation of evil. But with him that is conscious of no injustice in him, kindly hope, the nurse of age, as Pindar calls it, is always present. For that is **331** a beautiful saying of his, Socrates, that whoever has lived a righteous and holy life,

> She on his pilgrimage
> Fareth beside him, and his heart feedeth,
> Sweet hope, the nurse of age;
> Most surely she of all
> To its haven leadeth
> The many-turning mind
> Of human kind.

It is really a wonderfully fine description. Now here, I hold, lies the chief advantage of the possession of wealth, not perhaps for every one, but for the good man; for we can go to that other world without fear only if we are guiltless of even involuntary deceit or falsehood, and if we are quit of all our debts of sacrifice to God and of money to man, and to this result money largely contributes. It has indeed many other uses; but setting one thing against another, I should regard this as not the least of the uses of wealth to a man of sense."

"What you say, Cephalus, is excellent," I said. "But as to this justice, can we quite without qualification define it as truthfulness and repayment of anything that we have received; or are these very actions sometimes just and sometimes unjust? For example, if we had been given weapons by a friend when he was of sound mind, and he went mad and reclaimed them, it would surely be universally admitted that it would not be right to give them back. Any one who did so, and who was prepared to tell the whole truth to a man in that state, would not be just."

"You are right," he said.

"Then this is not the definition of justice—speaking the truth and restoring what we have received?"

"Yes, but it is, Socrates," broke in Polemarchus, "if we are to believe Simonides."

"Well, well," said Cephalus, "I leave the argument with you, for it is time for me to attend to the sacrifice."

"Well," said I, "is not Polemarchus your heir?"

"Certainly," he said smiling, and departed to sacrifice.

"Come, then," I said, "you who have inherited the argument, what is this saying of Simonides about justice of which you approve?"

"That to render to every man what is owing is just," said he, "and I for one think he was right in so saying."

"Well," I said, "Simonides is one whom we cannot

lightly disbelieve. He was a wise and godlike man. But as to what this saying means, you, Polemarchus, may know that; I certainly do not. For it clearly does not mean what we were just saying, repayment of what has been given to a man in pledge if the claimant is out of his senses. Yet surely what has been given in pledge is ³³² owing, is it not?"

"Yes."

"But we were certainly not to make repayment when the claimant is out of his senses."

"True," he said.

"Then Simonides apparently means something else when he says that to repay what is owing is just."

"But assuredly he does," he said, "for he thinks that friends owe to friends to do good and no evil."

"I understand," I said, "for what is repaid is not always what is owing; when, for example, a man repays money to one who has deposited it with him, if the repayment or acceptance is harmful and the repayer and the receiver are friends. Is that what you say Simonides meant?"

"Certainly."

"Then are we to repay to enemies whatever is owing to them?"

"Certainly we must pay them what is owing. But I imagine that from an enemy to an enemy evil of some sort is owing, because there evil is appropriate."

"Simonides then apparently, as poets will, made a riddle on the nature of justice. For he thought, as it appears, that to pay every man what is appropriate is just; but he called that, what is owing."

"Do you not agree?" he said.

"In heaven's name," I said, "what answer do you think he would have given us if we had asked him: "Simonides, what that is owing and appropriate does the art called medicine render, and to whom or what?"

"Clearly that it renders drugs and food and drink to bodies."

"And what that is owing and appropriate does the art called cookery render, and to whom or what?"

"Seasoning to dishes."

"Well, what then does the art called justice render, and to whom or what?"

"If, Socrates," he said, "we are to be consistent, it renders benefits and injuries to friends and enemies."

"Then does he mean by justice doing good to friends and evil to enemies?"

"I think so."

"But when people are ill, who, as regards health and disease, is most capable of doing good to friends and harm to enemies?"

"A doctor."

"And when they are on a voyage, as regards the dangers of the sea?"

"A ship captain."

"Then what about the just man? In what action and in what regard is he most capable of benefiting his friends and harming his enemies?"

"In wars and alliances, I imagine."

"Very good! But, my dear Polemarchus, a doctor is useless when men are not ill."

"True."

"And a ship captain when they are not on the sea."

"Yes."

"Then is the just man also useless when men are not at war?"

"I cannot think so."

"Then justice is useful in peace also?"

333    "It is."

"So is farming, is it not?"

"Yes."

"In the procuring of the fruits of the earth, that is to say?"

"Yes."

"And is shoemaking also useful?"

"Yes."

"In the procuring of shoes, you would say?"

"Certainly."

"Now, then, as to justice. What need does it satisfy or what benefit procure that makes it useful in peace?"

"It is useful in dealings, Socrates."

"By dealings, do you mean partnerships or something different?"

"Yes, partnerships."

"Then in a game of draughts is the just man or the draught player a good and useful partner?"

"The draught player."

"In bricklaying and masonry will the just man be a better and more useful partner than the builder?"

"Certainly not."

"Then as the harp player is a better partner than the just man in playing music, in what kind of partnership will the just man be better than the harp player or the builder?"

"In a money partnership, I imagine."

"Except, perhaps, Polemarchus, in using money, as when it comes to buying or selling a horse. There, I imagine, the man who knows horses is the better partner. Is he not?"

"Apparently."

"And in buying or selling a ship, the shipbuilder or the captain will be the better?"

"Probably."

"Then on which occasions of using silver and gold is the just man a more useful partner than others?"

"In cases of depositing and keeping money safe."

"Is not that as good as saying, when there is no need to use money, but only to keep it unused?"

"Yes."

"Then justice is useful in regard to money when money is useless?"

"It looks like it."

"And when a pruning knife is to be kept, justice is useful both in dealing with others, or for yourself; but when it is to be used, the art of vine-dressing is more useful?"

"Apparently."

"Would you say the same of a shield and a harp? When they are to be kept and not used, justice is useful; but when they are to be used, the arts of fighting and of music are more useful."

"That must be so."

"And is it not the same with everything else? When anything is to be used, justice is useless; and when it is not to be used, useful?"

"It looks like it."

"Justice, then, my friend, cannot be of any great moment if it is useful only for things that are useless. But let us consider this point. In any kind of fight, whether with fists or weapons, is not he who is cleverest in striking also cleverest in warding off blows?"

"Certainly."

"Moreover, is not he who is clever in warding off disease also cleverest in implanting it without being found out?"

"I think so."

"And he is an excellent guard of an army who is 334 clever in stealing the plans of the enemy and all their dispositions?"

"Certainly."

"Then whoever is a clever guarder of anything is also a clever thief of it?"

"Apparently."

"Then if the just man is clever at guarding money, he is also clever at stealing it?"

"That is certainly the drift of the argument," he said.

"Then the just man stands revealed as a clever thief, and you have probably learnt that from Homer, for he had a great liking for Odysseus' maternal grandfather, Autolycus, and says that he excelled all men in theft and perjury. Justice, then, according to you and Homer and Simonides seems to be a form of theft, for the advantage of friends and the harm of enemies. Have you not said so?"

"Good heavens, no!" he said; "but I do not know now what I have said. Still I am of the same opinion, that justice is to help your friends and harm your enemies."

"Do you define a man's friends as those who seem to him to be trustworthy, or as those who really are whether they seem so or not, and so with his enemies?"

"It is but likely," he said, "that a man should love those whom he thinks trustworthy, and hate those whom he thinks evil."

"But do not men make mistakes in this matter so that they think many men trustworthy who are not really so, and vice versa?"

"They do."

"Then to those men are not the good enemies and the bad friends?"

"Certainly."

"But nevertheless it is just for them in those circumstances to help the evil and harm the good, is it not?

"Apparently."

"But are not the good just, and such as do no injustice?"

"Yes."

"Then, according to your argument, it is just to do ill to those who do no injustice."

"Certainly not, Socrates," he said. "It is the argument that seems evil."

"Then is it just to harm the unjust and benefit the just?"

"That seems a fairer conclusion than the former."

"Then, Polemarchus," I said, "for the many who have been entirely mistaken about men, it will be just to harm their friends, for some of them are evil, and to help their enemies, for some of them are good. So we shall come to a conclusion exactly contrary to what we asserted to be Simonides' meaning."

"Yes," he said, "that is certainly the result. But let us change, for we probably did not define friend and enemy rightly."

"Where was the definition wrong, Polemarchus?"

"In defining the friend as him who seems to be trustworthy."

"And now," I said, "what change shall we make?"

"We shall say," he said, "that he is a friend who not only is thought to be but really is trustworthy, but he 335 who is only thought to be and is not really trustworthy is thought to be but is not really a friend. And the same change will apply to enemies."

'Then apparently according to the argument, the good man will be a friend and the bad an enemy."

"Yes."

"Then would you have us add to our definition of justice? In other words, whereas we said previously that it was just to do good to friends and harm to enemies, shall we now further say that justice is to do good to friends when they are good, and to harm enemies when they are bad?"

"Certainly," he said. "I think that is an excellent definition."

"Is it then," I said, "the nature of a just man to harm any human being whatever?"

"Why, certainly," he said. "He must harm those who are wicked and enemies."

"When horses are harmed, do they become better or worse?"

"Worse."

"Worse as horses, or worse as dogs?"

"Worse as horses."

"And, similarly, when dogs are harmed, do they become worse as dogs and not worse as horses?"

"Necessarily."

"Then, my good sir, shall we not say the same of men, that when harmed they become worse as men—that is, worse in human excellence?"

"Certainly."

"But is not justice a human excellence?"

"That, too, is indisputable."

"Then, my friend, it is also indisputable that men who are harmed become more unjust."

"Apparently."

"Now, can musicians, by the art of music, make men unmusical?"

"That is impossible."

"Or can horsemen by horsemanship make men worse riders?"

"No."

"Then can just men by justice make men unjust; or, in short, can good men by virtue make men bad?"

"No, that is impossible."

"It is not the function of heat, I imagine, to make cold, but of its opposite"

"Yes."

"Nor of dryness to make wet, but of its opposite?"

"Certainly."

"Nor of the good man to do harm, but of his opposite?"

"That is evident."

"And is not the just man good?"

"Certainly."

"Then to harm either his friend or any man is not the function of the just man, Polemarchus, but of his opposite, the unjust?"

"What you say seems to me indisputable, Socrates."

"Then if any man has said that it is just to restore to each man what is owing, and if that means that the just owes harm to his enemies and help to his friends, he was not a wise man, in that he said what was untrue. For we have discovered that it is never just to injure any man."

"I agree," he said.

"Then," I said, "you and I will take up arms together against any one who attributes this saying to Simonides, or Bias, or Pittacus, or any other wise and blessed man."

"I am quite ready to do my share of the fighting," he said.

"But do you know," I said, "whom I think to be the 336 author of the saying that it is just to help friends and harm enemies?"

"Whom?" he said.

"I fancy that it was Periander, or Perdiccas, or Xerxes, or Ismenias the Theban, or some man of wealth and fancied power."

"Yes, you are certainly right," he said.

"Very good," I said. "Now since this definition of justice and what is just has been rejected, what other definition can any one give?"

Now, while we had been talking, Thrasymachus had several times tried to interrupt the argument, but had been restrained by those next him who wished to hear it to the end. When we stopped for a moment, and I said these words, he could keep still no longer; but, gathering himself up, he sprang at us like a wild beast to make us his prey. Polemarchus and I shrank aside in fear. Then, speaking so that all could hear, he said:

"What nonsense has possessed you two all this time, Socrates? What do you mean by all your polite bowing and scraping to one another? If you have a genuine desire to know what justice is, don't confine yourself to asking questions, and making a show by refuting any answer that is given. You know that it is much easier to ask questions than to answer them. But answer yourself, and say how you define justice; and don't dare to tell me that it is the obligatory, or the expedient, or the profitable, or the lucrative, or the advantageous, but make your answer precise and accurate, for I will not have any rubbish of that kind from you."

When I heard this I was struck with amazement, and gazed at him, and began to be afraid. I think that if I had not looked at him before he looked at me, I should have been struck dumb. But when the argument began to exasperate him I had looked at him first, so that I was able to answer him:

"Thrasymachus," I said trembling, "don't be hard on us, for if Polemarchus and I have gone astray in our scrutiny of the argument, our sin has assuredly not been deliberate. If gold had been the object of our search, we could never have allowed our politeness to spoil our chance of finding it; and now, when we are seeking for justice, a thing more precious than much gold, never imagine that we should have given way to one another so weakly and foolishly, instead of making every effort to discover it. We are in earnest, my friend, believe me; but the task, I fancy, is beyond our powers; and therefore, you clever people should rather pity than scold us."

When he heard this he burst out laughing and said:

"O Heracles, this is our sly Socrates whom we all know so well. I knew how it would be, and I told the others that you would refuse to give an answer, but would take refuge in slyness or anything to excuse your answering a simple question."

"You are a wise man, Thrasymachus," I said, "and you know that if you asked someone what are the factors of twelve, and said to him: 'Don't dare, sir, to tell me that twelve is twice six, or three times four, or six times two, or four times three, for I will not have any such nonsense from you,' you could see, I fancy, that no one would answer that kind of question. If he said to you: 'Thrasymachus, what do you mean? Am I to give none of these answers? But what, my good sir, if one of them happens to be right? Am I then to give another answer than the true one? or what do you mean?' What would you have said to that?"

"Oh, well," he said, "the cases are so exactly parallel, are they not?"

"There is no reason why they should not be," I said. "But even if they are not, but one of those answers seems true to the person questioned, do you fancy that he will not answer as he thinks, whether we forbid him or not?"

"Then are you actually going to do that?" said he. "Will you give one of those answers which I have forbidden?"

"I should not be surprised," I said, "if on consideration I thought it right to do so."

"Well," he said, "what if I give you an answer about justice different from all these, and better? What penalty are you prepared to pay?"

"None," I said, "but the befitting penalty of ignorance. It is befitting surely to learn from wisdom. I am ready to pay that penalty."

"You are an entertaining fellow," he said. "Yes, you must learn, but you must pay in money also."

"Certainly, if I have any," I said.

"But that is all right," said Glaucon. "As far as money is concerned, Thrasymachus, you may say on, for we will all contribute for Socrates."

"Oh, yes," he said, "to let Socrates play his usual game, refuse to answer himself, but listen to another's answer, and then refute it."

"But, my good sir," I said, "How can a man answer when, in the first place, he is ignorant and confesses his ignorance, and when, secondly, even if he has any opinions on the subject, he has been forbidden to say what he thinks by a man of no mean authority? It is much 338 better that you should speak, for you say that you know and have an answer. Therefore don't refuse, but do me the favour of answering, and don't grudge instructing Glaucon here and the rest of us."

When I had said this, Glaucon and the others entreated him not to refuse. Now Thrasymachus was evidently eager to speak and win applause for the excellent answer he thought he had ready. But he pretended to insist on my answering. In the end he gave way and said:

"This is Socrates' wisdom. He refuses to teach, but goes about learning from others, and shows no gratitude for his lessons."

"It is perfectly true, Thrasymachus," I said, "that I learn from others. But it is untrue to say that I show no gratitude. I show all that I can, for I have no money. I can only give praise. When you answer, you will see at once how willingly I give that if I think an answer good, for I fancy that yours will be good."

"Listen, then," he said. "I declare that justice is nothing else than that which is advantageous to the stronger. Well, where is your praise? You refuse it?"

"I must first learn what you mean," I said. "As yet I do not know. You say that what is advantageous to the stronger is just. Now, what do you mean by that, Thrasymachus? For example, you surely do not assert that if Polydamas the athlete is stronger than we, and it is to his bodily advantage to eat meat, then for us also who are weaker this diet is advantageous, and consequently just?"

"You are shameless, Socrates," he said. "You conceive my meaning in the one way in which you can do most harm to the argument."

"Not at all, my good sir," I said, "but tell us your meaning more clearly."

"Do you mean to say you don't know," he said, "that in some cities a tyrant is master, in others a democracy, in others an oligarchy?"

"Surely."

"Then it is the government which is master in each city, is it not?"

"Certainly."

"Well, every government lays down laws for its own advantage—a democracy democratic, a tyranny tyrannical laws, and so on. In laying down these laws they have made it plain that what is to their advantage is just. They punish him who departs from this as a law-breaker and an unjust man. And this, my good sir, is what I mean. In every city justice is the same. It is what is advantageous to the established government. But the established government is master, and so sound reasoning gives the conclusion that the same thing is always just—namely, what is advantageous to the stronger."

"I have found out," I said, "what you mean. I shall try to find out whether it is true or not. But, Thrasymachus, you yourself have given the answer that the advantageous is just; yet you forbade me to give that answer, though indeed you have added the qualification, 'to the stronger.'"

"And that is an insignificant qualification, I suppose?" he said.

"It is not yet evident whether it is insignificant or important, but it is evident that we must examine whether your assertion is true; for I myself acknowledge that justice is in a sense advantageous, but you define the advantageous further by the addition of 'to the stronger.' I do not know about that. I must think."

"Think away," he said.

"That I will," I said. "Now tell me. Do you not also say that it is just to obey the rulers?"

"I do."

"Then are the rulers in every city infallible, or are they liable sometimes to make mistakes?"

"They are certainly liable to make mistakes," he said.

"Then in their legislation will they not lay down some right and some mistaken laws?"

"I fancy so."

"Are right laws those which are to their advantage, and mistaken laws those which are to their disadvantage?"

"Surely."

"And their subjects must do what they order and this is justice?"

"Yes."

"Then, according to your argument, not only is i' just to do what is advantageous to the stronger, but also to do the opposite, what is not advantageous."

"What are you saying?" he said.

"Just what you are, I imagine. But let us look more closely. Has it not been admitted that the rulers in pre-scribing certain acts to the governed sometimes mistake what is best for themselves, but that at the same time it is just for the governed to do what the rulers prescribe? Has not that been admitted?"

"I think so," he said.

"Think also," I said, "that you have admitted that it

is just to do what is to the disadvantage of those who govern and are stronger. The rulers unwittingly prescribe what is to their own hurt, and you say that it is just for others to do what they have prescribed. Then, my most wise Thrasymachus, must it not necessarily follow that it is thus just to do the opposite of what you say? For obviously the weaker are commanded to do what is to the disadvantage of the stronger."

340 "But, assuredly, Socrates," said Polemarchus, "that is perfectly plain."

"No doubt," put in Cleitophon, "if you are to give witness in his favour."

"What need is there of witness?" he said. "Thrasymachus himself acknowledges that the rulers sometimes prescribe what is to their own hurt, and that it is just for the governed to obey those commands."

"No, Polemarchus. Thrasymachus stated that it is just to do what the rulers command."

"Yes, and he also stated, Cleitophon, that what is to the advantage of the stronger is just, and in making these two statements he acknowledged that sometimes the stronger command the weaker over whom they rule to do what is to their disadvantage, and it follows from those admissions that what is advantageous to the stronger is no more just than what is disadvantageous."

"But," Cleitophon said, "by what is advantageous to the stronger he meant 'what the stronger thinks is to his advantage.' This is what the weaker must do, and this is his definition of justice."

"No, that is not what he said," Polemarchus replied.

"Well, Polemarchus," I said, "it does not matter. If Thrasymachus says so now, let us take him in that sense. Tell me, Thrasymachus, was this how you wished to define justice—namely, as that which in the judgment of the stronger is advantageous to the stronger whether it is really so or not? Are we to say that this is your meaning?"

"Most certainly not," he said. "Do you think that I call him who makes a mistake the stronger at the time of his mistake?"

"I certainly thought," I said, "that that was what you meant when you admitted that the rulers are not infallible, but sometimes make mistakes."

"Well, you are a quibbler, Socrates. When a doctor makes a mistake about this patients, do you at that moment in so far as he is mistaken call him a doctor? or do you call a man who makes a mistake in calculating an accountant at the moment of, and in respect to, his mistake? No. I fancy that is only our way of speaking. We say the doctor, or the accountant, or the writer made a mistake; but really none of these, so far as he is what we call him, ever makes a mistake. To speak precisely, since you are for being precise, every craftsman is infallible. He who makes a mistake does so where his knowledge fails him; that is, where he is no craftsman. As with craftsmen and wise men, so with a ruler; he is always infallible so long as he is a ruler, although in ordinary language we all say that the doctor made a mistake and the ruler made a mistake. In such ordinary language was my answer to you a moment ago. But this is the precise form of my statement. A ruler, so far as he is a ruler, is infallible, and being infallible he prescribes 341 what is best for himself, and this the subject must do. So that, as I said originally, to do what is advantageous to the stronger is just."

"Very good, Thrasymachus," I said. "So you think that I am a quibbler, do you?"

"Certainly," he said.

"And do you imagine that I ask those questions of you in deliberate intent to discredit you in the argument?"

"I know it," he said. "But it will not serve you. You will not cheat me by your tricks, nor will you oust me from the argument by open violence."

"I have no intention of trying, my dear sir," I said; "but that we may escape a similar confusion in the future, will you indicate precisely when you speak of the stronger whose advantage it is just for the weaker to serve, whether you mean 'the ruler and the stronger' in the popular sense or in that more precise sense which you have just now defined?"

"I mean a ruler in the most precise sense of the word," he said. "Try your tricks and your quibblings against that, if you can. I ask no quarter. But you are powerless."

"Do you imagine," I said, "that I should be as mad as to try to shave a lion or trick a Thrasymachus?"

"You tried it a moment ago," he said, "though you were no good at it."

"Well, enough of that," I said. "Answer me this. Is the doctor in the precise sense in which you have defined him a money-maker or a healer of the sick? Understand that I am asking about the real doctor."

"A healer of the sick," he said.

"What of the ship captain? Is the genuine captain a ruler of sailors or a sailor?"

"A ruler of sailors."

"The fact that he sails on a ship need not, I fancy, be taken into account, nor ought we to call him a sailor; for it is not because he is on board that he is called a ship captain, but because of his skill and his authority over sailors."

"True."

"Both for sick people and for sailors there is something which is advantageous, is there not?"

"Certainly."

"And is it not the natural end of the art to seek after and provide this?"

"It is," he said.

"But is there anything advantageous to an art, except that it should be as perfect as possible?"

"What is the meaning of your question?"

"This," I said. "If you were to ask me whether it is enough for a body to be a body, or whether it needs something more, I should reply: 'Certainly it needs something more. In fact, this is why the art of medicine has been discovered, because the body is defective, and it is not enough for it to be a body; and to provide what is advantageous to it this art is established.' Do you think that such a statement would be correct?"

"Quite correct," he said.

"Now is medicine itself defective? In other words, does any art whatsoever need some kind of virtue or power, as eyes need sight and ears hearing, so that what is advantageous to these powers must be discovered and provided by an art which presides over the eyes and ears? Is there any such defect in art as art, so that every art needs another to discover what is advantageous to it, and that discovering art another, and so on without end? or will each art seek its own advantage? or is it unnecessary that either itself or any other art should discover what is advantageous to it and will supply its deficiency? For in truth no art is subject to any defect or mistake, and it is not the office of an art to seek the advantage of anything except its subject. So long as an art, which is strictly an art, is true to its own nature, it is correct, and is therefore without defect or blemish. Remember that we are using the words in their strict sense. Is that a true description or not?"

"It seems true," he said.

"Then," I said, "medicine seeks what is advantageous not to medicine, but to the body."

"Yes," he said.

"And horsemanship what is advantageous not to horsemanship, but to horses; and no art seeks its own advantage (for it needs nothing), but the advantage of its subject."

"So it appears," he said.

"But, Thrasymachus, the arts govern and are masters of their subject."

To this he agreed, though very reluctantly.

"Then no science either prescribes or seeks the advantage of the stronger, but the advantage of the weaker over which it rules?"

This also he admitted in the end, though he tried to make a fight of it. When he had made the admission, I said:

"Then does any doctor, so far as he is a doctor, prescribe or seek the advantage of the doctor rather than of the patient? For the doctor, in the strict sense of the word, has been admitted to be a ruler of bodies, and not a money-maker. Have we not admitted that?"

He agreed.

"And is not the ship captain, in the strict sense of the word, a ruler of sailors rather than a sailor?"

"That has been admitted."

"Then such a captain and ruler will not prescribe and seek the advantage of the captain, but of the sailors over whom he rules."

He agreed reluctantly.

"Then, Thrasymachus, no one in any kind of government will, so far as he is a ruler, prescribe or seek his own advantage but that of the subject of his craft over which he rules; all that he says and does is said and done with the subject in view, and for his advantage and good."

343     When we had reached this stage in the argument, and it was plain to all that the definition of justice had been turned upside down, Thrasymachus, instead of answering, said:

"Tell me, Socrates, have you a nurse?"

"Why this?" I said. "Should you not answer rather than ask questions of that kind?"

"Because," he said, "she lets you go on snivelling, and doesn't wipe your nose when you need it, for you have not learnt from her to distinguish sheep and shepherd."

"What, in particular, makes you say that?" I said.

"You imagine that shepherds or herdsmen look after the good of their sheep or cattle, and fatten and tend them with some other end in view than the good of their masters and themselves, and you actually think that rulers in cities, who are really rulers, do not regard their subjects just as a man his sheep, and do not night and day seek how they may profit themselves, and that only. So profoundly wise are you concerning the just and justice, and the unjust and injustice, that you are unaware that justice and the just is really the good of another, the advantage of the stronger who rules, but the self-inflicted injury of the subject who obeys; that injustice is the opposite, and rules those very simple just souls; that the governed serve the advantage of the stronger man, and by their obedience contribute to his happiness, but in no way to their own. My most simple Socrates, you must see that a just man always comes off worse than an unjust. Take, first, the case of commercial dealing, when a just and an unjust man are partners. At the dissolution of the partnership you will never find the just man with more than the unjust, but always with less. Then in politics, where there are taxes to pay, out of equal incomes the just man pays more, the unjust less; where there is money to be got, the just man gets nothing, the unjust much. Then, again, when they are in office, the just man, apart from other losses, ruins his own business by neglect, while his justice prevents his making a profit out of the public; and, in addition, he incurs the dislike of his kinsfolk and acquaintances by refusing to be unjust for their advantage. With the unjust man it is the opposite in every particular. For I am speaking, in accordance with my recent explanation, of him who is capable of aggrandizement on a large scale. If you wish to decide how much more advantageous for the individual injustice is than justice, consider such a man. For if you take the most perfect injustice, you will most easily see that it makes the doer of injustice the happiest of men; but those who suffer and will not do unjustly, the most miserable. This is tyranny. It plunders by fraud and force alike the goods of others, sacred and holy things, private and public possessions, and never pettily but always on a grand scale. Individual cases of these crimes are on detection visited with punishment and utter disgrace, and petty offenders of this sort are called temple-breakers, kidnappers, burglars, swindlers, and thieves. But those who not only despoil the citizens of their money, but capture and enslave their persons, get no such ugly names, but are called happy and blessed men, not only by their citizens, but by all who hear of their complete injustice. Men revile injustice, not because they fear to do it, but because they fear to suffer it. Therefore, Socrates, injustice, when great enough, is mightier and freer and more masterly than justice; and, as I said at the start, justice is to the advantage of the stronger, but injustice is profitable and advantageous to oneself."

Having so spoken, Thrasymachus was going to depart after having, like a bathman, flung a great flood of words about our ears; but the company would not suffer this, but insisted on his staying and giving account for what he had said. And I myself entreated him earnestly, saying:

"My good Thrasymachus, are you going to depart after throwing a speech like that at us, before you have thoroughly taught us or learnt yourself whether or no such things be? Or do you think it a small matter to undertake to decide on the whole course of life which each of us must follow if we would live most profitably."

"Do you mean that I don't think it a serious matter?" said Thrasymachus.

"Apparently," I said, "or else you are perfectly indifferent about us, and care nothing whether our ignorance of the knowledge you profess leads us to live worse or better lives. But, my dear sir, take the trouble to convince us as well as yourself. You will not suffer for having <sup>345</sup> helped so many of us. For I may tell you my own opinion. I am not convinced, and I do not think that injustice is more profitable than justice even if it is given free play, and may do what it will without hindrance. No, my dear sir, a man may be unjust, and may be able to practise injustice either by escaping detection, or by overpowering opposition; nevertheless, he cannot convince me that it is really more profitable than justice. Perhaps some others of the company besides myself may feel the same. So, my good friend, give us satisfactory proof that we are wrong in prizing justice above injustice."

"Well," he said, "how am I to persuade you? If you are not convinced by what I have just said, what more can I do for you? Am I to take the doctrine and feed you with it?"

"God forbid!" I said, "not that. But firstly, abide by what you have said, or, if you change your mind, do so openly and don't deceive us. For as it is, Thrasymachus, to look back at the argument, observe that though you began by defining the genuine doctor, you did not think the same accuracy necessary afterwards when you came to the genuine shepherd. You thought that he, so far as he is a shepherd, fattens his sheep without considering what is best for them, but with an eye to good eating, like a gourmand who is giving a banquet, or with an eye to profit, like a money-maker, not a shepherd. But surely the art of shepherding is only concerned with how it may provide what is best for that over which it presides? As for its own interests, all that can contribute to its excellence has been already provided, so long as it is not unfaithful to its nature. This made me think that we must admit that any government, so far as it is a government, considers what is best only for that which it governs and tends, whether the government be public or private. Now, do you think that those who rule in cities, who are genuine rulers, do so willingly?"

"No, I don't think so. I know it," he said.

"How is that, Thrasymachus?" I said. "Do you not notice that in the ordinary offices of state there are no voluntary rulers? They demand to be paid on the assumption that their holding office benefits not themselves, but 346 the governed. And tell me this. Is not the test by which we always distinguish one art from another its possession of different powers? Please, my dear sir, do not answer against your convictions, as we want to get on."

"Yes," he said, "that is the distinguishing test."

"And does not each of these arts give us a distinctive, not a common benefit?—medicine health, for example; navigation safety on a voyage, and so on?"

"Certainly."

"And the art of wages gives wages, does it not? For this is its power. For you do not call medicine and navigation the same art, do you? Speaking precisely, as you suggested, if a sea captain becomes healthy because being at sea suits him, that doesn't make you call his art medicine, does it?"

"Surely not," he said.

"Nor do you call the art of wages medicine, I imagine, if a man gets well while earning wages?"

"Certainly not."

"Well, would you call medicine the art of wages if a man earned wages in medical practice?"

"No," he said.

"Then we have agreed that the benefit of each art is confined to that art?"

"We have."

"Then if there be any benefit which all craftsmen enjoy in common, that will clearly come from their all using as well something which is common to them all?"

"Apparently," he said.

"We assert, therefore, that craftsmen who earn wages derive that benefit from their use of the additional art of wages."

He agreed reluctantly.

"Then in the case of each art this benefit, the receiving of wages, does not come from the art. If we consider carefully we shall see that health is given by the art of medicine, fees by the art of wages; a house is provided by the art of architecture, and pay by the accompanying art of wages, and so on with all the arts. Each fulfils its own function and benefits its subject. But is a craftsman benefited by his art if he does not get pay in addition?"

"Apparently not," he said.

"Then the voluntary performance of his art does not benefit him?"

"I think not."

"Then, Thrasymachus, it is now clear that no art or government provides what is for its own benefit, but, as we said long ago, it provides and prescribes what is for the benefit of the subject, seeking the advantage of him who is weaker, not the advantage of the stronger. It was for this reason, my dear Thrasymachus, that I said a moment ago that no one of his own will becomes a ruler and undertakes to set straight the misfortunes of others. The ruler demands wages, because he who is going to <sup>347</sup> practise his art aright, and is prescribing in accordance with his art, neither practises nor prescribes what is best for himself, but for the subject. For these reasons, naturally, it is right that those who are going to consent to rule should be paid either in money or in honour, or by escaping a penalty which the refusal to rule involves."

"What do you mean by that, Socrates?" said Glaucon. "The first two kinds of wages I know, but I do not understand the penalty you mention which you describe as a kind of wages."

"Do you not understand," I said, "what are the wages of the best men, which induce the most virtuous to rule when they consent to do so? Do you not know that ambition and love of money are held to be, and actually are, something to be ashamed of?"

"I do," he said.

"For that reason," I said, "neither money nor honour will make the good men consent to be rulers. They are unwilling to be called hirelings for openly exacting wages for their office, or to get the name of thieves by fraudulently enriching themselves from it. Nor will honour move them, for they are not ambitious. Therefore if they are to consent to rule the compulsion of a penalty must be laid upon them (this may be why to take office without compulsion is considered disgraceful) ; and the greatest penalty is to be ruled by an inferior if you will not rule yourself. When virtuous men take office I think they are prompted by this fear; and then they approach it not as a blessing or with any prospect of good fortune: they face it as a compulsory task because they can find none superior or equal to themselves to whom they might entrust it. Were there a city of good men, it is probable that men would contend to escape office as they now contend to gain it, and it would then be clearly shown that a true ruler is in reality one who seeks not his own advantage but the advantage of the subject, so that every man of understanding would prefer to be benefited by another rather than labour for another's benefit. Therefore I in no way agree with the statement of Thrasymachus that justice is the advantage of the stronger. But this we shall consider again. I attach much greater importance to Thrasymachus' present position, that the life of the unjust man is superior to that of the just man. And you, Glaucon? Which side do you take? Which statement do you consider the truer?"

"I think that the life of the just man is more profitable."

"Have you heard," I said, "the list of blessings which **848** Thrasymachus has just assigned to the life of the unjust man?"

"I have," he said, "but I am not convinced."

"Then shall we convince him, if we can possibly find a way of proving his statements are untrue?"

"Yes, let us," he said.

"Now," I said, " if we match ourselves against him and give speech for speech, enumerating the advantages of justice, and he speaks a second time, and we speak yet again, then we must add up and measure the advantages enumerated by each party in each speech, and we shall need a jury to decide between us. But if we follow our previous form of inquiry, arguing till we come to an agreement, then we shall be at the same time jury and advocates."

"Certainly," he said.

"Then have which you will," I said.

"Let us have the second way," he said.

"Come, then, Thrasymachus," I said, "answer us from the beginning. You say that perfect injustice is more profitable than perfect justice?"

"Certainly I do," he said, "and I have given reasons why it is so."

"Well, then, how do you deal with this question on the subject? I suppose you call one of them a virtue and the other a vice?"

"Surely."

"Justice a virtue, and injustice a vice?"

"That is likely, my dear good fellow, when I say that injustice is profitable, but justice not."

"Well, what else?"

"The opposite," he said.

"Do you call justice a vice?"

"No, but certainly sublime good nature."

"Then do you call injustice ill nature?"

"No, I call it good policy."

"Then, Thrasymachus, do you actually think that the unjust are sagacious and good?"

"Certainly," he said; "those who are capable of perfect injustice, who can bring cities and nations under their dominion. But perhaps you imagine that I was talking of pickpockets? Such injustice indeed," he went on, "is, if undetected, profitable in its way. But it is not worth considering beside that which I have described."

"I understand," I said, "that that is what you mean, but I marvelled that you should class injustice with virtue and wisdom and justice with their opposites."

"Well, that is exactly what I do."

"This is a much more stubborn position," I said, "and it is hard to know what to say to it. For if you had said that injustice is profitable, but admitted that it is a vice and evil, as certain people do, then we should have had something to say in accordance with ordinary notions about it; but now it is evident that you will say that it 349 is also beautiful and strong, and you will give it all the attributes which we used to give to justice, since you have actually dared to class it with virtue and wisdom."

"You are a most true prophet," he said.

"Nevertheless," I said, "I must not shrink if I may take it that this is your real opinion, but must take thought and attack the argument; for I imagine, Thrasymachus, that you are really not scoffing, but are saying what is your opinion of the truth."

"What difference does it make to you," he said, "whether this is my real opinion or not? Can you refute the argument?"

"You are right," I said; "but will you try to answer this further question? Do you think that the just man is ready to outdo the just man in anything?"

"Certainly not," he said. "If he was, he would not be the pretty good-natured fellow that he is."

"Then will he outdo the just action?"

"No, not the just action either," he said.

"Would he presume to outdo the unjust man, or would he or would he not think that just?"

"He would think so," he said, "and he would presume, but he would not manage it."

"That," I said, "is not my question. I asked whether the just man presumes and wishes to outdo not the just, but the unjust man."

"It is as you suggest," he said.

"Then what of the unjust? Does he presume to outdo the just man and the just action?"

"What else?" he said, "seeing that he presumes to outdo all the world."

"Will he not also outdo the unjust man and action, and strive to get the most of everything for himself?"

"That is the case."

"Then let us put it in this way," I said. "The just outdoes not the like but the unlike; the unjust man both the like and the unlike."

"You have expressed it excellently," he said.

"And of course," I said, "the unjust is sagacious and good, but the just is neither."

"That is also excellent," he said.

"Then the unjust resembles the sagacious and good, but the just does not?"

"Yes," he said; "the former, being what he is, must be

like those who are of the same nature with himself, and
the latter unlike."

"Good! Then is each man of the same nature as those
whom he is like?"

"What else?"

"Very good, Thrasymachus. Now do you call one man
musical and another unmusical?"

"I do."

"Which do you call wise and which unwise?"

"The musical man, of course, I call wise, the unmusical
unwise."

"Then do you also say that a man is good in the same
respects as he is wise, and evil in the same respects as he
is unwise?"

"Yes."

"And do you say the same of a medical man?"

"Yes."

"Now, my excellent friend, do you think that a musician in tuning a harp would wish to outdo or would presume to get the better of a musician in tightening or
loosening the strings?"

"No."

"But would he outdo the unmusical man?"

"Of necessity," he said.

350    "What of the medical man? In the prescription of food
or drink, would he seek to outdo a medical man in the
practice of medicine?"

"Of course not."

"But would he outdo the non-medical man?"

"Yes."

"Then consider knowledge and ignorance in general,
and tell me whether you think that any expert would
choose to outdo either the actions or the words of another
expert? Would he not rather say or do the same as his
fellow in the same case?"

"Perhaps," he said, "it must be as you suggest."

"But what of the ignorant man? Would he not outdo the expert and the ignorant man with equal indifference?"

"Perhaps."

"And is the scientific man wise?"

"He is."

"And is the wise man good?"

"He is."

"Then the man who is good and wise will not try to outdo his like, but his unlike and opposite?"

"Probably," he said.

"But the man who is bad and unlearned will outdo both his like and his opposite?"

"Apparently."

"But, Thrasymachus," I said, "does not our unjust man outdo both his like and his unlike? Did you not say so?"

"I did."

"While the just man will outdo not his like but his unlike, will he not?"

"Yes."

"Then," I said, "the just man is like the good man and wise, but the unjust man like the bad and unlearned?"

"That seems likely."

"And we agreed that if two men are like one another, they are of the same nature?"

"We did."

"Then the just man is revealed to us as good and wise, but the unjust man as unlearned and bad?"

Thrasymachus made all these admissions, not in the easy way in which I repeat them, but reluctantly, after great resistance and with floods of perspiration, for the weather was hot. Then too for the first time I caught Thrasymachus blushing.

As we had now agreed to rank justice with virtue and wisdom, and injustice with vice and ignorance, I said:

"So much for that point. But we also said that injustice is strong. Have you forgotten, Thrasymachus?"

"No, I remember," he said; "but I am not satisfied with your arguments, and I have something to say on those points. Only if I said it, I know that you would accuse me of speechifying. So either let me say as much as I want, or if you wish to ask questions, ask them; but I shall treat you as we treat garrulous old women, say Yes! Yes! and nod or shake my head as occasion requires."

"Please," I said, "don't assent to what you don't believe."

"Anything to please you," he said, "since you won't let me speak. What else do you want?"

"Nothing in the world," I said. "If this is your desire, follow it, and I shall ask questions."

"Ask."

"Then I shall repeat the question which I asked before, 351 that we may go on where we left off in our inquiry into the relative advantages of justice and injustice. A statement was made that injustice is more powerful and stronger than justice. But," I said, "now that justice is ranked with wisdom and virtue, it will, I imagine, easily be seen to be stronger than injustice, since injustice is ranked with ignorance. No one could any longer fail to recognize that. However, I have no desire, Thrasymachus, to settle the matter in such an off-hand way. I would rather examine it in some such manner as this: Is it not a fact that unjust cities exist, that they attempt to subdue other cities unjustly, that they enslave them and hold many of them in subjection?"

"Surely," he said, "and this will be peculiarly the work of the best city, of that which is most perfectly unjust."

"I understand," I said, "that was your theory. But this is what I am considering. Will the city which becomes master of another attain the position without the aid of justice, or in such a case is justice indispensable?"

"If your recent statement that justice is wisdom be true," he said, "then justice is indispensable; but if mine be true, then injustice."

"I am delighted, Thrasymachus, that you are not content to nod and shake your head, but give most excellent answers."

"I do it to please you," he said.

"It is very good of you. But please me still more by telling me whether you think that a city, or an army, or a band of robbers or thieves, or any other company which pursue some unjust end in common, would be able to effect anything if they were unjust to one another?"

"Of course not," he said.

"What if they were not unjust? Would they effect more?"

"Certainly."

"The explanation is, I suppose, Thrasymachus, that injustice and hatred make men quarrel and fight with one another, while justice makes them friendly and of one mind. Is not that the case?"

"Let us suppose so," he said, "as I don't want to differ from you."

"It is very good of you, my friend; but tell me this: Is it the function of injustice to implant hatred wherever it be? Whether it makes its appearance among freemen or slaves, will it not make them hate and quarrel with one another, and make them incapable of joint action?"

"Certainly."

"What if it makes its appearance in a company of two? Will they not disagree and hate and be enemies one of the other and of the just?"

"They will," he said.

"Then, my admirable friend, if injustice appears in a single individual, will it lose its power or retain it unimpaired?"

"We will suppose that it retains it," he said.

"Then, does not injustice seem to have some such power as this? Wherever it appears, whether in city, tribe, army, or anywhere else, by arousing dissension and division it makes that which possesses it, firstly, incapable of united action; secondly, the enemy of itself, of everything that opposes it, and of the just. Is not that so?"

"Certainly."

"And I fancy that when it exists in an individual it will do the same, and produce its natural effect. Firstly, it will make him at strife and not of one mind with himself, and incapable of action. Secondly, it will make him the enemy of himself and of the just. Is that the case?"

"Yes."

"And the gods are just, my friend?"

"We may presume so," he said.

"Then the unjust man, Thrasymachus, will be the enemy, the just the friend of the gods."

"Feast on your argument," he said, "and be of good cheer. I shall certainly not oppose you. I don't want to displease the company."

"Come, then," I said, "crown my feast for me by answering as you are doing. Certain things we have discovered. The just are shown to be the wiser, the better, and the more capable in action; the unjust are unable even to act together. And when we say that any vigorous joint action is the work of unjust men, our language is not altogether accurate. If they had been thoroughly unjust, they could not have kept their hands off one another. Clearly they must have possessed justice of a sort, enough to keep them from exercising their injustice on each other at the same time as on their victims. They did what they did by reason of their justice, and their injustice partially disabled them in the pursuit of their unjust purposes. For the thorough villains who are perfectly unjust, are also perfectly incapable of action. That I see to be true. The truth of your original statement I

do not see. But now we have to consider what we postponed for subsequent discussion, whether the just live
better and are happier than the unjust. Now this is, I
think, already proved by what we have said. Nevertheless we must consider it more fully. For the subject of our
argument is no trifling matter. It is the question of the
right manner of life."

"Consider, then," he said.

"I am doing so," I said. "Tell me, do you think that a
horse has a function?"

"I do."

"Would you define the function of a horse or of anything else as that work for which it is the indispensable
or the best instrument?"

"I do not understand," he said.

"Let me explain. Can you see with anything but your
eyes?"

"Of course not."

"Or hear with anything but your ears?"

"Certainly not."

"Then could we not justly describe seeing and hearing
as the functions of eyes and ears?"

"Certainly."

"Again, could not a vine shoot be cut with a carving- 353
knife or with a chisel or with many other instruments?"

"Undoubtedly."

"But with no instrument so well, I imagine, as with a
pruning-knife, which is made for the purpose?"

"True."

"Then shall we not call vine-dressing the function of
the pruning-knife?"

"We shall."

"Now, I fancy, you will understand better what I
wanted a moment ago when I asked whether the function
of each thing is that for which it is the indispensable or
the best instrument."

"Yes," he said, "I understand, and I agree with that definition."

"Good," I said. "Now do you not think that everything which has a function has also a corresponding virtue? To revert to our previous instances. We say that the eyes have a function, have they not?"

"They have."

"Then have not the eyes a virtue also?"

"They have."

"Again, the ears were found to have a function, were they not?"

"Yes."

"Then they have a virtue also?"

"They have."

"Can we say the same of everything else?"

"Yes."

"Come now, could the eyes perform their proper function well if they were without their proper virtue, but had the corresponding vice instead?"

"How could they?" he said. "You mean probably blindness instead of sight."

"I mean," I said, "whatever their virtue be. I am not inquiring into that here. My question is whether things perform their own function well by reason of their proper virtue, badly by reason of the corresponding vice?"

"It is as you say," he said.

"Then if ears are deprived of their proper virtue, will they not perform their proper function badly?"

"Certainly."

"Then may we make this principle of general application?"

"I think so."

"Come, then, consider this point next. Has the soul a function which nothing else upon earth can perform save itself? For example, to superintend and rule and advise and so on. Is there anything except the soul to which we could assign these acts as its peculiar functions?"

"Nothing."

"Then what of life? Shall we declare it to be a function of the soul?"

"Assuredly," he said.

"And do we say that the soul has a virtue?"

"We do."

"Then, Thrasymachus, could the soul, if deprived of its proper virtue, perform its proper functions well? Or is that impossible?"

"It is impossible," he said.

"Of necessity an evil soul must rule and superintend badly, but a good soul will do all these things well?"

"Of necessity."

"But have we not agreed that justice is a virtue of the soul, and injustice a vice?"

"Yes, we have."

"Then the just soul and the just man will live well, but the unjust badly?"

"Apparently," he said, "according to your argument."

"Again, he that lives well is blessed and happy, he that 354 lives badly the opposite?"

"Agreed," he said.

"But it is not profitable to be miserable, but to be happy?"

"Undoubtedly."

"Then, my noble Thrasymachus, injustice is never more profitable than justice?"

"Well, Socrates," he said, "let that be your entertainment for the feast of Bendis."

"I have you to thank for it, Thrasymachus," I said, "since you became gentle with me, and stopped being disagreeable. But I have no satisfaction in my feast. That is my fault, not yours. I am like those greedy fellows who before they have properly enjoyed what is before them leave it to snatch at and taste every dish that comes their way. I have done the same. We left the original object of our inquiry, the definition of justice, before we had discovered it, and went off to consider whether it is a vice and ignorance, or wisdom and virtue. Then another argument appeared, to the effect that injustice is more profitable than justice. And I could not refrain from leaving what we were at for this further point, so that now the result of our conversation is that I know nothing. For when I do not know what justice is, I am hardly likely to know whether it is a virtue or not, or whether he that possesses it is unhappy or happy."

# BOOK II

WITH these words I thought that I had finished. But this, it appeared, was after all only a prelude, for Glaucon with his usual fearlessness would not accept Thrasymachus' refutation, but said:

"Socrates, are you content with the appearance of conviction, or do you wish really to convince us that to be just is in every way better than to be unjust?"

"I should certainly prefer," I said, "really to convince you if I could."

"Well," he said, "you do not effect your desire. Tell me now, how do you classify things we call good? Do you think that there are some which we would gladly have, not for their consequences, but because we appreciate them for their own sake; as, for example, enjoyment and those harmless pleasures which produce no further effects beyond the mere pleasurable experience?"

"I certainly think," I said, "that there are some like that."

"Secondly, there are some which we prize both for themselves and for their consequences; as, for example, thought and sight and health. These and similar good things we appreciate for a twofold reason."

"Yes," I said.

"Do you recognize a third class of good things, which includes gymnastic exercises, the undergoing of medical treatment, the practice of medicine, and the other forms of money-making? These are things which we call troublesome but advantageous. We should never take them for themselves, but we accept them for the sake of the rewards and other consequences which they bring."

"There is certainly," I said, "a third class of that description. What then?"

"In which class," he said, "do you place justice?"

358 "In the fairest class, I fancy," I said, "amongst those which he, who would be blessed, must love both for their own sake and for their consequences."

"That is not the opinion of most people," he said. "They place it in the troublesome class of good things, which must be pursued for the sake of the reward and the high place in public opinion which they bring, but which in themselves are irksome and to be avoided."

"I know that people think so," I said. "It is on these grounds that Thrasymachus has always criticized justice and praised injustice. But I am apparently a slow pupil."

"Well," he said, "as Thrasymachus has spoken, let me speak also, and see then whether you are still of the same opinion. Thrasymachus you charmed like a snake, I think, and he gave in sooner than he need have done, but I am not yet satisfied with the exposition either of justice or injustice. I want to know what each is, and what power each has of itself when existing by itself in the soul; their rewards and their consequences may be left out of account. And if you agree, I shall proceed in this way. I shall renew Thrasymachus' argument. First, I shall state what is said to be the nature and origin of justice. Then, secondly, I shall assert that all who practise it do so unwillingly, and that they do so not because justice is good, but because it is indispensable. And, thirdly, that this conduct of theirs is reasonable; for the life of the unjust man is far better than that of the just, according to their statement. I myself, Socrates, am not at all of this opinion. But I get confused; my ears are dinned with the arguments of Thrasymachus and countless others; but from none have I heard as yet

the argument in defence of justice, and its superiority to
injustice, as I want to hear it. For I want to hear the
praises of justice for its own sake, and I have the greatest hopes that I shall do so from you. I shall speak
vehemently therefore in favour of the unjust life, and
in doing so I shall show you the way in which I want
to hear you condemning injustice and praising justice.
Now, do you like my proposal?"

"Most certainly I do," I said, "for on what subject
would a man of sense more gladly converse time and
again?"

"I am delighted to hear you say so," he said. "Listen,
then, and I shall begin as I proposed with the nature
and origin of justice. By nature, men say, to do injustice is good, to suffer it evil, but there is more evil in
suffering injustice than there is good in inflicting it.
Therefore when men act unjustly towards one another,
and thus experience both the doing and the suffering,
those amongst them who are unable to compass the one
and escape the other, come to this opinion: that it is
more profitable that they should mutually agree neither 359
to inflict injustice nor to suffer it. Hence men began to
establish laws and covenants with one another, and they
called what the law prescribed lawful and just. This,
then, is the origin and nature of justice. It is a mean
between the best—doing injustice with impunity— and
the worst—suffering injustice without possibility of re-
quital. Thus justice, being a mean between those extremes, is looked upon with favour, not because it is
good, but because the inability to inflict injustice makes
it valuable. For no one who had the power to inflict
the injustice and was anything of a man would ever
make a contract of mutual abstention from injustice
with any one else. He would be mad if he did. Such,
Socrates, is the nature of justice, and such is its origin,
according to the popular account."

"Now, that those who practise justice do so unwillingly and from inability to inflict, will be seen most clearly
if we make the following supposition. Suppose we take
the just and the unjust man and give each power to do
whatever he will, and then follow them and see where
each is led by his desires. We shall catch the just man
following undisguisedly the very same road as the unjust. He would be led on by his desire to outdo his
fellows: every nature naturally pursues that as good,
though law compels it to turn aside and reverence equality. The impunity I refer to would be best exemplified if
they could have the power possessed by the ancestors of
Gyges the Lydian in the story. For they say that he was
a shepherd, a servant of the reigning king of Lydia.
There was a great storm of rain and an earthquake
where he was feeding his flock: the ground was rent,
and a chasm appeared. In amazement he looked in, then
descended into the chasm, and saw there many marvellous things which the story enumerates. Among them
was a horse of bronze, hollow, with windows in its sides.
He looked in and saw inside a dead body, which seemed
of almost superhuman size. On the hand was a golden
ring. He took this and nothing besides, then came away.
When the shepherds held their monthly gathering at
which they arranged for the sending of their report on
the flocks to the king, he came with the ring on his
finger. As he was sitting with the others he happened to
turn round the bezel of the ring till it came to the inside of his hand. On his doing so he became invisible
360 to his companions, and they talked of him as of an
absent man. In astonishment he touched his ring again
and turned the bezel back to the outside of his hand.
As he turned it he became visible again. Then having
noticed thus he tried whether this power really lay in
the ring, and he found that he became invisible when
he turned the bezel inwards, visible when he turned it

outwards. When he had made this discovery he at once
contrived to be one of the messengers sent to the king.
Arriving at the palace he seduced the queen, plotted
with her against the king, killed him, and so obtained
the crown.

'Now, if there were two such rings, and the just
man took one and the unjust the other, no one, it is
thought, would be of such adamantine nature as to abide
in justice and have the strength to abstain from theft,
and to keep his hands from the goods of others, when
it would be in his power to steal anything he wished
from the very market-place with impunity, to enter men's
houses and have intercourse with whom he would,
to kill or to set free whomsoever he pleased; in short,
to walk among men as a god. And, in so doing, the just
man would act precisely as the unjust. Both would follow the same path. This, surely, may be cited as strong
evidence that no man is just willingly, but only on compulsion. Justice is not a good to the individual, for
every one is unjust whenever he thinks injustice possible. Every man thinks that injustice is more profitable
to the individual than justice, and thinks rightly, according to the supporters of this theory; for if any man
who possessed this power we have described should yet
refuse to do unjustly or to rob his fellows, all who knew
of his conduct would think him the most miserable
and foolish of men, but they would praise him to each
other's faces, their fear of suffering injustice extorting
that deceit from them. So much, then, for that. Now
this question concerning the life of these two men we
shall be able to decide aright only by contrasting the
extremes of justice and injustice. How shall we make
our contrast? In this way. Let us abstract nothing from
the injustice of the unjust or from the justice of the
just; each shall be perfect in his own way of life. Firstly,
then, the unjust man shall be like a clever craftsman.

The skilful captain or doctor can discern what is possible and what is impossible in his art. He attempts the one and leaves the other alone; and if by any chance he makes a mistake, he is able to retrieve it. Similarly the unjust man, if he is to be thoroughly unjust, shall show discernment in his unjust deeds, and shall not be found out. If he is caught, we must consider him a failure; for it is the last word in injustice to seem just without being it. To the perfectly unjust man, then, we must give perfect injustice, and abstract nothing from it. We must allow him to do the fullest injustice and be reputed truly just. If ever he makes a mistake, he must be able to retrieve it. If any of his unjust deeds are brought to light, his eloquence will be convincing in his favour. He will be able to use force where force is needed, thanks to his courage, his strength, and his resources of friends and wealth. Such is the unjust man. Beside him, in accordance with the argument, let us place our just man, a simple and noble character, one who, as Aeschylus says, desires not to seem, but to be good. The semblance, indeed, we must take from him; for if he is reputed just, he will enjoy the honours and rewards that such a reputation earns, and thus it will not be apparent, it is objected, whether he is just for justice' sake or the honours' and rewards' sake. He must be stripped of everything except justice, and made the very counterpart of the other man. He shall do no injustice, and be reputed altogether unjust, that his justice may be tested as being proof against ill repute and its consequences, and he shall go on his way unchanged till death, all his life seeming unjust but being just. Thus these two will have come to the extremes of justice and of injustice, and we may judge which of them is the happier."

"Hallo, my dear Glaucon," I said, "how energetically you are scouring these two for judgment, as if they were a pair of statues."

"I am doing my best," he said. "Well, given two such characters, it is not difficult now, I fancy, to go on to discover what sort of life awaits each of them. Let me describe it. If my description is rather harsh, remember, Socrates, that those who praise injustice above justice are responsible, and not I. They will say that our just man will be scourged, racked, fettered, will have his eyes burnt out, and at last, after all manner of suffering, will be crucified, and will learn that he ought to desire not to be but to seem just; for those words of Aeschylus applied much more truly to the unjust man. For it is the unjust man in reality, they will say, who, as his practice is akin to truth and his life not ruled by appearances, desires not to seem but to be unjust,

> And from the deep-ploughed furrow of his heart
> Reaps harvest rich of goodly purposes.

For, firstly, his semblance of justice brings him rule in his city. Then he may marry and give in marriage as he pleases; he may contract or enter into partnership with whom he will, and since he has no scruples against unjust dealings, he can besides make large profits. Therefore, when he enters into a contest, whether public or private, he comes out victorious and gets the better of his enemies. By so doing he becomes rich, helps his friends and harms his enemies, and on the gods he bestows sacrifices and offerings fitting and magnificent. Far better than the just man can he serve the gods or whatsoever man he pleases. So that even the love of the gods is more appropriately his than the just man's. Thus they say, Socrates, that at the hands of gods and men life is made richer for the unjust than for the just."

After Glaucon had spoken, I was going to say something in reply, when his brother Adeimantus said:

"You do not imagine, I hope, Socrates, that the argument has been adequately expressed?"

"Why, has it not?" I said.

"What most needed saying has been omitted," he said.

"Well," I said, "you know the proverb, 'Let brother help brother.' So if Glaucon falls short, you must come to his aid. I must admit he has said enough to throw me and make me quite incapable of coming to the aid of justice."

"Nonsense," he said. "But listen to what I have to say. For we must also examine the arguments on the other side, those which praise justice and condemn injustice, and we shall see more clearly what I think Glaucon means. For parents and all who have any one to care for, when they exhort their children and say that it is right to be just, do not praise justice itself, but the reputation it brings. Their desire is that their children may seem just, and may thus obtain the rewards that reputation brings to the just man—offices of state and advantageous marriages, and all the benefits which Glaucon has been enumerating. Even higher than this do these persons rate the importance of seeming; for they cast the esteem of the gods into the scale, and can tell of countless benefits which they say the gods give to the pious. The noble Hesiod and Homer are with them here. The first tells what the gods do for the just. First of their oak trees:

> Acorns grow on the branches, and honey is found in the tree trunks;
> Rich in wool are their flocks, bowed down by the weight of their fleeces,

and they have many other similar blessings. And Homer says much the same. Talking of someone he speaks of him as:

> Like a never ill-deserving king,
> Whose equal hand impartially doth temper
> Greatness and Goodness: to whom therefore bears
> The black earth store of all grain, trees confers

Cracking with burthen, long-lived herds creates,
All which the sea with her sorts emulates;

and still more delightful than these are the blessings
which Musaeus and his son bestow on the just men from
the gods; for they take them in their story to Hades,
where they seat them on couches and prepare a banquet
for the saints, making them spend all their time gar-
landed and drunken, as though they thought an eternity
of drunkenness the fairest reward of virtue. Others
make out the rewards of the gods to be even more far-
reaching than these; for they say that a man who is
holy and abides by his oath, leaves children's children
for a posterity behind him. In these and other similar
ways they sing the praises of justice. But the wicked
and unjust they bury in a muddy mire in Hades, and
make them carry water in a sieve. In life, too, they
bring them into ill repute; and all the punishments
which in Glaucon's description were suffered by those
who are just but reputed to be unjust, all these, they
say, fall upon the unjust. More than that they do not
say. This is their praise and their condemnation of
each.

"Further, Socrates, consider another way of speaking
of justice and injustice which we find in ordinary conversation and in poetry. All in unison sing that temperance and justice are beautiful, but hard and troublesome, whilst their opposites are pleasant and easy of at-
tainment, and only bad in appearance and by legal
convention. Unjust deeds, they say, are on the whole
more profitable than just. They have no hesitation in
pronouncing wicked men happy if they are rich and
powerful, or in giving them honours, both public and
private; while they dishonour or slight all who are
weak and poor, though they acknowledge them to be
the better men. The stories they tell of the attitude of
the gods towards virtue are the most astonishing of

all. They say that the gods have actually given misfortunes and a life of sorrow to many good men, and the opposite to many evil. Mendicant priests and soothsayers go the round of rich men's doors and persuade them that they have power from the gods, whereby, if any sin has been committed by a man or his ancestors, they can heal it by charms and sacrifices performed to the accompaniment of feasting and pleasure, and if any man wishes to injure an enemy, at a small cost he may harm just and unjust indifferently; for with their incantations and magic formulae they say they can persuade the gods to serve their will. To support all these assertions they quote the poets. Some tell of the easiness of vice in such passages as this:

> Easy of choice is evil and pleasant it is in the choosing,
> Very smooth is the way and close beside us it lieth.
> But sweat the gods have ordained must be ours in the getting of virtue,

and a long journey too on a rough and uphill road. Others quote Homer to prove that men can turn the gods from their will, as when he says:

> The gods themselves are flexible:
> Perfumes, benign devotions, savours of offerings burned,
> And holy rites the engines are with which their hearts are turned
> By men that pray to them, whose faith their sins have falsified.

And they produce a crowd of books by Musaeus and Orpheus, the descendants of the moon and the Muses, as they say. These are their liturgies, and they persuade not only individuals, but whole cities, that there are modes of redemption and purification from sins for the 365 living and for the departed also, by means of sacrifices and pleasurable amusements which they call mysteries. These redeem us from the evils of the other world; if they are neglected, peril awaits us. Now, my dear Socra-

tes," he said, "when concerning the way in which gods
and men honour virtue and vice, we find statements
such as these made repeatedly and in the same tenor,
what can we think will be their effect on the souls of
those who hear them, young men of good natural dispositions who, like bees, fly from one statement to another, gather from them all an answer to the question:
What must a man be, and what paths must he take, if
he would live the best possible life? Naturally he will
say to himself in the words of Pindar. 'Shall I by justice
or by crooked wiles ascend the higher wall' and so
fortify myself for life? For what do men say? If I am
just, unless I also seem just, I gain no advantage, but
manifest toil and pains. But if I am unjust and have acquired the appearance of justice, a heavenly life, they
say, is mine. Well, then, since seeming, as the wise men
show me, does violence even to truth and is the lord of
happiness, I must turn to it with all my heart. The
fore-court of my house of life I must adorn with the
presentment of virtue, but behind the walls I shall hide
the crafty subtle Reynard whom that wise Archilochus
loved. 'But,' someone says, 'it is not easy to be bad and
never be found out.' No, we answer, and nothing else
that is great is easy. Still, if we would be happy, this is
the path we must follow. The tracks of the argument
point this way. That we may not be found out, we shall
organize clubs and fellowships, and there are masters of
persuasion who impart the wisdom of the public assembly and of the law courts. By their help persuasion and
force will be our weapons, and we shall pay no penalty
for our aggrandizement. 'But the gods you can neither
cheat nor force.' But if they do not exist, or if they
have no concern with men, why should we care whether
we cheat them or not? while if there are gods who concern themselves with men, we know and have heard
nothing of them save from the lore and the genealogies

of the poets, and it is they who say that they can be turned from their will and persuaded 'by prayer, slaying of victims and offerings,' and we must believe them altogether or not at all. If we are to believe them, it is best to practise injustice and then make sacrifice from our ill-gotten gains. For if we are just, all that we shall get is immunity from the penalties of heaven, but we shall lose the gains of injustice. But if we are unjust, we shall make those gains ours, and by making entreaty for our sin and transgression we shall persuade the gods and get off without punishment. 'But in Hades we shall be punished for our unjust deeds of this life, we or our children's children.' But the young man will make his calculations and reply: My dear sir, the mysteries and the gods of redemption are of great power. So say the greatest of cities and the poets who are the children of gods, and the prophets who came from the gods and tell us that such things be."

"Now, on what grounds can we still prefer justice to the greatest injustice? For if we combine injustice with a spurious decorum we shall fare according to our mind with gods and men alike, both in life and death. That is the report of the many and of the best authorities on the subject. Now after all that has been said, Socrates, how can it be contrived that a man should wish to honour justice if he has any power of mind, or wealth, or body, or birth? Will he not smile when he hears its praises? So that if any man can prove the falsehood of what we have said and has certain knowledge that justice is best, still he will surely be very ready to excuse those who are unjust, and will not be angry with them. He knows that a man may by divine grace of nature dislike injustice or may have acquired knowledge and so avoid it, but that apart from these no one is just of his own will, and it is by reason of cowardice or age or some other weakness that men condemn the injustice which they cannot practise. The truth of this is manifest. Of such men the first to attain to power is the first to practise injustice to the measure of his ability. And the cause of it all is nothing else than this, to put it in the words which Glaucon used to you at the beginning of the argument, Socrates: 'Excellent sir, of all you who profess yourselves praisers of justice, from the heroes of old whose words have come down to us, to the men of to-day, not one of you has ever condemned injustice or praised justice for anything but their reputations, their values in men's eyes, and their rewards. But what each does of itself by the power of its own nature, when dwelling in the heart of him who possesses it, hidden from gods and men alike: that no one has ever thoroughly considered either in poetry or in prose: nor shown that injustice is the greatest of evils that the soul contains within herself, and justice the greatest good. Had you all from the beginning spoken in that 367 strain, and so persuaded us even from our youth, we should not be all watching our neighbours to prevent them from committing injustice. Each man would himself be his own best guard, in his fear lest by doing unjustly he should have portion with the greatest of evils.' That, Socrates, and even more perhaps, is what Thrasymachus, and possibly others with him, would say concerning justice and injustice, ignorantly, as I conceive, reversing the inherent power of each. Now I, for I have no wish to deceive you, have put their case as vehemently as I can, from a desire to hear you contradict them. So do not be content with proving to us in your argument that justice is stronger than injustice, but show what effect each has in him who possesses it, that makes the one in itself and for itself good, and the other bad. Abstract the reputation of each, as Glaucon urged. For unless you abstract from each its proper reputation, and give it one that does not belong to it, we shall say that you are praising not the reality but the appearance of justice, and condemning not the reality but the appearance of injustice; that your advice is that we should be unjust and not be found out; and that you agree with Thrasymachus that justice is the good of another, the advantage of the stronger, while injustice is advantageous and profitable to oneself, but disadvantageous to the weaker. Now you have agreed that justice belongs to the class of the greatest goods, those that are worthy of acquisition for the sake of their consequences, but very much more for their own sake. You have ranked it with sight, hearing, thought, health, and with all other goods which are genuine and real, good in their own nature, not for the reputation they bring. Now therefore praise justice in this; show how in itself and by itself it benefits its possessor, and how injustice harms him, and leave rewards and reputations for others to praise. For I can put up with others praising justice and condemning injustice in this way, eulogizing and reviling the respective reputations and rewards they bring, but not with your doing so, unless you insist on it, for you have spent all your life in this one inquiry. Therefore do not be content with proving to us that justice is stronger than injustice, but show what effect they each have on their possessors that makes them in themselves and by themselves, whether or not they be hid from gods and men, the one good and the other bad."

I have always admired the characters of Glaucon and Adeimantus, but when I had heard this I was quite extraordinarily pleased, and said: "Well named was your father, and happily did Glaucon's lover describe you in the opening line of the verses he wrote, when you had distinguished yourselves at the battle of Megara:

Sons of Ariston, children divine of a famous father.

That seems to me very true, my friends. For there is assuredly something divine in you, if you are not persuaded that injustice is better than justice when you can speak so eloquently on its behalf. And I think that you really are not persuaded. I conclude so from your general character. For to judge by your arguments alone I should distrust you. But the greater my confidence in you, the less do I feel that I know how to meet the situation. I cannot come to the rescue. I do not think it is in me. Indeed you convince me of it. For I thought I had proved that justice is better than injustice in my argument with Thrasymachus, which you have rejected. And yet I cannot refuse to come to the rescue. I fear it would be impious were I to stand by and refuse aid while justice was being reviled, and did not come to her rescue so long as there was breath in my body, and I had voice to speak. It is best therefore that I should succour her as well as I can."

Glaucon and the others implored me by all means to come to the rescue, and not let the argument drop, but to investigate what justice and injustice are, and what is the truth about their advantages. So I said what seemed to me best.

"The search in which we are engaged is no easy matter, but needs sharp eyes, I see. Therefore, as we are not clever people, I think," I said, "that we had best adopt a method of this kind. If persons of not very sharp eyesight were given the task of reading small letters at a considerable distance, and one of them noticed that the same inscription was written up elsewhere in larger letters and on a larger space, they would, I imagine, consider it a lucky find, and would first read the larger letters and then examine whether the smaller ones were the same."

"That is certainly true," said Adeimantus. "But, Socrates, what do you see in our search after justice that is analogous to that?"

"I shall tell you," I said. "Justice, we say, is the attribute of an individual, but also of a whole city, is it not?"

"Certainly."

"And is not a city greater than an individual?"

"It is."

"Then perhaps justice may exist in greater proportions in the greater space, and be easier to discover. So 369 if you are willing, we shall begin our inquiry as to its nature in cities, and after that let us continue our inquiry in the individual also, looking for the likeness of the greater in the form of the less."

"I think your proposal is excellent," he said.

"Now," I said, "if in our argument we were to watch a city in the making, should we not see its justice and injustice in the making also?"

"Very probably," he said.

"And when we have done this, may we not hope that we shall more easily see that which we are seeking?"

"Yes, surely."

"Then do you think we should proceed with our attempt? I warn you that, in my opinion, it will be no small task, so take care how you make up your minds."

"They are made up" said Adeimantus; "will you please proceed?"

"The origin of a city," I said, "is, in my opinion, due to the fact that no one of us is sufficient for himself, but each is in need of many things. Or do you think there is any other cause for the founding of cities?"

"No," he said, "none,"

"Then men, being in want of many things, gather into one settlement many partners and helpers; one taking to himself one man, and another another, to satisfy their diverse needs, and to this common settlement we give the name of city. Is not that so?"

"Certainly."

"And when they exchange with one another, giving or receiving as the case may be, does not each man think that such exchange is to his own good?"

"Certainly."

"Come, then," I said. "Let us in our argument construct the city from the beginning. Apparently it will be the outcome of our need?"

"Surely."

"But the first and greatest of our needs is the provision of food to support existence and life?"

"Yes, assuredly."

"The second the provision of a dwelling-place, and the third of clothing, and so on?"

"That is so."

"Come, then," I said, "how will our city be able to supply a sufficiency of all those things? Will it not be by having one man a farmer, another a builder, and a third a weaver? Shall we add a shoemaker, and perhaps another provider of bodily needs?"

"Certainly."

"Then the city of bare necessity will consist of four or five men?"

"Apparently."

"Well, then, should each of these men place his own work at the disposal of all in common? For example, should our one farmer provide corn for four and spend fourfold time and labour on the provision of corn, and then share it with the rest; or should he pay no attention to the others, and provide only a fourth part of the corn for himself in a fourth of the time, and 370 spend the other three-fourths of his time in providing a house, clothes, and shoes? Should he not have the trouble of sharing with the others, but rather provide with his own hands what he wants for himself?"

Adeimantus answered: "The first alternative, Socrates, is perhaps the easier."

"Well, it is certainly not strange that it is. For as you were speaking, I myself was thinking that, in the first place, no two of us are by nature altogether alike. Our capacities differ. Some are fit for one work, some for another. Do you agree?"

"I do."

"Well, then, would better work be done on the principle of one man many trades, or of one man one trade?"

"One man one trade is better," he said.

"Yes, for I fancy that it is also evident that, in work, opportunities which we pass by are lost."

"That is evident."

"I fancy that things to be done will not wait the good time of the doer. Rather the doer must wait on the opportunity for action, and not leave the doing of it for his idle moments."

"He must."

"And so more tasks of each kind are accomplished, and the work is better and is done more easily when each man works at the one craft for which nature fits him, that being free from all other occupations he may wait on its opportunities."

"That is certainly the case."

"Then, Adeimantus, we need more citizens than four to provide the above-mentioned necessities. For the farmer, naturally, will not make his own plough if it is to be a good one, nor his mattock, nor any of the other farming tools. No more will the builder, who also needs many tools. And the same will hold of the weaver and the shoemaker, will it not?"

"True."

"Then carpenters and smiths and many other artisans of that kind will become members of our little city, and make it populous?"

"Certainly."

"Yet it would not be so very large if we added herdsmen and shepherds and others of that class, that the farmers may have oxen for ploughing, and both builders and farmers may have yoke animals for their carting, and that the weavers and shoemakers may have skins and wool."

"Nor so very small if so well provided."

"Again," I said, "it will be almost impossible to have our city so situated that it will need no imports."

"Yes, that will be impossible."

"Then it will need more men still to bring it what it needs from other cities?"

"It will."

"And if they are to get what they need from other people, their agent must take with him something that 371 those others want. If he goes empty-handed, he will return empty-handed, will he not?"

"I think so."

"Then the workers of our city must not only make enough for home consumption; they must also produce goods of the number and kind required by other people?"

"Yes, they must."

"Then our city will need more farmers, and more of all the other craftsmen?"

"Yes."

"And among the rest it will need more agents who are to import and export the different kinds of goods. These are merchants, are they not?"

"Yes."

"We shall need merchants, then?"

"Certainly."

"And if the commerce is over sea, we shall need a host of others who are experts in sea-trading."

"Yes, there will be many of them."

"Again, in the city itself how will men exchange the produce of their labours with one another? For this was the original reason of our establishing the principle of community and founding a city."

"Clearly," he said, "by selling and buying."

"This will give us a market-place, and money as a token for the sake of exchange."

"Certainly."

"Then if the farmer or any other craftsman brings his produce into the market-place, and meets there none who wish to exchange their goods with him, is he to sit idle in the market-place when he might be working?"

"Certainly not," said he. "There are men who have taken note of this, and devote themselves to this service. In well-governed cities they are usually those who are weakest in body, and incapable of any other work. They have to stay there in the market-place and exchange money for goods with those who want to sell, and goods for money with those who want to buy."

"Then," I said, "this necessity brings shopkeepers into our city. We give the name of shopkeepers, do we not, to those who serve buyers and sellers in their stations at the market-place, but the name of merchants to those who travel from city to city?"

"Certainly."

"Then are there not other agents also who have no mental gifts to make them at all worthy to share in the community, but who have bodily strength sufficient for hard labour? They sell the use of their strength, and the price they get for it being called hire, they are known, I fancy, as hired labourers?"

"Certainly."

"Then these hired labourers, too, serve to complete our city?"

"I think so."

"Then, Adeimantus, has our city now grown to its perfection?"

"Perhaps."

"Then, where in it shall we find justice and injustice? With which of the elements we have noticed did they make their entry?"

"I cannot see how they came in, Socrates," he said, 372 "unless we find them somewhere in the mutual needs of these same persons."

"Well," I said, "perhaps you are right. But let us consider the matter and not draw back. And first, let us consider what will be the manner of life of men so equipped. Will they not spend their time in the production of corn and wine and clothing and shoes? And they will build themselves houses; in summer they will generally work without their coats and shoes, but in winter they will be well clothed and shod. For food they will make meal from their barley and flour from their wheat, and kneading and baking them they will heap their noble scones and loaves on reeds or fresh leaves, and lying on couches of bryony and myrtle boughs will feast with their children, drink wine after their repast, crown their heads with garlands, and sing hymns to the gods. So they will live with one another in happiness, not begetting children above their means, and guarding against the danger of poverty or war."

Here Glaucon interrupted and said: "Apparently you give your men dry bread to feast on."

"You are right," I said; "I forgot that they would have a relish with it. They will have salt and olives and cheese, and they will have boiled dishes with onions and such vegetables as one gets in the country. And I expect we must allow them a dessert of figs, and peas and beans, and they will roast myrtle berries and acorns at the fire, and drink their wine in moderation. Leading so peaceful and healthy a life they will naturally attain to a good old age, and at death leave their children to live as they have done."

"Why," said Glaucon, "if you had been founding a city of pigs, Socrates, this is just how you would have fattened them."

"Well, Glaucon, how must they live?"

"In an ordinary decent manner," he said. "If they are not to be miserable, I think they must have couches to lie on and tables to eat from, and the ordinary dishes and dessert of modern life."

"Very well," I said, "I understand. We are considering, apparently, the making not of a city merely, but of a luxurious city. And perhaps there is no harm in doing so. From that kind, too, we shall soon learn, if we examine it, how justice and injustice arise in cities. I, for my part, think that the city I have described is the true one, what we may call the city of health. But if you wish, let us also inspect a city which is suffering from inflammation. There is no reason why we should not. Well, then, for some people the arrangements we have made will not be enough. The mode of living will not satisfy them. They shall have couches and tables and other furniture; rich dishes too, and fragrant oils and perfumes, and courtesans and sweetmeats, and many varieties of each. Then again we must make more than a bare provision for those necessities we mentioned at the first, houses and clothes and shoes. We must start painting and embroidery, and collect gold and ivory, and so on, must we not?"

"Yes," he said.

"Then we must make our city larger. For the healthy city will not now suffice. We need one swollen in size, and full of a multitude of things which necessity would not introduce into cities. There will be all kinds of hunters and there will be the imitators; one crowd of imitators in figure and colour, and another of imitators in music; poets and their servants, rhapsodists, actors, dancers and theatrical agents; and makers of all kinds of articles, of those used for women's adornment, for example. Then, too, we shall need more servants; or do you think we can do without footmen, wet-nurses, dry-nurses, lady's maids, barbers, and cooks and confectioners, besides? Then we shall want swineherds too; we had none in our former city—there was no need—but we shall need them along with all the others for this city. And we shall need great quantities of all kinds of cattle if people are to eat them. Shall we not?"

"Surely."

"Then if we lead this kind of life we shall require doctors far more often than we should have done in the first city?"

"Certainly."

"Then I dare say even the land which was sufficient to support the first population will be now insufficient and too small?"

"Yes," he said.

"Then if we are to have enough for pasture and ploughland, we must take a slice from our neighbours' territory. And they will want to do the same to ours, if they also overpass the bounds of necessity and plunge into reckless pursuit of wealth?"

"Yes, that must happen, Socrates," he said.

"Then shall we go to war at that point, Glaucon, or what will happen?"

"We shall go to war," he said.

"And we need not say at present whether the effects of war are good or bad. Let us only notice that we have found the origin of war in those passions which are most responsible for all the evils that come upon cities and the men that dwell in them."

"Certainly."

"Then, my friend, our city will need to be still greater, and by no small amount either, but by a whole 374 army. It will defend all the substance and wealth we have described, and will march out and fight the invaders."

"Why," he said, "are they not capable of doing that themselves?"

"Certainly not," I said, "if you and the rest of us were right in the principle we agreed upon when we were shaping the city. I think we agreed, if you remember, that it was impossible for one man to work well at many crafts."

"True," he said.

"Well," I said, "does not the business of war seem a matter of craftsmanship?"

"Yes, certainly," he said.

"Then ought we to be more solicitous for the craft of shoemaking than for the craft of war?"

"By no means."

"But did we not forbid our shoemaker to attempt to be at the same time a farmer or a weaver or housebuilder? He was to be a shoemaker only, in order that our shoemaking work might be well done. So with all the others: we gave each man one trade, that for which nature had fitted him. Nothing else was to occupy his time, but he was to spend his life working at that, using all his opportunities to the best advantage and letting none go by. And is not efficiency in war more important than anything else? Or is it such a simple profession that a farmer or a shoemaker, or any other craftsman, can be a soldier in the intervals of his craft, though no one in the world would find that practice in his leisure moments or anything short of studying the game from his youth would make him a good draught or dice player? Is he to take up a shield, or any other of the weapons and tools of war, and in a single day to become an efficient antagonist in a heavy-armed engagement or in any other kind of battle, though the mere handling of any other tools will never make a craftsman or an athlete, and though tools are useless to the man who has not acquired the special knowledge and gone through the proper training for their use?"

"Yes, tools that taught their own use would be worth having."

"Then," I said, "because the work of our guardians is the most important of all, it will demand the most exclusive attention and the greatest skill and practice."

"I certainly think so," he said.

"And will it not need also a nature fitted for this profession?"

"Surely."

"Then it will be our business to do our best to select the proper persons and to determine the proper character required for the guardians of the city?"

"Yes, we shall have to do that." 375

"Well, certainly it is no trivial task we have undertaken, but we must be brave and do all in our power."

"Yes, we must," he said.

"Do you not think, then," I said, "that so far as their fitness for guarding is concerned, a noble youth and a well-bred dog are very much alike?"

"What do you mean?"

"I mean, for example, that both must be sharp-sighted, quick of foot to pursue the moment they perceive, and strong enough to make captures and overcome opposition when necessary."

"Yes," he said; "all these qualities are required."

"And since they are good fighters, they must certainly be brave."

"Surely."

"But will either horse or dog or any animal be brave if it is not spirited? Have you not observed that spirit is unconquerable and irresistible? Every soul possessed by it will meet any danger fearless and unshrinking."

"I have noticed that."

"Then we are quite clear as to what must be the bodily characteristics of our guardians?"

"Yes."

"And as to their mental qualities, we know they must be spirited."

"Certainly."

"Then, Glaucon," I said, "with such natures as these, how are they to be prevented from behaving savagely towards one another and the other citizens?"

"By Zeus," he said, "that will not be easy."

"Still we must have them gentle to their fellows and fierce to their enemies. If we can't effect that, they will prevent the enemy from destroying the city by doing it first themselves."

"True," he said.

"What then are we to do?" I said. "Where shall we find a character at once gentle and high-spirited? For a gentle nature is surely the antithesis of a spirited one?"

"So it appears."

"Nevertheless, if either is lacking, we shall certainly not have a good guardian. But this combination is apparently unattainable, and so you see it follows that a good guardian is an impossibility."

"It looks like it," he said.

I was perplexed, but reflecting on what had gone before I said, "We certainly deserve to be in difficulties, for we have forsaken the simile we set before ourselves."

"What do you mean?"

"Have we not noticed that natures are to be found

possessed of those opposite qualities, for all that we thought them non-existent?"

"Where?"

"In many animals, but perhaps best in that with which we compared our guardian. Well-bred dogs, you surely know, are naturally of that disposition—as gentle as possible to their friends and those whom they know, but the very opposite to strangers."

"Yes, I know that."

"Then," I said, "we may assume that the character we seek in our guardian is possible, and not contrary to nature?"

"I think we may."

"Do you think, then, that there is another quality indispensable to the guardian? The spirited element is not enough; he must be of a philosophical nature as well."

"What are you saying?" he said. "I don't understand." 376

"You will notice this other quality in dogs," I said. "It certainly is surprising in the creatures."

"What quality?"

"Why, when dogs see a stranger, without any provocation they get angry; but if they see someone they know, they welcome him, even though they have received no kindness at his hands. Have you never wondered at that?"

"I have hardly thought of it before. But that certainly is how they behave."

"Well, but this instinct in the dog is a very fine thing, and genuinely philosophical."

"In what way?"

"Why, he distinguishes between a friendly and an unfriendy face, simply by the fact that he knows the one and is ignorant of the other. Now, how could the creature be anything but fond of learning when knowledge and ignorance are its criterion to distinguish between the friendly and the strange?"

"How, indeed?"

"Well, but is it not the same thing to be fond of learning and to be philosophical?" I asked.

"It is," he said.

"Then shall we confidently apply this to man? If he is to be gentle to his friends and acquaintances, he must be by nature philosophical and fond of learning."

"Let us do so," he said.

"Then he who is to be a good and noble guardian of our city will be by nature philosophical and spirited, and quick and strong."

"Yes, he will be all those things," he said.

"This, then, will be his original character. Now, how shall we rear and educate these guardians? Will this inquiry help us in discovering the object of all our search, namely, how justice and injustice arise in a city? We don't want to miss anything, and yet we mustn't be tedious."

Glaucon's brother answered: "I for one most certainly anticipate that a consideration of this question will help us."

"In that case, my dear Adeimantus," I said, "we must certainly go on with it, even though it should prove rather lengthy."

"Yes, we must."

"Come, then, we shall be like idle story-tellers in a story, and our tale shall be the education of these men."

"Yes, by all means."

"Well, what is our system of education to be? Is it not difficult to improve on what has been worked out through long generations? We have gymnastics for the body, and music for the soul."

"Yes."

"Then we shall begin our education with music before gymnastics, shall we not?"

"Surely."

"Do you include literature in music, or not?" I said.

"I do."

"Are there not two kinds of literature—true and false?"

"Yes."

"Must our education include both, or should we begin with the false?"

377

"I don't understand what you mean," he said.

"Do you not understand," I said, "that we begin by telling stories to children? These surely are, as a general rule, false, though there may be some truth in them. But we tell the children stories before we give them gymnastic exercises."

"Yes."

"But that is what I said—literature is to come before gymnastics."

"You were right," he said.

"Then do you know that the most important part of every task is the beginning of it, especially when we are dealing with anything young and tender? For then it can be most easily moulded, and whatever impression any one cares to stamp upon it sinks in."

"Most certainly."

"Then shall we carelessly and without more ado allow our children to hear any casual stories told by any casual persons, and so to receive into their souls views of life for the most part at variance with those which we think they ought to hold when they come to man's estate?"

"No, we shall certainly not allow that."

"Our first duty then, it seems, is to set a watch over the makers of stories, to select every beautiful story they make, and reject any that are not beautiful. Then we shall persuade nurses and mothers to tell those selected stories to the children. Thus will they shape their souls with stories far more than they can shape their bodies with their hands. But we shall have to throw away most of the stories they tell now."

"What kind do you mean?" he said.

"In the big stories we can discern the little; for both big and little must bear the same form, and have the same effect. Do you not agree?"

"I do," he said; "but I don't see any more what you mean by the big stories."

"Those," I said, "that Hesiod and Homer and the other poets have told us; for surely they have composed untrue stories, and have told, and do tell them, to men."

"But what kind do you mean, and what fault do you find in them?"

"A fault," I said, "that deserves immediate and emphatic condemnation, especially if the untruth have no beauty in it."

"What is that?"

"When any man in describing the character of gods and heroes does it badly, like an artist whose drawing is absolutely unlike the things he wishes to draw."

"Well," he said, "it is certainly right that stories of that kind should be condemned; but what do you mean, and to what do you refer?"

"Well, firstly, the poet, who told the greatest of falsehoods of the greatest of beings, told a falsehood with no beauty in it, when he said that Ouranos did 378 what Hesiod said he did, and that Kronos, took vengeance on him. And as for the deeds of Kronos, and what he suffered at his son's hands, even if these stories are true, I should not think we could so lightly repeat them to the young and foolish. It were best to be silent about them, or if they had to be told, it should be done under the seal of silence to as few hearers as possible, and after the sacrifice not of the mystic pig but some great and almost unprocurable victim, so that very few would hear the story."

"Yes," he said, "those are certainly hard stories."

"Yes, Adeimantus," I said, "and stories that are not to be told in our city. We must not let a young man hear that in committing the most awful crimes or in requiting an unjust father's misdeeds with every conceivable cruelty, he would be doing nothing extraordinary, but only acting like the chiefest and greatest of the gods."

"No, certainly not," he said. "I too think it inexpedient to tell such stories."

"And we shall strictly forbid," I said, "all stories of gods making war on or plotting against or fighting other gods. To begin with, they are not true; and besides, those who are to guard our city must think it the most deadly sin to quarrel easily with one another. The fights of the giants and the other many and varied strifes of gods and heroes with kinsfolk and friends must not be told them in story or woven on their tapestry. But if we can in any way find stories to persuade them that no citizen has ever hated another, and that such a thing is impious, it is these rather that our old men and women must tell to the young children, and when they grow older, the poets must be compelled to make stories for them of a like nature. But the binding of Hera by her son, or the hurling of Hephaestus from heaven by his father, when his mother was being beaten and he tried to defend her, and all the tales of the battles of the giants that Homer has made, these stories we shall not receive into our city, whether their purport be allegorical or not. For the child is unable to discriminate between what is allegory and what is not; whatever he receives and believes at that early age is apt to become permanent and indelible, For these reasons, perhaps, we must do everything in our power to contrive that the first stories our children are told shall teach virtue in the fairest way."

"Yes," he said, "that is reasonable. But if any one were to ask us for examples of these stories and in what works they are told, how should we reply?"

I answered, "Adeimantus, you and I at this juncture 379 are not poets, but founders of a city. The founders ought to know the canons in accordance with which the poets should tell their stories, and which they are not to be allowed to transgress, but they need not themselves compose stories."

"True," he said, "but this is just what I wish to know. What are the canons for stories about the gods?"

"Something like this," I said. "If a poet tells of God in epic, lyric, or tragedy, he must surely represent him as he actually is."

"Yes, he must."

"But is not God truly good, and must he not be described as such?"

"Yes. Why do you ask?"

"Well, nothing that is good is harmful, is it?"

"I think not."

"And does that which is not harmful do harm?"

"Certainly not."

"And does that which does no harm, do any evil?"

"No."

"Then would that which does no evil cause any evil?"

"How could it?"

"Well, is the good beneficial?"

"Yes."

"And does it cause good fortune?"

"Yes."

"Then the good does not cause all things; it is re-

sponsible for the things that are good, but not responsible for the evil?"

"That is certainly true," he said.

"Nor can God," I said, "since he is good, cause all
things, as most people say. He is responsible for a few
things that happen to men, but for many he is not, for
the good things we enjoy are much fewer than the evil.
The former we must attribute to none else but God;
but for the evil we must find some other causes, not
God."

"That seems to me very true," he said.

"Then," I said, "we must have nothing to do with
the mistake of Homer or of any other poet who makes
the foolish misstatement that

> Two tuns of gifts there lie
> In Zeus' gate, one of good, one ill,

which when Zeus mixes for any man

> One while he frolics, one while mourns,

but as for the man who gets no mixture but only of the
second,

> Sad hunger in th' abundant earth doth toss him to and fro;

nor with the statement that Zeus is to us

> The giver both of woe and weal

And we shall not praise any one who says that Zeus and
Athene were responsible for Pandarus' violation of the
oaths and treaties, or that Themis and Zeus caused strife 380
and division among the gods, nor shall we allow the
young to hear the words of Aeschylus, when he says

> God sends a curse on mortals
> When he would utterly destroy a house.

But if any one makes a poem of the sufferings of Niobe,
as is the play from which those lines are taken, or of the
history of the children of Pelops, or the Trojan war, or

any similar story, either he must not be allowed to say that these were the deeds of God, or if he says that, he must find some such explanation as we are now looking for. He must say that God did what was just and good, and the sufferers were benefited by punishment. We must not allow the poet to say that those who were punished were miserable, and that God made them so. But we must allow them to say that the bad were miserable because they needed punishment, and were benefited by being punished at God's hand. We must contend with all our might against the assertion that God, who is good, is the author of evil to any man. No one shall say that in our city if it is to have good laws, and no one shall hear it, neither young nor old. Neither in metre nor without shall it be told. For to tell such things is impious, and they are neither to our advantage nor self-consistent in the telling."

"I vote with you for this law. I like it," he said.

"This, then," I said, "will be one of our canons concerning the gods, in accordance with which our speakers must speak and our poets compose, namely, that God is not the author of all things, but of the good alone."

"Yes, that is sufficiently proved."

"Well, what of this for the second? Do you think that God is a magician of deliberate purpose appears in different forms at different times; that sometimes he actually leaves his own form and passes into many different shapes, and at other times deceives us and creates in us illusions of that kind; or do you think that God is simple, and of all beings abides most steadfast in his own form?"

"I can't answer all at once," he said.

"Well, answer me this. If anything departs from its own form, must not the change arise in itself or be caused by something without?"

"It must."

"Well, are not the most perfect things least altered and moved by any outside influence? Take, for example, the alterations effected in the body by food and drink and exertion, or in every plant by sun and wind and similar causes. Does not the healthiest and strongest body suffer least alteration?"

"Surely."

"Then would not the bravest and wisest soul be least disturbed or altered by any outside effect?"

"Yes."

"And, again, the same holds good of manufactured articles—furniture, houses, and clothes. Those that are well made and in good condition suffer least alteration from time or other influences?"

"That is so."

"Then everything that is at its best, either in nature or in art, or both, suffers least change from without?"

"So it appears."

"But surely God and the divine nature are in every way perfect?"

"Surely."

"Therefore God would least of all take on many shapes through external influence?"

"Yes, least of all."

"Then would he change and alter himself?"

"If he changes at all," he said, "that must clearly be the manner of it."

"Then would God in changing himself become better and fairer, or worse and uglier?"

"He must become worse," he said, "if he changes at all. For we certainly cannot say that God is lacking in any excellence or beauty."

"You are perfectly right," I said. "That being so, Adeimantus, do you think that any one, God or man, would deliberately make himself in any way worse than he was before?"

"That is impossible," he said.

"Then," I said, "it is also impossible for a god to wish to alter himself, but as is natural, every god having the utmost beauty and excellence, abides ever simple in his own shape."

"That seems to me conclusively proven."

"Then, my good sir, let none of the poets tell us that

> Like such poor stranger pilgrims do the gods,
> All shapes assuming, glide through towns and towers,

and let no one tell us lies about Proteus and Thetis, or introduce either in tragedy or other poetry Hera transformed, disguised as a priestess collecting alms

> For the life-giving of Inachus, river of Argos.

And we will have nothing to do with the many other lies of that sort. And the mothers are not to be persuaded by the poets into frightening their children with evil stories that forsooth there are certain gods that go about at night in many strange shapes. If they do, they will both blaspheme the gods and make their children cowardly."

"No, that must not be allowed," he said.

"But," I said, "are the gods such that while they do not really change, they make themselves appear to us to have different forms, deceiving us by their magic?"

"Possibly," he said.

"What!" I said; "would God wish to lie by spoken or acted illusion?"

"I do not know," he said.

"Do you not know," I said, "that all gods and men hate the true lie, if we may use the expression?"

"What do you mean?" he said.

382 "This," I said; "no one deliberately wishes to lie in the most vital part of him about the most vital matters.

Every one fears above all to harbour a lie in that quarter."

"I don't yet understand," he said.

"That is because you think I am uttering some mysterious truth. All I am saying is that to lie, and be the victim of a lie, and to be ignorant in the soul concerning reality, to hold and possess falsehood there, is the last thing any man would desire. Men hate falsehood in such a case above all."

"Certainly," he said.

"But this that I have just mentioned may be most accurately called the true lie, namely, the ignorance in the soul of him who is deluded. For the spoken lie is an imitation of this state in the soul, an image of it which arises afterwards and is not a wholly unmixed lie. Is it not so?"

"Certainly."

"Then the real lie is hated not only by the gods, but also by men?"

"I think so."

"Then what of the spoken lie? Is it sometimes useful to certain people, and therefore not deserving of hatred? Is it not useful against enemies, and a good remedy to divert so-called friends from any evil intention they may form in madness or folly? Again, in the stories of which we have just been speaking, when we do not know the truth of those ancient happenings, but make the falsehood as near the truth as possible, is our action not useful?"

"Yes, certainly that is true."

"And for which of these reasons is falsehood useful to God? Will he be seeking to make a lie like the truth because he does not know ancient history?"

"That would be ridiculous," he said.

"There is nothing of the lying poet in God, then?"

"I think not."

"Would he lie from fear of his enemies?"

"Far from it."

"Or because of the folly or madness of his friends?"

"No," he said, "no fool or madman is a friend of the gods."

"Then there are no reasons why God should lie?"

"None."

"Then the nature of gods and spirits is altogether apart from falsehood?"

"Most assuredly," he said.

"In that God is simple and true in word and deed, he does not change himself; nor does he delude others, either in phantasies or words, or by sending signs, whether in waking moments or in dreams?"

383 "I think so myself," he said, "after what you have said."

"Then do you agree," I said, " that our second canon determining all speaking and writing about the gods is that they are not magicians, and do not change themselves, or deceive us by lies, either in word or deed?"

"I agree."

"Then though we find much to praise in Homer, we should not praise him for his story of the sending of the dream to Agamemnon by Zeus; nor shall we praise the passage in Aeschylus where Thetis says that Apollo sang at her wedding, dwelling on her happy motherhood:

> The span of life from sickness free,
> And telling all my fate that gods had blest,
> He sang a song of gladness to my heart.
> I dreamed the lips of Phoebus could not lie
> Being divine, touched with the seer's skill.
> But he the singer, he the wedding guest,
> The same who sang these words, is he who slew
> My own dear son.

When any one says such things about the gods we shall be angry, and shall not give him a chorus; nor shall we allow our teachers to use his poen.s to instruct the young, if our guardians are to be god-fearing and godlike so far as man may be?"

"Decidedly," he said, "I agree with those canons, and would use them as laws."

# BOOK III

"So much, then," I said, "for stories of the gods. We have settled, it seems, which of them our young children may hear and which they may not, if they are to grow up to honour the gods and their parents, and to hold friendship dear."

"Yes," he said, "and I think that our conclusions are right."

"Come, then, if they are to be brave, must they not be told such stories as will make them have no fear of death? Or do you think that any man was ever brave who had this fear in his heart?"

"No, indeed," he said, "not I."

"Well, but do you think that any one who believes that Hades exists, and is a terrible place, will be without this fear, and that he will be ready in battle to choose death rather than defeat and slavery?"

"Certainly not."

"Then, it seems, we must prescribe for intending poets concerning those stories also, and tell them that they must not simply abuse Hades, but rather praise it. For their stories, as ordinarily told, are neither true nor useful to those who are to be warriors."

"Yes, we must do that," he said.

"Then we shall begin with the following verse and score out all passages like it:

> I rather wish to live on earth a swain,
> Or serve a swain for hire that scarce can gain
> Bread to sustain him, than, that life once gone,
> Of all the dead sway the imperial throne;

or
>           And so his house so dim,
>     So loathsome, filthy, and abhored of all the gods beside,
>     Should open both to gods and men;

and
>           O ye gods, I see we have a soul
>     In th' under-dwellings, and a kind of man-resembling idol;
>     The soul's seat yet, all matter left, stays with the carcass
>           here;

and
>           That he alone
>           May sing truth's solid wisdom, and not one
>     Prove more than shade in his comparison;

and
>           His soul took instant wing,
>     And to the house that hath no lights descended, sorrowings
>     For his sad fate, to leave him young and in his ablest age;

and                                                          387
>           Like matter vaporous
>     The spirit vanished under earth and murmured in his stoop;

and
>           And as amid the desolate retreat
>           Of some vast cavern, made the sacred seat
>           Of austere spirits, bats with breasts and wings
>           Clasp fast the walls, and each to other clings,
>           But swept off from their coverts, up they rise
>           And fly with murmurs in amazeful guise
>           About the cavern: so these, grumbling, rose
>           And flockt together.

We shall bid Homer and the other poets not be angry if
we strike out these passages and all like them, not that
they are not poetic, or that they are not enjoyed by most
people, but that the more poetic they are, the less must
they be heard by boys and men who are to be free, fearing slavery more than death."

"Certainly."

"Then we must also get rid of all the fearful and terrifying titles belonging to those subjects, 'wailing Cocytus,' and 'loathed Styx,' 'infernals,' and 'sapless dead,' and all the words of that type, the very sound of which is enough to make men shiver. These will probably be useful enough for other purposes, but for our guardians we are afraid that this shivering fear will make them more emotional and softer than they ought to be."

"Yes," he said, "your fear is justifiable."

"Shall we strike them out, then?"

"Yes."

"And must we speak and write in the opposite strain?"

"Clearly."

"Then shall we also strike out the weepings and wailings of famous men?"

"These must go with the others," he said.

"But consider," I said, "whether we are justified in striking them out. We assert that the good man will not think that death is terrible for another good man who is his comrade."

"We do."

"Then he will not weep for him as for one who has suffered any terrible thing?"

"No."

"We may even say this, that such a man most of all has within himself that which makes a good life possible. Far better than ordinary people can he do without others."

"True," he said.

"Then for him of all people there is least that is terrible in losing a son or a brother, or in the loss of money, or any other of his possessions?"

"Yes, least for him."

"When any such misfortune comes upon him, he does

not bewail it as other men do, but bears it as patiently as may be?"

"Certainly."

"Then may we justifiably strike out the lamentations of famous heroes, and give them to women, to bad women and cowardly men, that those whom we are bringing up to guard our city may be ashamed to imitate them?" **388**

"You are right," he said.

"Again, we shall request Homer and the other poets not to represent Achilles, the son of a goddess,

> As lying prostrate, now his side and now his face upturned,
> Now on his bosom fallen,

then starting upright and wandering unsteadily by the shore of the harvestless sea; nor as lifting with both his hands the black mould and pouring it on his head; nor as weeping and lamenting on the many other occasions and in the diverse manners depicted by Homer; nor are they to describe Priam, who was closely descended from the gods:

> Entreating, and all filed with tumbling, calling on
> Each man by name.

Still more earnestly we shall request them not to represent the gods making lament and saying:

> Hapless I brought forth unhappily
> The best of all the sons of men.

But if they speak of the gods, they must not dare so to misrepresent the greatest of the gods, as to make him say:

> Oh, ill sight!
> A man I love much, I see forced in most unworthy flight
> About the city. My heart grieves;

or

> Ah, woe is me since fate decrees that this Menoetius' son
> Shall slay Sarpedon whom I hold of all mankind most dear.

For, my dear Adeimantus, if our young were to take such passages seriously, instead of laughing at them as bad poetry, unworthy of their subjects, it would be difficult to make them feel that they themselves, who are but men, are above those actions, or to make them rebuke themselves if it should occur to them also to say or do such things. They would lose their sense of shame and their hardihood, and weep and lament loudly over the most trifling misfortunes."

"That is most true," he said.

"And that we must prevent, as our argument has taught us, and we shall follow it till someone shows us a better."

"Yes, it must be prevented."

"Next, our guardians ought not to be ready laughers; for when any man indulges in excessive laughter, it is almost always followed by an equally violent reaction."

"So I think," he said.

"Then we must not allow any poet to represent men 889 of repute as overcome by laughter, much less to represent gods in such a case."

"Yes, much less," he said.

"Then we shall not allow Homer to speak thus of the gods:

> A laughter never left,
> Shook all the blessed deities, to see the lame so deft
> At that cup service.

Your argument will not allow that."

"Well, if you like to call it mine," he said, "it will not."

"Further, a high value must be placed upon truth. For if we were right in what we said a little while ago, and falsehood is really useless to the gods, and useful to men only as a medicine, clearly the use of medicine must be confined to our doctors. Laymen must have nothing to do with it."

"That is clear," he said.

"Then it pertains to the guardians of the city, and to

them alone, to tell falsehoods, to deceive either enemies
or citizens for the city's welfare. To all other persons such
conduct is forbidden, and we shall say that, for a private
citizen to tell a falsehood to such rulers as these, is a crime
more serious but the same in principle as for a patient to
deceive his doctor, or a pupil his training-master concerning his bodily health, or for a sailor to tell his captain
an untruth about the ship or the crew in describing his
own condition or that of his shipmates."

"Most true," he said.

"Then if the governor finds any private person in the
city telling falsehood, any

> Of such as craftsmen are
> A seer, a doctor or a carpenter,

he will punish him as the introducer of a practice as
subversive and destructive of a city as of a ship."

"He will," he said, "if his deeds answer to his words."

"Next, will our young men need to be temperate?"

"Surely."

"Speaking generally, is not this the greater part of
temperance, that men should be subject to the rulers, and
make subject to themselves the pleasures of drink and
love and food?"

"I think so."

"Then I fancy that we shall approve of such speeches
as that which Homer puts into the mouth of Diomedes:

> Suppress thine anger's powers,
> Good friend, and hear why I refrained,

and the verses which follow:

> The Greeks charged silent, and like men, bestowed their
>    thrifty breath,
> Their silence uttering their awe of those that them controlled,

with other passages of a like nature?"

"Excellent."

"Well, what of this verse:

Thou ever steeped in wine, dog's face, with heart but of a hart,

890 and those that follow it, and all the impertinences of private men to rulers, whether actually spoken or related in poetry, are they excellent?"

"They are not."

"No. I do not fancy the hearing of them will help young men to be temperate. It may give them pleasure of another kind. That would not surprise me. How do you think about it?"

"As you do," he said.

"Again, when the wisest of men is represented as saying that the finest sight in the world to him is

A wine-page waiting; tables crowned with meat,
Set close to guests that are to use it skilled;
The cupboards furnisht, and the cups still filled,

do you think that is calculated to induce self-control in the young man who hears it, any more than the verse

To die
The death of Famine is a misery
Past all death loathsome;

or the story that Zeus, when all the other gods and men were sleeping, kept awake to carry out what he had purposed, and then forgot all in the eagerness of his lust, and was so maddened by the sight of Hera that he would not wait till they returned into their chamber, but wished to enjoy her there and then, saying that he had never been so hot with desire, not even in their first stolen meetings which were hidden from their dear parents; or the story of the binding of Ares and Aphrodite by Hephaestus in a similar affair?"

"On my word," he said, "I think such stories are not conducive to self-restraint."

"But if there be any needs of perfect endurance," I said, "done by famous men among us, or told of them in poetry, these we must see and hear, as, for example,

> He chid his angry spirit, and beat his breast,
> And said, 'Forbear, my mind, and think on this:
> There hath been time when bitterer agonies
> Have tried thy patience.'"

"Most certainly," he said.

"Our heroes, again, must not be fond of money, or men who would take a bribe."

"Certainly not,"

"Then they shall not be told that

> Gifts persuade gods, gifts reverend kings persuade;

nor must we praise Phoenix, Achilles' tutor, nor allow that he spoke wisely when he advised him to help the Achaeans if they gave him gifts, but without the gifts not to relent from his wrath; nor shall we suppose nor admit of Achilles himself that he was so fond of money as to take gifts from Agamemnon, or to be willing to restore the body of Hector only if he were paid for it?"        391

"It is certainly not just," he said, "to praise deeds of that description."

"Though," I said, "my admiration for Homer makes me hesitate to say it, nevertheless it is impious to speak such things of Achilles, or to believe them on the report of others, or to believe that he said to Apollo,

> It is thou
> That putt'st dishonour thus on me, thou worst of deities.
> Held I the measure in my hand, I should requite thee dear;

or that he resisted obstinately, and was ready to fight with the river, who was a god; or that he said of his hair, which was sacred to the other river, Spercheius.

> My friend's hands shall to the Stygian shore
> Convey these tresses,

when his friend Patroclus was dead: that he said and did thus, we must not believe. And as for the dragging of Hector's body round the tomb of Patroclus, and the slaughter of the prisoners on the pyre, all these tales we shall declare to be unture. We shall not suffer our guardians to believe that Achilles, whose parents were a goddess and Peleus the wisest of men and the grandson of Zeus, and who had been educated by the sage Chiron, was so full of confusion that in his heart were two most contrary diseases, meanness and love of money, and overweening contempt of gods and men."

"You are right," he said.

"Further," I said, "let us neither believe nor allow men to say that Theseus, the son of Poseidon, and Peirithous, the son of Zeus, ever attempted such terrible rapes, or that any son of god or hero dared to do the terrible and impious deeds of which those false stories tell. Rather let us compel our poets to say either that they were not the authors of those deeds, or that they were not the sons of gods—one or other. They are not to try to persuade our young men that the gods beget evil, or that heroes are no better than common men. As we said originally, these stories are both impious and untrue; for we have proved that evils cannot come from the gods."

"We have."

"And these stories are also harmful to those who hear them; for every man will excuse his own wickedness, being persuaded that like deeds have been, and are now, done by

> The gods' own offspring,
> Near kin to Zeus, who high on Ida's mount
> To Zeus, their father, feed the altar flame,
> And still within their veins runs blood divine.

For these reasons we must stop such stories lest they breed in our young men a ready disposition to evil."

"Certainly," he said.

"Then what class of literature is still left for this discussion of ours as to what may and what may not be treated of in poetry? We have stated how the poets must write of the gods and of the lesser deities and heroes, and of those in Hades?"

"Yes."

"Then does not the remaining class consist of stories about men?"

"That is evident."

"But it is impossible for us, my friend, to lay down rules for them at present."

"Why?"

"Because I fancy that we shall say that in what they tell of men, poets and makers of stories are most wrong when they say that many unjust men are happy, many just men miserable, that injustice is profitable if it be not detected, and justice the good of another, but a man's own loss. I fancy, too, that we shall forbid them to make statements of that kind, and shall order them to make songs and stories to the contrary effect. Do you not think so?"

"I am certain of it," he said.

"Well, if you admit that I am right, shall I say that you admit what we have been after all this time?"

"Your assumption is correct," he said.

"When we have discovered the nature of justice, and have found that it is naturally profitable to him who possesses it, whether he have the reputation of a just man or no, shall we not then agree that stories which deal with men must be of the nature we have indicated?"

"Most true," he said.

"Then that may suffice for the subject-matter. We must now, I fancy, examine the question of diction, and then we shall have thoroughly examined both what the poets are to say and how they are to say it."

Adeimantus said, "I don't understand what you mean by that."

"But we must see that you do," I said. "Perhaps you will grasp it better in this way. Is not everything which is said by story-tellers or poets a narration of past, present, or future events?"

"What else?" he said.

"Then do they not use either simple narration or imitative narration, or both?"

"That again," he said, "I need to have explained to me."

"I am evidently a ridiculously obscure teacher," I said. "But as poor speakers do, I shall leave the general principle alone, and taking a particular example try to make my meaning clear to you. You know the beginning of the Iliad where the poet says that Chryses asks Agamemnon to ransom his daughter and he angrily refuses, and then Chryses, since his request is refused, prays to the god 393 against the Achaeans?"

"I do."

"Well, you know that up to the lines

> And made suit to all, but most to the commands
> Of both th' Atrides who most ruled,

the poet speaks in his own person, and does not try to make us think that the speaker is any one but himself; but in the passage after that he speaks as though he were himself Chryses, and tries as hard as he can to make us think that the speaker is not Homer, but the old priest. And all the rest of the narrative concerning the events in Ilium and in Ithaca, and all the Odyssey is written in much the same way."

"Certainly," he said.

"And is it not narrative when the poet presents each speech and the parts in between?"

"Surely."

"But when he speaks in the person of another, shall we not say that he then always makes his style as nearly as possible like that of the man whom he has announced to be speaking?"

"We shall, of course."

"But if a man makes himself either in voice or in look like another man, does he not imitate that man?"

"Of course."

"Then in such cases, it appears, Homer and the other poets carry on the narration by means of imitation?"

"Certainly."

"Now if the poet never concealed his own person, his whole poem and narration would be without imitation. To prevent you from saying that you still don't understand, I shall tell you how this would work out. After Homer has told how Chryses came bearing gifts to ransom his daughter, and how he made supplication to the Achaeans, and especially to the chiefs, if after that he had spoken, not as if he had been transformed into Chryses, but as if he were still Homer, that, you know, would not have been imitation, but simple narration. It would have gone in some such way as this. I shall not put it in metre, as I am no poet. The priest came and prayed that the gods might grant to them the capture of Troy and a safe return, and entreated them to ransom his daughter, taking the gifts he offered in fear of the god. And when he had spoken, the others reverenced his words and gave assent; but Agamemnon was angry and told him to go away and not to come back, or his sacred staff and the fillets of the god would not protect him. He said that Chryses' daughter should grow old with him in Argos before he would ransom her, and told Chryses to go away and to not make him angry if he wanted to get 394 home safe. The old man when he heard this was afraid and went away in silence; but when he left the army behind him, he prayed earnestly to Apollo, calling on the god by his titles, and putting him in remembrance, and asking to be repaid if ever he had made him an acceptable offering by building his temple or sacrificing victims. In return for these services, he prayed that the Achaeans might be made to pay for his tears by the arrows of the god. Thus, my friend," I said, "it becomes simple narration without imitation."

"I understand," he said.

"You will understand then," I said, "that we have the opposite form to this, when the words of the poet between the speeches are struck out, and only the alternating dialogue is left."

"Yes," he said, "I understand. That happens in tragedy."

"Your supposition," I said, "is quite correct, and I fancy that now I can make you see what before I could not, namely that all poetry and story-telling may be said to be in one of three forms: the first, where imitation is employed throughout, is, as you suggest, tragedy and comedy; in the second, the poet tells his own story—the best example of that is perhaps the dithyramb; in the third, both imitation and simple narration are used— it is found in epic and in several other kinds of poetry. I hope that you follow me."

"Yes, I now understand what you meant."

"Then let me remind you that we have said before that we were agreed as to the proper subjects of poetry, but had still to consider its proper manner."

"Yes, I remember."

"Well, then, this is what I was trying to say, that we must come to an agreement as to whether we should allow our poets to make their narrations by means of imitation, or partly by imitation and partly by the other method, in which case we should have to determine where each method should be used, or whether we should forbid imitation altogether."

"I think," he said, "that you are considering whether we shall admit tragedy and comedy into the city or not."

"Possibly," I said, "but possibly even more than that. I don't myself know as yet. We must go where the wind of the argument carries us."

"Yes," he said, "you say well."

"Then, Adeimantus, consider whether our guardians ought to be imitative or not. Does not the answer follow from what we have said already, that each man can practise well one profession but not many, and that if he attempts more, and meddles with many, he will fail in all to attain creditable distinction?"

"That is certainly the case."

"Then will not the same argument apply to imitation? The same man cannot imitate many things as well as one."

"No, certainly not."

"Then he will hardly be able to practise any worthy 395 profession and at the same time imitate many things and be imitative, since as a matter of fact the same persons are not successful even in two forms of imitation that seem very closely allied, in writing tragedy and comedy, for example. Did you not describe these as forms of imitation?"

"I did, and you are right. The same writers are never successful in both."

"Nor can any one be both a rhapsodist and an actor with any success."

"True."

"We even find that tragedy and comedy cannot be played by the same actor. And all these are forms of imitation, are they not?"

"They are."

"Then, Adeimantus, human nature seems to me to be split up into even smaller subdivisions, so that a man is unable to imitate many things well, or to do well the things themselves of which the imitations are likenesses."

"That is perfectly true," he said.

"Then if we are to be faithful to our original position, that our guardians must be released from all other handicrafts to be in all earnestness craftsmen of the freedom of the city, and must do nothing that does not contribute to this end, then they must neither do nor imitate anything else. And if they imitate, they must imitate from childhood subjects befitting their vocation, brave, temperate, pious, free men, and the like; but meanness and any other ugly thing they must neither do nor be able to imitate, lest from the imitation they become infected with the reality. Have you not noticed that the practice of imitation, if it is begun in youth and persisted in, leaves its impress upon character and nature, on body and voice and mind?"

"Yes, certainly," he said.

"Then we shall not allow persons for whom we say we care, who are men, and men who must grow up good, to imitate a woman, whether she be young or old, either railing at her husband, or striving and vaunting herself against the gods, thinking that she is happy, or overcome by misfortune, or grief, or tears; much less shall we allow them to imitate one who is ill, or in love, or in labour."

"Most certainly not," he said.

"Nor may they imitate slaves, male or female, doing servile actions."

"No, they may not."

"Nor, it would follow, may they imitate bad men or cowards, or men doing actions of the contrary nature to those we described, reviling and caricaturing one another, using abominable language, whether drunk or sober, or committing any other faults of speech or action characteristic of that class of men in their personal demeanour and their relations with others. I think, too, that they must not get into the habit of making themselves resemble madmen, either in word or action. They must know madmen and bad men and women, but they must neither do nor imitate any of their actions."

"Most true," he said.

"Further," I said, "may they imitate smiths or any other craftsmen at their trade, or men rowing in triremes or their boatswains, or anything else of that kind?"

"How should they," he said, "when they are not to be allowed even to pay attention to any of those things?"

"Then will they imitate horses neighing, and bulls bellowing, and rivers gurgling, and seas crashing, and thunder, and all those things?"

"No," he said, "we have already forbidden them to be mad or to make themselves like madmen."

"Then," I said, "if I understand your meaning, there is one form of diction and narration which would be used by the truly noble and good man when he needed to say anything, and another different form which a man of the opposite nature and breeding would find congenial, and which he would use."

"What are these?" he said.

"The man of measured character in the first place, when he came in his narration to the speech or action of a good man, would, I think, wish to speak in the good man's person, and would not be ashamed of that kind of imitation. He would imitate the good man with especial thoroughness in his cautious and wise actions, less carefully and to a less degree when he was overcome by disease, or love, or by drunkenness, or any other misfortune. But when he comes to someone unworthy of him, he will not be willing to liken himself seriously to his inferior. He may for a little when he is doing a good action, but apart from that he will be ashamed, partly because he is not in the way of imitating such people, but also from a repugnance to moulding and conforming himself to the morals of inferior men whom he deliberately despises; unless it be for mere amusement."

"That is likely," he said.

"Then he will use the form of narration which we described a little while ago, which is used in Homer. His manner of speech will partake both of imitation and simple narration, and only a small part of the whole will be imitation. Am I not right?"

"Yes, certainly," he said, "such must be the model for such a speaker."

397 "Then," I said, "as for the man of different character, the more contemptible he is, the more will he imitate everything without discrimination and think nothing beneath him, so that he will attempt in sober earnest, and before a large audience, to imitate everything, as we said a moment ago—thunder and the noise of the wind, and of hail, and of axles and of pulleys; the notes of trumpets and flutes, and fifes and all manner of instruments; the barking of dogs and the bleating of sheep, and the cries of birds. And so his manner of speech will all involve imitation of voice and form, with possibly a little simple narration."

"Yes," he said, "that is inevitable."

"Then these," I said, "are the two classes of diction?"

"They are," he said.

"Then of the two, may we not say that the first involves no violent changes, and if it be given a musical mode and rhythm in accord with the diction, it may be performed correctly in almost the same mode throughout; that is, since character is so uniform, in one musical mode, and also in a similarly unchanging rhythm?"

"Yes," he said, "that is certainly the case."

"Then what of the other kind? Does it not require just the opposite for its proper expression, all musical modes and all different rhythms, so many and manifold are its transitions?"

"Yes, that is very true."

"Do not all poets and writers hit upon one or other of those modes of diction, or on a mixture of both?"

"That is inevitable," he said.

"What then shall we do?" I said. "Shall we admit into our city all those different styles, or one or other of those primary styles, or the mixture?"

"If my opinion prevails," he said, "we shall admit the simple imitator of the good man."

"But, Adeimantus, the mixed style is certainly attractive, while the opposite style to that which you have chosen is much the most popular with children and their attendants, and with the vulgar mass."

"Popular it may be."

"But perhaps," I said, "you will say that it is not befitting in our city where no man is twofold or manifold, since each does his own work, and that only."

"No, it is not befitting."

"Therefore is this not the only city where we shall find the shoemaker actually a shoemaker, and not sea-captain and maker of shoes in one; the farmer a farmer, and not adding jury work to his farming; and the soldier a soldier, and not money-maker and soldier in one, and so with them all?"

"True," he said.

"Then apparently if there comes to our city a man so 398 wise that he can turn into everything under the sun and imitate every conceivable object, when he offers to show off himself and his poems to us, we shall do obeisance to him as to a sacred, wonderful, and agreeable person; but we shall say that we have no such man in our city, and the law forbids there being one, and we shall anoint him with myrrh, and crown him with a wreath of sacred wool, and send him off to another city, and for ourselves we shall employ a more austere and less attractive poet and story-teller, whose poetry will be to our profit, who will imitate for us the diction of the good man, and in saying what he has to say will conform to those canons which we laid down originally when we were undertaking the task of educating the soldiers?"

"Yes," he said, "we shall do that, if it lies in our power."

"Here, then," I said, "we have apparently completely finished with that branch of music which relates to literature and stories. We have discovered both subject and manner."

"Yes, I think with you," he said.

"Then after that," I said, "we have left the manner of song and melody."

"Obviously."

"Well, would not any one without further consideration see what we should have to say as to the proper nature of these elements, if we are to be consistent with what has gone before?"

"Then, Socrates," said Glaucon, laughing, "I am apparently no one; for at this moment I can't infer with any assurance what kinds we ought to allow, though I have my suspicions."

"Well, in any case," I said, "you can at least say with assurance that a song is composed of three elements—words, musical mode, and rhythm."

"Yes," he said, "that is so."

"Well, as for the words, will they in any way differ from words that are not to go with music so far as concerns their conformity to those canons of subject and manner which we announced a little while ago?"

"No, they will not."

"And should not the musical mode and rhythm accord with the words?"

"Of course."

"But we said that in our poems we want no weepings and lamentations."

"No, certainly not."

"What are the wailful modes? Tell me. You are musical."

"Mixed Lydian and Hyperlydian, and some other similar ones."

"Then these we must dismiss, must we not?" I said. "For even in the training of virtuous women they are useless, much more so in the training of men."

"Certainly."

"Then are not drunkenness, effeminacy, and idleness most unseemly in guardians?"

"Surely."

"Which are the soft and convivial modes?"

"There are Ionian and Lydian modes which are called slack."

"Then, my friend, shall we use those for men who are **399** warriors?"

"By no means," he said. "You seem to have Dorian and Phrygian left."

"I do not know these modes," I said; "but leave us the mode which will fittingly imitate the tones and accents of a man who is brave in battle and in every difficult and dangerous task, who, if he fails, or sees before him wounds or death, or falls into any other misfortune, always grapples with his fate, disciplined and resolute. Another shall imitate a man in the actions of peace, where his choice has scope and he is free from compulsion: when he is persuading or entreating a god in prayer, or a man by instruction and advice, or when he is attending to the requests, or instruction, or persuasion of another. It shall imitate a man who in all these circumstances acts according to his liking, never puffing himself up, but in all his actions, and in his acceptance of their consequences, is ever prudent and restrained. These musical modes, two in number, one of compulsion, the other of free will, which imitate in the fairest manner the tones of the unfortunate and the fortunate, of the prudent and the brave, these you may leave to us."

"But,' he said, "you are asking for just those which I mentioned a little while ago."

"Then," I said, "we shall not require for our songs and melodies a variety of strings or sudden changes of modulation?"

"I think not," he said.

"Then we shall not maintain the makers of harps and dulcimers, and of all instruments which are many-stringed and many-keyed?"

"I think not."

"Then will you allow flute makers and flute player into the city? Has not the flute more notes than any othe instrument, and are not those many-keyed instrumen really imitations of the flute?"

"Obviously," he said.

"You have left," I said, "the lyre and the zither, whic will be useful in town, and in the fields the herdsmer may have a pipe."

"So the argument tells us," he said.

"We are making no innovation," I said, "when we prefer Apollo and Apollo's instruments to Marsyas and his instruments."

"No, by Zeus," he said, "I think we are not."

"Now, by the dog," I said, "here have we been purging the city which we said before was too luxurious, and we never noticed it."

"Well, it was very wise of us," he said.

"Come, then," I said, "and let us finish our purgation. After musical modes comes the canon of rhythm, according to which we must not aim at a variety of rhythms with all kinds of metrical feet, but must discover what are the rhythms of an orderly and brave life. When we have done so, we must make our metre and our melody to suit the words describing such a life, and not make

words to suit metre and melody. Which these rhythms  400
are, it is your business to tell us, as you told us of the
musical modes."

"But, my good sir," he said, "I can't tell you. I know
that there are three kinds of rhythm from which the
measures are woven, just as in tones I could on examination discover four kinds which are the basis of all musical
modes. But which imitate which kind of life I can't tell
you."

"Well," I said, "we shall consult Damon on this subject, and ask him which metrical feet are fitter to express
meanness and pride, or madness or other evil, and which
rhythms must be kept to express the opposite qualities.
I fancy that I have heard him using the expressions 'warlike,' 'complex,' 'dactyl,' and 'heroic,' of a rhythm.
He arranged it in a way I do not understand, and showed
the balance of the rise and fall of the feet as the rhythm
passed from short to long, and I fancy that he called one
foot an iambus and another a trochee, and assigned them
longs and shorts. In some of them I think his praise and
blame referred to the tempo of the separate foot as much
as to the whole rhythm, or perhaps it was to the combined
effect of both; I cannot say definitely. But these matters,
as I said, we may leave to Damon, for to settle them
would take a great deal of discussion; or do you think
otherwise?"

"Not I, assuredly."

"But this you can settle, that grace and awkwardness
accompany a good and a bad rhythm, can you not?"

"Surely."

"But goodness and badness of rhythm follow the diction. The good rhythm is assimilated to a beautiful style,
and bad rhythm to the opposite; and so with goodness
and badness of music, since, as we said, rhythm and musical mode conform to the words, not the words to them."

"Yes," he said, "they must follow the words."

"Then what of the style and the subject? Do they not conform to the character of the soul?"

"Surely."

"And the others conform to the style?"

"Yes."

"Then good speech and good music, and grace and good rhythm, follow good nature, not that silliness which we call good nature in compliment, but the mind that is really well and nobly constituted in character."

"Most certainly," he said.

"Then if our young men are to do their own work, must they not follow after these?"

"They must."

401 "But painting and all craftmanship are, we know, imbued with these; so are weaving and embroidery, architecture and the making of all other articles; so too is the body and other living things. All these show either grace or absence of grace. And absence of grace and bad rhythm and bad harmony are sisters to bad words and bad nature, while their opposites are sisters and copies of the opposite, a wise and good nature."

"That is certainly the case."

"Then we must speak to our poets and compel them to impress upon their poems only the image of the good, or not to make poetry in our city. And we must speak to the other craftsmen and forbid them to leave the impress of that which is evil in character, unrestrained, mean and ugly, on their likenesses of living creatures, or their houses, or on anything else which they make. He that cannot obey must not be allowed to ply his trade in our city. For we would not have our guardians reared among images of evil as in a foul pasture, and there day by day and little by little gather many impressions from all that surrounds them, taking them all in until at last a great mass of evil gathers in their inmost souls, and they know it not. No, we must seek out those craftsmen who have the happy gift of tracing out the nature of the fair and graceful, that our young men may dwell as in a health-giving region where all that surrounds them is beneficent, whencesoever from fair works of art there smite upon their eyes and ears an affluence like a wind bringing health from happy regions, which, though they know it not, leads them from their earliest years into likeness and friendship and harmony with the principle of beauty."

"A nobler manner of education," he said, "there could not be."

"Then, Glaucon," I said, "is not musical education of paramount importance for those reasons, because rhythm and harmony enter most powerfully into the innermost part of the soul and lay forcible hands upon it, bearing grace with them, so making graceful him who is rightly trained, and him who is not, the reverse? Is it not a further reason that he who has been rightly trained in music would be quick to observe all works of art that were defective or ugly, and all natural objects that failed in beauty? They would displease him, and rightly; but beautiful things he would praise, and receiving them with joy into his soul, would be nourished by them and become noble and good. Ugly things he would rightly con- 402 demn, and hate even in his youth before he was capable of reason; but when reason comes he would welcome her as one he knows, with whom his training has made him familiar."

"Yes," he said, "I think that those are the purposes of education in music."

"Now, in learning to read," I said, "we had become fairly proficient by the time that we could recognize the few letters that there are, in all the different words in which they are scattered about: when we never passed them over, either in a big word or a small, as though they were not worth noticing, but were anxious to distinguish them everywhere, knowing that we should be no scholars until we had got thus far."

"True."

"Is it not also true that we shall not know the images of letters, supposing they are to be seen in water or in mirrors, before we know the letters themselves? The same skill and practice is needed in either case?"

"Most certainly."

"Then by heaven, is it not true that in the same way neither we ourselves shall become musical, nor will the guardians whom we say we have to educate, until we can recognize the forms of temperance and courage and liberality and highmindedness, and those which are akin to them, and also their opposites, wherever they are scattered about, until we discern them wherever they are to be found, both the forms and their images, never slighting them in big things or in small, but believing that the same skill and practice is needed to discern both form and image?"

"That certainly follows," he said.

"Then," I said, "could he that has eyes to see have ever a fairer sight than a man in whom beautiful gifts of soul are combined with the expressions of those gifts in outward form, corresponding and harmonious to them because made in the same mould of beauty?"

"No, never," he said,

"And that which is fairest is most to be beloved, is it not?"

"Surely."

"Then the truly musical person will love them who come nearest to this ideal, but him in whom there is dissonance they will not love."

"No," he said, "at least not if there be any defect in his soul, but if it be a bodily defect, he may manage almost to welcome it."

"I understand," I said; "you say so because you have

or have had a favourite of this kind, and I acquiesce. But
tell me this. Has excess of pleasure anything in common
with temperance?"

"How could it have?" he said. "It unsettles the mind
as surely as pain."

"With other virtue, then?"

"Certainly not."

"With insolence and wantonness, perhaps?"

"Yes, that it has."

"Can you name any pleasure more excessive and more
intense than sexual pleasure?"

"I cannot, nor any more maddening either."

"But does not true love really consist in loving in a
temperate and musical spirit that which is orderly and
beautiful?"

"Yes," he said.

"Then nothing that is maddening or touched with
licentiousness must be brought near true love, must it?"

"It must not."

"Then the pleasure we have mentioned must not come
near the lover and his favourites, nor must they partake
of it if they love and are loved truly?"

"By Zeus, no, Socrates," he said, "it must not come
near them."

"It seems, then," I said, "that in the city we are founding you will lay down a law that the lover may kiss his
beloved, may frequent his society and embrace him, as
though he were his son, if he so persuade him, for beauty's
sake, but in all else his relations with the person he affects
shall be such that they shall never be suspected of going
beyond this. If he acts otherwise, he shall draw upon himself the reproach of bad taste and vulgarity."

"Yes," he said.

"Then," I said, "do you agree with me that our discussion of music is finished? And it has come to an end at

408

the proper place. For music surely ought to end with the love of the beautiful?"

"I agree," he said.

"After music, the young men are to be trained in gymnastic?"

"Yes."

"Well, in this as well as in music they must be carefully trained all their lives from their earliest years. The true view of the case, as I think, is more or less this. See whether you agree with me. It is not my opinion that a healthy body by its excellence makes the soul good. The opposite is the case. A good soul by its excellence makes the body as good as it can be. What is your opinion?"

"I think the same," he said.

"Then if, when we have carefully looked after the understanding, we leave to it the settlement of the details of bodily training, and content ourselves with laying down general principles, shall we not have acted rightly? That will be shorter."

"Certainly."

"We have already said that drunkenness is to be avoided. The last thing we can allow is that a guardian should be drunk and not know where in the world he is."

"Yes," he said, "it is absurd that a guardian should need to be guarded."

"What about food? Our heroes are athletes entered for the greatest of contests, are they not?"

"Yes."

"Then will the habit of body of the ordinary trained athlete suit them?"

"Possibly."

404 "'Well," I said, "theirs is a sleepy kind of regimen, and dangerous to the health. Do you not notice that those trained athletes sleep their whole life through, and contract serious and severe illnesses whenever they depart in the smallest respect from their prescribed diet?"

"I do."

"Then for our warrior athletes," I said, "we need some more subtle system of training, for they must be sleepless as watch-dogs, and of very sharp sight and hearing. In their campaigns they will have to put up with frequent changes in the water they drink and the food they eat; with changes, too, in the weather, from sultry heat to storms. They must not, then, be of delicate health."

"I think with you."

"Then will not the best gymnastic be sister to the simple music which we described a little while ago?"

"What do you mean?"

"A good gymnastic, especially that assigned to warriors, must surely be simple?"

"Yes."

"And that is a lesson that we may learn from Homer. For you know that when his heroes are on active service he does not provide fish for their banquets, and that though they were encamped by the sea at the Hellespont; nor does he give them boiled dishes, but only roasted meats, which would be, of course, most convenient for soldiers; for you may say it is everywhere easier to use the fire alone than to carry pots about."

"Of course."

"Homer, too, I fancy, has never mentioned sauces. And all other trainers know this too, do they not? If you want to be in good condition you must abstain from all dainties of that sort?"

"Yes, and they do well in knowing and abstaining."

"Then if you think so, you will not, I imagine, recommend Syracusan living and the Sicilian variety of foods?"

"I think not."

"And you will say that the damsels of Corinth should not be too dear to men who purpose to keep in good condition?"

"Most certainly."

"Will you find fault also with the reputed delicacies of Athenian confectionery?"

"Of necessity."

"Yes, I fancy that we should not go wrong in comparing such manners of eating and living to the music and singing produced on many-keyed instruments and in all rhythms."

"Indeed, we should not."

"And may we not say that diversity, as it there engendered licentiousness, here engenders disease, while simplicity in music breeds temperance in souls, and in gymnastic health in bodies?"

405        "That is most true," he said.

"And when licentiousness and disease are rife in a city, do not the courts of justice and the dispensaries have their doors always open; and do not law and medicine begin to give themselves airs, when great numbers even of free men are their eager devotees?"

"No doubt."

"But when not only the lower and working classes in a city, but even those who have pretensions to a liberal education, require skilled doctors and lawyers, is not that the strongest possible proof that a vicious and ugly system of education rules there? Does it not seem disgraceful, and a sure sign of lack of culture, that they should be compelled to resort to justice which they get from others whom they make their masters and judges, and that they should not rely on their own resources?"

"Yes," he said, "it is most disgraceful."

"But do you not think one thing even more disgraceful, namely, when a man not only spends the greater part of his life in the law courts as either defendant or plaintiff, but is so vulgar as to be actually persuaded to plume himself on the fact, believing himself to be a clever villain, so well up to every turn and trick of the game, that he can wriggle out triumphantly in the end and get off scot-free; when he does all this for trifling and unimportant ends, not knowing how much nobler and better it is so to lead one's life as never to be dependent on a drowsy juryman?"

"You are right," he said; "that is even more disgraceful."

"And do you not think it disgraceful when men need medical treatment, not for wounds or because of epidemics, but because the idle, dissolute manner of life which we have described fills them with humours and winds till they are like pools of water, and the smart sons of Asclepius have to invent new names for diseases—'flatulence' and 'catarrh'?"

"Yes," he said, "those really are new and extraordinary names for illnesses."

"And of a kind," I said, "that were not, I imagine, used by Asclepius. My evidence for that is, that his sons at Troy found no fault with the maiden who gave the wounded Eurypylus a potion of Pramnian wine with barley and scraped cheese sprinkled on it, though that certainly sounds inflammatory, nor did they rebuke Patroclus, who was curing him, for allowing it." 400

"Yes," he said, "it is certainly an extraordinary potion for a wounded man."

"Not so extraordinary," I said, "if you observe that the sons of Asclepius, according to report, did not until the time of Herodicus resort to this coddling of diseases which is characteristic of modern medicine. Herodicus was a trainer who fell into bad health, and by a combination of gymnastic and medicine worried away to nothing first and chiefly himself, and then many others after him."

"How?" he said.

"By making death a long process," I said. "His disease was mortal, and he could not, I imagine, cure himself, but he kept dancing attendance on it, gave up all his business, and spent his life in cures, worrying to death at the smallest departure from his regular diet, so that through his science he came to old age and died hard."

"Well," he said, "that was a fine reward for his skill."

"It was natural enough," I said, "for a man who did not know that it was neither from ignorance nor want of practical experience that Asclepius did not reveal this form of medicine to his descendants, but because he knew that in all well-regulated communities each man has a special work assigned to him in the state, which he must do, and no one has time to spend life in being ill and being cured. We see how absurd this is in the case of artisans, but we don't see its absurdity in the case of those who are supposed to be happy—the rich."

"What do you mean?" he said.

"When a carpenter is ill," I said, "he expects his doctor to give him medicine which will expel the disease by vomiting or purging, or to cauterize or cut the wound and set him right. If any one prescribes him a long course of treatment with head bandages and so on, he says at once that he has no time to be ill, and that it does not pay him to live like that, giving all his attention to his illness and neglecting his proper work. At that he bids that doctor good-day, and goes back to his ordinary way of life, regains his health, and lives on doing his work; or if his body is not strong enough to carry him through, he dies, and is released from troubles."

"Yes," he said, "that is the medical treatment befitting a man of that class."

407 "And is not the reason for it," I said, "that he has work to do, and if he is not doing it, it doesn't pay him to live?"

"Clearly," he said.

"Then the rich man, as we say, has no such proper work which he must do if he is to find life worth living."

"So they say."

"Then you do not listen to Phocylides, when he says that as soon as a man has got a means of livelihood he ought to practise virtue."

"I think he should begin even before that," he said.

"Well," I said, "we need not quarrel with him on that point, but let us assure ourselves whether this practice of virtue is incumbent on the rich, so that life is not worth living to the man who does not practise it, or whether valetudinarianism, while it makes carpentering and other crafts which require attention of mind impossible, does not stand in the way of following the advice of Phocylides."

"But assuredly it does," he said. "This excessive care of the body, which goes beyond what gymnastic admits, is perhaps worse than anything. It is equally harassing to a man in business, in a campaign, or in magisterial office at home."

"And the worst part of it is, that it makes a man ill disposed for any kind of study, for reflection and inward meditation. It causes constant suggestions of headaches and dizziness, for which philosophy is blamed, so that it is always in the way in so far as virtue is practised and tested by study. It is always making a man fancy himself ill and be continually worrying about his health."

"That is true enough," he said.

"Then shall we say that Asclepius knew this and revealed the science of medicine for men who had naturally sound bodies and who lived a sound life, but who had some specific isolated malady? He expelled their maladies by drugs or by surgery, and ordered them to go on living in their usual way so that the affairs of state should take no harm. But he was not prepared to deal with bodies that were diseased through and through; he would not attempt special courses of treatment, draining off a little here, and pouring in a little there, which would give a man a long and miserable life, and let him beget chil-

dren, probably as diseased as himself. He was of opinion
that it was not right to treat a man who could not live
in his ordinary round of duties, such a man being useless
to himself and to the state."

"You make Asclepius a statesman," he said.

"Obviously," I said; "and don't you observe that because he was so, his sons showed themselves good fighters
at Troy, and practised medicine in the way I describe?
Do you not remember how they treated the wound which
Menelaus got from Pandarus:

> How first from it the clottered blood they sucked,
> Then medicines, wondrously composed, applied;

but they gave him no more instructions than they did
Eurypylus, as to what he should eat or drink afterwards?
Their medicines, they thought, would cure men who,
before they got their wound, had been healthy and orderly
in their manner of life, even if they happened to drink
the next moment a compound of meal and wine and
cheese; but the lives of the constitutionally diseased and
intemperate they considered useless to the patients themselves and to the rest of the world. Their art was not
meant for such people, and they were not to be treated,
though they were richer than Midas."

"You make out the sons of Asclepius to have been fine
fellows," he said.

"That is but right," I said, "though the tragedians and
Pindar disregard us, and say that Asclepius was the son
of Apollo, but was induced by an offer of money to raise
to life a rich man who was already dead, for which deed
he was struck by a thunderbolt. But in accordance with
what we said before, we shall not believe both these
statements of theirs. If he was the son of a god, he was
not, we shall say, greedy of gain; and if he was greedy
of gain, he was not the son of a god."

"That is perfectly right," he said. "But what do you

say to this, Socrates? You must get good doctors in your
city, must you not? Well, surely the best doctors will be
those who have had the largest practice among both the
healthy and the diseased, and similarly the best judges
will be those who have associated with men of every type
of character?"

"Certainly, if they are really good. But do you know to
whom I think that term applies?"

"Perhaps you will tell me," he said.

"Well, I shall try," I said; "but you have applied the
same argument to two quite different things."

"How?" he said.

"You would certainly," I said, "make very clever doctors of men who from their earliest years, besides acquiring scientific knowledge, had come in contact with very
many cases, including those which were very much diseased, and who had themselves suffered from every malady, and were not constitutionally very healthy. Because
they do not, I fancy, cure the body with the body. If
that were so, it would not do for their own bodies to
be unhealthy or for them to become ill; but they cure
the body with the mind, and if the mind is evil, or has
become so, it cannot cure anything properly."

"You are right," he said.

"But the judge, my friend, rules mind with mind, and
that we cannot allow to be trained from earliest years in
company with minds that are evil, and to have itself
committed all manner of iniquity, in order that it may
draw sharp inferences as to the guilt of others from its
own self-knowledge, as is allowable in the case of bodily
diseases. No, if a man's mind is to be noble and good,
and to judge just deeds in a sound way, he must from
early years have been without experience of or part
in evil dispositions. It is for this reason that good men
show themselves in youth to be simple-minded and easily
deceived by the wicked, because there is nothing in their

own hearts of like nature to the thoughts of evil men, with which they might compare them."

"Yes," he said, "that is markedly their experience."

"And for that reason," I said, "a good judge must not be young, but old, one who has learned late in life the nature of wickedness, not from taking note of the wickedness dwelling in his own heart, but from having learned to understand wickedness in the hearts of others, so that he has knowledge, though not personal experience, of how evil it is."

"Such a man," he said, "would be a most noble judge."

"And a good one also," I said, "which was the point of your question; for he that has a good mind is good. But that clever and suspicious fellow, who has himself done many evil deeds, and thinks himself a wise rascal, appears a master of cunning whilst he has to deal with men of his own kidney, thanks to those inward patterns by which he judges; but when he comes into contact with good men older than himself, he appears but a fool, stupidly incredulous and ignorant of a healthy moral character, since he has no pattern of any such thing in his heart. But as he comes across bad more often than good, he is thought by himself and other people to be more a wise man than a fool."

"That is very true," he said.

"Then," I said, "for a good and wise judge we must look not to this man, but to the other. For vice can never know both virtue and herself, while virtue in a well-educated nature will in course of time attain to scientific knowledge at once of herself and of vice. So the virtuous man, it appears to me, and not the wicked makes the wise judge."

"I think with you," he said.

"Then along with such judges you will give the city 410 doctors such as we described, and the two professions will tend the souls and bodies of such of your citizens as are of sound nature; but for the rest, they will permit the unsound in body to die, and actually put to death those who are incurably corrupt in soul."

"Yes," he said, "we have seen that that is best both for the sufferers themselves and for the city."

"Your young men, it is clear," I said, "will be chary of incurring any need of law, since they will be trained in that simple music which, we have declared, engenders temperance."

"Surely," he said.

"And he that is trained in music will follow the same path in his pursuit of gymnastic, and may, if he will, be independent of medicine except in extreme cases."

"I think so."

"Unlike other athletes who diet and exercise themselves to gain strength of body, he will endure the exercises and toils of gymnastic rather to stimulate the spirited part of his soul than to make himself strong."

"You are right," he said.

"Then, Glaucon, may we say that the purpose of those who established a joint education in music and gymnastic was not, as some people think, that they might tend the body with the one and the soul with the other?"

"What was it then?" he said.

"It is more likely," I said, "that both music and gymnastic are meant especially for the soul."

"How?"

"Have you never noticed," I said, "how a lifelong training in gymnastic without music affects the character, or what is the effect of the opposite training?"

"To what do you refer?" he said.

"To fierceness and hardness on the one hand," I said, "and softness and gentleness on the other."

"I know," he said, "exclusive devotion to gymnastic turns men out fiercer than need be, while the same devotion to music makes them softer than is good for them."

"Yes," I said, "It is the spirited element in their nature that produces the fierceness; well trained it would be bravery, but if it is strained over much it will turn into hardness and surliness, and naturally enough."

"I agree with you," he said.

"Then is not gentleness involved in the philosophic nature; but if it relaxes too much into gentleness, the temperament will be made too soft, while the right training will make it both gentle and orderly, will it not?"

"It will."

"Now we assert that our guardians must have both those elements of character?"

"They must."

"Then must not these be made to accord with one another?"

"Surely."

"And when this accordance has been reached, is not the soul both temperate and brave?"

411 "Certainly."

"But when there is discord, is not the soul cowardly and boorish?"

"Yes."

"Then when any man lets music flute his soul away, and pour flooding into his mind through his ears, as through a funnel, those sweet and soft and mournful melodies which we have described, till he spends his whole life piping and cloying himself with sound, that man at first tempers the spirited element in him, as steel is tempered, and makes it useful instead of useless and hard; but if he continues without ceasing to beguile that element, after a time he begins to dissolve and melt it away, till he pours out his spirit in a stream, cuts as it were the sinews of his soul, and makes of it 'a feeble warrior.'"

"That is very true," he said.

"And if," I said, "he has at the beginning received from

nature a spiritless soul, this process is rapid; if a spirited, he makes his spirit weak, and easily swayed this way and that, provoked and extinguished quickly and by trifles. Such men instead of spirited become cross and irritable, full of bad temper."

"Most certainly."

"But what is the result of hard gymnastic exercise and good living, with no participation in music and philosophy? Is not the first result that a man being sound in body is filled with understanding and spirit and becomes braver than he has ever been before?"

"It is."

"But what if he continues exclusively in this course, and has no fellowship whatever with the Muses? If there were ever in his soul any love of learning, then since it is starved of all knowledge and inquiry, and is debarred from discourse and all music, does it not become weak and deaf and blind, being never roused and never fed, and having its senses unpurged?"

"That is so," he said.

"Then such a man, I fancy, becomes a hater of reason, and unmusical. He no longer uses the persuasiveness of discourse, but accomplishes all his ends by violence and fierceness, like a brute beast, and lives in ignorance and ineptitude, devoid of all rhythm and grace."

"That is precisely what happens," he said.

"Then seemingly for those two elements of the soul, the spirited and the philosophic, God, I should say, has given men the two arts, music and gymnastic. Only incidentally do they serve soul and body. Their purpose is to tune these two elements into harmony with one 412 another by slackening or tightening, till the proper pitch be reached."

"So it would appear."

"Then we shall rightly name as the perfect master of music and understander of harmony not him who can attune the strings, but him who can most fairly mix music and gymnastic and apply them in the most perfect measure to the soul."

"Yes, and with reason, Socrates."

"Then, Glaucon, shall we not need such a one in our city to be always our minister, if the constitution is to be preserved?"

"Yes, we can have no greater need than that."

"So much, then, for our outlines of education and upbringing; for why need we lay down for these men laws for their dances, for hunting and the chase, and for their gymnastic contests and their horse-racing? It is surely clear enough that these must be in accord with what we have already prescribed. To work that out is now no difficult matter."

"Perhaps not," he said.

"Good," I said. "Now what is the next question we have to settle? Is it not who of these citizens are to rule, and who are to be ruled?"

"Yes."

"Well, is it not obvious that the older men must rule, and the younger be ruled?"

"It is."

"And the best of the older men?"

"Yes."

"Are not those who are best at farming the best of the farmers?"

"Yes."

"Then in the present case, since we must have the best of guardians, must we not have those who are best at guarding the city?"

"Yes."

"For this purpose must they not be intelligent and capable, and, moreover, careful of the city?"

"They must."

"A man cares best for what he loves?"

"Inevitably."

"And a man will be most likely to love that whose interests he thinks are bound up with his own, whose prosperity he fancies entails his own prosperity, whose adversity his adversity?"

"Yes," he said.

"Then from among the guardians we must select those men who we think, on inquiry, have excelled all their life long in doing zealously whatever they thought was for the city's interests, and in refusing resolutely to do what they thought was to its harm?"

"Yes, these are the men we want," he said.

"We must watch them, I think, at every stage of life and see that they hold fast to their doctrine, that neither witchcraft nor violence makes them forget and abandon the belief that they must do what is best for the city."

"Of what abandonment do you speak?" he said.

"I shall tell you," I said. "The loss of belief by the mind may be willing or unwiling. A man who has learnt better, loses his false belief willingly; all true beliefs, on the other hand, are lost unwillingly." 413

"I understand voluntary loss; involuntary loss you must explain to me."

"Don't you understand," I said, "or do you not think with me, that men lose good things unwillingly, bad things willingly; or that to be deceived as to the truth is bad, and to think what is true is good? Or do you not think that to believe what is, is to think truly?"

"Yes," he said, "you are right, and I think that men lose a true belief unwillingly."

"It is taken from them by theft, or witchcraft, or violence, is it not?"

"Again," he said, "I fail to understand."

"My language, I am afraid, is high-flown and obscure. I call it theft when men are persuaded out of their opinion, or when they forget it; for time in the one case, and argument in the other, robs them of their belief without their knowing what is happening. Now, do you understand?"

"Yes."

"Then I call it violence when pain or suffering makes men change their beliefs."

"That too I understand," he said, "and you are right."

"Then I fancy that you would say with me that the bewitched are those who change their beliefs under the beguilement of pleasure or the pressure of fear?"

"Yes," he said, "all things that deceive may be said to bewitch."

"Then, as I said a moment ago, we must discover who are the best guardians of the doctrine that is in them, that they must do whatever they think at any time best for the city. We must watch them from their earliest childhood, and set them tasks in which there are the strongest temptations to forget or to be cheated out of their devotion to the city. We must select those that are tenacious of memory and hard to deceive, the others we must reject. Do you agree?"

"Yes."

"We must impose upon them, too, labours, and vexations, and contests, and watch for the same things there."

"You are right," he said.

"Then," I said, "we must prepare for them a contest of the third kind, a trial in resistance to witchcraft, and watch them then. As men try whether colts are easily frightened by taking them near noises and alarming sounds, so we must bring our men, while still young, into the midst of terrors, and then again plunge them into pleasures, testing them more hardly than gold is tested in the fire; and if one appears in all things gracious and a resister of enchantment, if he is a good guardian of himself and the music he has learnt, if he bears himself in all his trials with rhythm and harmony, such a man would be of the greatest service to himself and to the city. Therefore we must elect as ruler and guardian of the city him who as boy and youth and man has been tested and has come out without stain, and render him honours **416** in life and after death, giving him the highest rewards of public burial and other memorials. The others we must reject. Some such method as that, Glaucon," I said, "seems to me the best for the election and appointment of rulers and guardians. I give the outline only without accurate details."

"My opinion is much the same," he said.

"Then is it really most correct to give these the name of perfect guardians, inasmuch as they watch over both enemies without and friends at home, taking care that the first shall be unable, and the second unwilling, to do harm; and to call the young men, whom we formerly counted as guardians, auxiliaries, and upholders of the doctrines of the rulers?"

"I think so," he said.

"Well, then," I said, "can we contrive anything in the way of those necessary lies of which we spoke a little while ago, so that by means of one noble falsehood we may convince, preferably the rulers themselves, but in any case the rest of the citizens?"

"What do you mean?" he said.

"It is no novelty," I said, "but of Phoenician origin, and has happened in many places before this, according to the accredited stories of the poets, but we have never had it, and I am not sure whether we could. It would need a great deal of persuasion to get it believed."

"You seem very shy of divulging it," he said.

"You will understand why I am shy," I said, "when I have told it you."

"Out with it," he said, "and don't be afraid."

"Well, I will, though I don't know how I am to find the courage or the words to tell you; and I shall try first to convince the rulers themselves and the soldiers, and then the rest of the city, that all our training and education of them, all those things which they thought they experienced, were only dreams. In reality all that time they were under the earth, being fashioned and trained, and they themselves, their arms and all their possessions, were being manufactured, and when they had been made quite ready, this earth, their mother, sent them up to the surface. Now, therefore, they must watch over the land in which they dwell, as their mother and nurse, and defend her against all invaders, and look upon the other citizens as their brothers and children of the same soil."

"You had reason," he said, "to be so long ashamed of telling your falsehood."

415 "Yes," I said, "you are no doubt right; but still listen to the rest of the tale. 'You in this city are all brothers,' so we shall tell our tale to them, 'but God as he was fashioning you, put gold in those of you who are capable of ruling; hence they are deserving of most reverence. He put silver in the auxiliaries, and iron and copper in the farmers and the other craftsmen. For the most part your children are of the same nature as yourselves, but because you are all akin, sometimes from gold will come a silver offspring, or from silver a gold, and so on all round. Therefore the first and weightiest command of God to the rulers is this—that more than aught else they be good guardians of and watch zealously over the offspring, seeing which of those metals is mixed in their souls; if their own offspring has an admixture of copper or iron, they must show no pity, but giving it the honour proper to its nature, set it among the artisans or the farmers; and if on the other hand in these classes children are born with an admixture of gold and silver, they shall do them honour and appoint the first to be guardians, the second to be auxiliaries. For there is an oracle that the city shall perish when it is guarded by iron or

copper' Can you suggest any contrivance by which they may be made to believe this story?"

"No," he said, "I see no hope of succeeding with your original citizens, but possibly their sons and their descendants, and subsequent generations, might believe it."

"Well," I said, "even that would have a good effect in making them care more for the city and for each other; for I think I understand what you mean."

"This will be as the popular voice shall determine. But for our part, now that we have armed these children of the soil, let us lead then forth with the guardians at their head. They shall march forth and examine which is the best place in the city for a camp, selecting a site from which they can at once control any disobedience to the law within the city, and repel all attacks from without if any enemy comes upon them like a wolf on the fold. Let them make their camp, offer sacrifices to the proper gods, and then make their arrangements for sleeping. Do you agree?"

"I do," he said.

"Their sleeping places should suffice to protect them from storms and heat, should they not?"

"Surely," he said. "For you are talking of their houses."

"Yes," I said, "but the houses of soldiers, not of money-grubbers."

"What is the difference you imply?" he said. 4li

"I shall try to tell you," I said. "You know how terrible and disgraceful it is for shepherds to keep dogs to guard their flocks which are so badly bred or trained that from want of discipline or hunger, or from some other evil in their nature, they will dare to worry the sheep, and act like wolves rather than dogs?"

"It is terrible," he said. "Certainly."

"Then we must take every precaution against our auxiliaries acting in this way to the citizens, since they are stronger than they, and behaving like fierce masters rather than loving allies?"

"We must," he said.

"Is not a really noble education the best possible precaution?"

"Well, they have that," he said.

"Well," I replied, "we need not go into that now, my dear Glaucon, but we must insist on what I have just mentioned, namely, that they must have the right kind of education, whatever that may be, if they are to have what will do more than anything else to make them gentle to one another and to those they guard."

"Yes, you are right," he said.

"But besides this education, any man of sense will tell us that their houses and their other arrangements must be so regulated as in no way to discourage them from being the best of guardians, or to incite them to maltreat the rest of the citizens."

"And he will tell us rightly," he said.

"Consider, then," I said, "whether their manner of life and their dwelling-places must be of some such fashion as this if they are to answer our description. In the first place, no one shall have any private property, unless it is absolutely necessary. Secondly, no one shall have dwelling-place or storehouse which any one who pleases may not freely enter. To supply the proper necessities of men who are warrior athletes, and both prudent and courageous, they shall receive from the other citizens a fixed reward for their guardianship, large enough to support them for a year and leave nothing over. They shall live in common, taking their meals at the public tables, as in an army. As for silver and gold, we shall tell them that they have the divine metals always in their hearts, given them by the gods, and have no need of men's silver and gold; nay, that it is an act of impiety to pollute their possession of the divine gold by conjoining it with the mortal; for many unholy deeds are done for the common currency, but the coinage in their souls is unsullied. They alone in all the city are not allowed to handle or touch silver and gold, or to be under the same roof with it, or hold it in their hands, or drink out of gold and silver vessels; this will be their salvation, and the salvation of the city. But if at any time they acquire land or houses or money of their own, and are men of business and farmers instead of guardians, they will become the hated masters instead of the allies of the other citizens. They will live their life, hating and being hated, plotting and being plotted against, always in greater and more intense fear of the citizens within than of the enemies without, rushing to the very brink of destruction, and the city with them. "For all those reasons," I said, "shall we not say that this is the manner in which our guardians must be provided with houses and other necessaries, and shall we legislate accordingly?"

"Certainly," said Glaucon.

# BOOK IV

419 HERE Adeimantus interposed with the remark: "How, Socrates, will you answer a possible objection that you are not making these men so very happy, and that this unhappiness is their own fault? Really the city belongs to them, and yet they enjoy none of the advantages of other rulers. These own lands, build fine and magnificent houses, which they furnish with an equal magnificence; they make their own sacrifices to the gods and indulge in hospitality, and, briefly, to come to what you mentioned, are in possession of silver and gold and everything that is thought essential to a state of blessedness. But your rulers, the objector will say, seem es-
420 tablished in the city just like paid auxiliaries, nothing but a garrison."

"Yes," I said, "and you may go on and say that they only get their food, and no wages in addition to it, like the other citizens; so that if they want to travel at their own expense, they will be unable; they will have nothing to give a mistress, no money to spend on anything they may happen to want, like the men who are ordinarily thought happy; you omit these counts and many like them from your indictment."

"Well," he said, "let those be added."

"Then, you ask, how shall I reply?"

"Yes."

"I fancy," I said, "that we shall find what to say, if we proceed along the path we have followed up to now. For we shall say that while it would not surprise us if even under these conditions these men were extremely happy, still our purpose in founding the city was not

to make any one class in it surpassingly happy, but to
make the city as a whole as happy as possible. For it
was our idea that in such a city we should most certainly find justice, as we should find injustice in the worst
governed city, and by inspecting both we hoped to decide our old question. And now we are, we think, constructing the happy city, not in a partial way by making
happy a few people in it, but by making the whole city
happy. When we have done we shall examine the opposite city. If we were painting a statue and someone
came and criticized us on the grounds that we were not
putting the most beautiful colours on the most beautiful parts of the statue—for the eyes, which are the most
beautiful part of the body, would not be painted purple, but black—we should be thought to reply reasonably
to such a critic if we said: 'My dear good sir, don't imagine that we ought to paint eyes so beautiful that they
don't look like eyes at all, or paint any of the other
limbs in that manner. You must consider if, by giving
each part its proper colour, we make the whole beautiful. Just so in the case before us, do not force us to
give the guardians happiness of a kind that will make
them anything rather than guardians. For we know
quite well that we might clothe the farmers in glorious
robes, and set crowns of gold on their heads, and tell
them to cultivate the land at their pleasure; and we
might have the potters recline in a graceful row by the
fire, drinking and feasting, and turning their wheel
when they felt inclined to do their work, and put all
the others in a similar state of rapture; so making the
whole city, no doubt, quite extraordinarily happy. Give
us no advice of that kind, because if we take it, the
farmer will not be a farmer, nor the potter a potter; **421**
no one in all the professions of which the state is made
up will follow his profession. But the consequences in
these cases are less important. For that cobblers should

degenerate and be corrupt, and pretend to be what they are not, inflicts no very serious harm on the city, but if the guardians of the laws and the state are such in seeming only, not in reality, then you may be sure that they will utterly destroy the whole city just as they alone have power to make it prosperous and happy.' We, that is, are making true guardians, who will be the last to harm the city; your objector offers us men like farmers, fitted not for a state but to be merry revellers at some congenial gathering, and cannot be speaking of a city at all. We then have to consider whether in establishing the guardians we are to aim at giving them as much happiness as possible, or whether we ought rather to turn our attention to giving happiness to the whole city, in which case we must compel the auxiliaries and guardians to second our efforts, and we must persuade them to be as skilful at their own business as lies in their power, and similarly with all the others. And when the whole city is thus increasing and prosperous, we may allow each class to partake of such happiness as their nature allows."

"Your words," he said, "seem to me excellent."

"Then," I said, "will you equally approve of the companion remark I make to that?"

"What is that?"

"Consider whether this is what corrupts the other craftsmen, so that they become not only corrupt, but bad workmen."

"To what do you refer?"

"Riches and poverty," I said.

"In what way?"

"In this way. Do you think that a potter who has come into money will want to go on with his craft?"

"Certainly not,"

"Will he not become more idle and careless than he was before?"

"Yes, much more."

"And that will make him a worse potter?"

"Yes; a much worse potter too."

"Then, to take the other case, if poverty prevents him from buying tools or anything else required for his craft his work will be inferior, and he will make worse craftsmen of his sons or apprentices?"

"Surely."

"Then both poverty and riches produce worse handicraft and worse craftsmen?"

"Evidently."

"Then it seems we have found some other things against whose secret entrance into the city the guardians must take every precaution."

"What are they?"

"Riches and poverty," I answered; "for the one pro- 422 duces luxury and idleness and revolution, the other revolution and meanness and villainy besides."

"Certainly," he said. "But, Socrates, think of this: How will our city be able to carry on war if it has no money, especially if it is forced to fight a city which is large and rich?"

"Clearly," I said, "to fight one such city will be rather hard, but to fight two will be easier."

"What do you mean?" he said.

"Well," I said, "in the first place you will allow that our men will be warrior athletes fighting against rich men?"

"Yes, of course," he said.

"Well, Adeimantus," I said, "don't you think that one perfectly trained boxer is an easy match for two fat wealthy men who can't box?"

"Not for both at once, perhaps," he said.

"Not if he can start to run away and then wheel round and plant a blow on the man who happens to be in front, and go on repeating these tactics in the stifling heat? Would not such a fighter beat more than two such opponents?"

"Indeed," he said, "it would not be surprising."

"And do you not think that the rich know more, both theoretically and practically, about boxing than about war?"

"I do," he said.

"Then the chances are that our athletes will be an easy match for two or three times their number?"

"I agree," he said. "I think what you say is just."

"Then suppose they send an embassy to one of the cities and quite truthfully say, 'We do not use gold or silver; we are not permitted to possess them, but you are. Ally yourselves with us therefore, and you may have the wealth of the other city.' Do you imagine that any man who heard this proposal would prefer to fight against the lean and wiry dogs rather than to fight with them against fat and tender sheep?"

"No, I think not. But," he went on, "take care that the amassing of the wealth of all the other cities by one does not involve danger to the city without wealth."

"It is certainly a happy idea of yours," I said, "to think that we can give the name of city to any but such a one as we have been organizing."

"Why not?" he said.

"You must give the others a grander title," I said. "For each of them, as the saying runs, is no city, but cities upon cities; two at the least, each other's enemies, the city of the poor and the city of the rich; and in either of these is a vast number of cities which you will be entirely wrong to treat as one. But if you treat them as many, and hand over to one class the property and offices, and even the persons of the other classes, you will always have many allies and few enemies. And so long as your city is governed wisely on the lines we have laid down, it will be the largest of all. I don't mean the most famous, but really the largest, even though it have only a thousand fighting men. For you will not easily find any one city of this size among Hellenes or barbarians, though you will find many that seem to be many times the size. Do you agree with me?"

"Most assuredly," he said.

"Our guardians, then," I said, "will find here the fairest standard by which to regulate the size of the city. They may then set apart land in proportion, and let the rest alone."

"What standard?" he asked.

"This, in my opinion," I said. "The city may go on increasing so long as it can grow without losing its unity, but no further."

"Yes, that is excellent," he said.

"Then we shall lay this further command upon the guardians, that they take every precaution that the city be neither small nor of illusory greatness, but of sufficient size and unity."

"Well, that is certainly a trifling task," he said.

"Here is another," I said, "still more trifling. We mentioned it before, when we said that it would be necessary to remove any inferior child that was born to the guardians and place it in another class, and to promote to the guardian class any noble children born among the other classes. This was intended to show that the other citizens as well as the guardians must be set each to the task for which nature has fitted him, one man one task, that so each citizen doing his own particular work may become one man and not many, and thus the whole city may grow to be not many cities, but one."

"Yes," he said, "that is a smaller affair than the former."

"Really, my good Adeimantus," I said, "those tasks we are imposing upon them are not numerous or great, as any one would allow, but quite trifling, so long as they observe the proverbial one great thing: I should rather call it sufficient than great."

"What is that?" he said.

"Education," I said, "and upbringing. For if they are all educated and become reasonable men, they will easily understand all those matters and all the other details which we now pass over—the possession of wives, and questions of marriage and the begetting of children: in all these things they will see that the proverb, 'Friends' goods are common goods,' must be realized as far as possible."

"Yes, that must be perfectly right," he said.

"Then," I said, "once our city is well started, it goes on growing as a circle round itself; for an honest upbringing and education by their preserving force create good natures, and honest natures laying hold on such an education grow better and better, and, like other animals, their breeding qualities improve at the same time."

"That is likely enough," he said.

"In a word, the overseers of the city must devote themselves to this principle, preserving it from secret destruction, and guarding it with all care—the principle, namely, that there shall be no innovation of the established order in gymnastic and music. They must watch over this with all possible care, fearing when they hear such words as

> For men more praise
> That which is newest of the minstrel's lays,

lest, perchance, someone thinks the poet means, not new songs, but a new fashion of songs, and praises that. But he must neither praise such a novelty nor understand this to be the poet's meaning. He must beware of changing to a new kind of music, for the change always involves far-reaching danger. Any alteration in the modes of music is always followed by alteration in the most fundamental laws of the state. So says Damon, and I believe him."

"You may put me down also as a believer," said Adeimantus.

"Then," I said, "here it would seem, in music, the guardians must erect their guard-house."

"The first beginnings of lawlessness in music are very hard to detect," he said.

"Yes, it is looked on as an amusement which can do no harm."

"All it does," he said, "is gradually to establish and quietly to insinuate itself into manners and customs. From these it issues in greater force and penetrates men's mutual dealings; from mutual dealings it advances, with the utmost insolence, Socrates, to laws and constitutions, till in the end it overturns all things public and private."

"Well," I said. "Is that the case?"

"I think so," he said.

"Then, as we were trying to say at the beginning, must not our children be set to more law-inspired amusements? For when amusements are lawless the children are the same, and it is impossible that they 421 should grow up law-abiding and good men."

"Surely," he said.

"Then when the children make a good start in their amusements, and through music are inspired with loyalty, the result is the very reverse of that which you have described. Loyalty pervades the whole state, fostering its growth and restoring any institutions that may have fallen into decay."

"Yes, that is true," he said.

"And this new generation bring to light those regulations that are thought unimportant, which their predecessors had allowed to fall into neglect."

"Which?"

"Such, for example, as to exact of young men a proper silence in presence of their elders, befitting behaviour in offering seats to others, and in rising to make room for them, and attention to parents, along with other rules concerning the mode of wearing the hair, concerning dress, shoes, and the other details of personal appearance. Do you agree with me?"

"I do."

"To lay down laws on such matters would, I think, be foolish. They are not established or maintained by force or written legislation."

"No."

"The probability is, Adeimantus," I said, "that the direction given by education will determine the course of all that follows. Does not like always call like after it?"

"Yes."

"And the end I think we may expect to be some one, complete, and grand result, whether good or the reverse."

"Surely," he said.

"Then for these reasons," I said, "I should not attempt to legislate on such matters."

"And quite rightly," he said.

"Then in heaven's name," I said, "what of those market troubles about contracts which the various classes make with one another in the market, and, if you please, about the contracts of craftsmen; what of libels, assaults, the bringing of lawsuits, and the empanelling of juries, and all such exaction or payment of dues as may be necessary in markets and harbours, and, in a word, all market, city, and harbour regulations, and the like—are we to venture to legislate in these matters?

"No," he said, "in these matters there is no need to dictate to true men. They will easily find for themselves most of the legislation required."

"Yes, my friend," I said, "if God grant them the preservation of those laws which we have already enumerated."

"Without that good fortune," he said, "they will spend their lives always legislating on such-like things, and always making reforms, ever hopeful of attaining the ideal."

"You mean," I said, "that they will be like men who are ill and too intemperate to consent to give up their unhealthy mode of life?"

"Certainly."

"Such men truly live a charming life. They are doctored and get no better, but only add to the complications and extent of their disease, always hopeful that some doctor will recommend a remedy which will make them well." 426

"Yes," he said, "those are just the symptoms of that type of invalid."

"Further," I said, "is not this a delightful trait of theirs, that they consider as their worst enemy him who tells them the truth, that until they give up their drunkenness and gluttony and chambering and idleness, no drugs or cauteries or surgery, no incantations or charms or anything else will be of any use to them?"

"Not very delightful," he said. "There is nothing delightful in being angry when you are given good advice."

"You are not an admirer of those men apparently?" I said.

"No, not I."

"Then neither will you admire the city as a whole which behaves as we have been describing. Do you not think that such invalids find their counterpart in those

badly governed cities in which citizens are warned on
pain of death against disturbing the whole constitution
of the city, but in which any one who serves them most
agreeably under their existing constitution, who pleases
them by servility and by anticipating and by cleverly executing their wishes, will be taken for a good man and
profoundly wise, and will be held in honour by them?"

"Yes," he said, "they seem to me to be the counterpart, and I don't in any way praise them."

"What of those individuals who are willing and eager
to serve such cities? Do you not admire their courage
and irresponsibility?"

"I do," he said, "except when they are deluded by
them and fancy themselves genuine statesmen, because
the mob praises them."

"What do you mean?" I said. "Can you not excuse
these men? Do you think it possible if a man who
knows nothing of measurement, that when many other
equally ignorant persons tell him he is a six-footer, he
should not adopt their opinion of him?"

"No," he said, "that is impossible."

"Well, don't be vexed with them, for surely the most
delightful of all are the public who go on legislating as
we described and setting things to rights, always imagining that they will find some way of stopping fraud
in contracts and those other difficulties which I mentioned a moment ago, not knowing that they are but
beheading the Hydra."

427 "Yes," he said, "that is exactly what they are doing."

"I, for my part," I said, "should not have thought that
the genuine legislator need trouble himself with those
branches of law and constitution either in an ill or in a
well governed city. In the first, because they are useless,
and effect nothing; in the second, because some of them
are discoverable by any one, and the rest result naturally
from the original institutions."

"Then," he asked, "what still remains for us in the way of legislation?"

"For us," I replied, "nothing; but for the Delphian Apollo, the first, and chiefest, and fairest objects of legislation."

"Which?" he said.

"Building of temples, and sacrifices, and other service of gods and daemons and heroes, and burials of the dead, and all the rites which we must fulfil to propitiate the departed. For of such matters we ourselves know nothing, and in founding our city, if we are wise, we shall take no advice and ask for no guidance save from our national guide. For surely this god, as he gives his guidance from his seat on the Omphalos in the centre of the earth, is the national guide of all men."

"Your words are good," he said. "Let us do as you suggest."

"Then, son of Ariston, your city is now established. The next step is to search within it, getting light for your purpose whence you may. You must look yourself, and summon your brother and Polemarchus and the rest to help you, in the hope that we may see where justice is and where injustice, and how they differ from one another, and which must be chosen by him who would be happy, whether his actions be hid or revealed to all gods and men."

"You are talking nonsense," said Glaucon. "For you promised to conduct the search, saying that it would be an act of impiety on your part to refuse to help justice with all the means at your command."

"That is true," I said. "I must do as I promised, but you must help too."

"But of course," he said.

"I hope," I said, "to make the discovery in this way. I imagine that our city, as it has been rightly established, is perfectly good?"

"Inevitably," he said.

"Then obviously it is wise, and brave, and temperate, and just?"

"Obviously."

"Then if we discover any of those virtues in the city, the undiscovered will make up the remainder?"

428        "Surely."

"Just as with any other four, if we were looking for one of them in something, we should be satisfied if we recognized that one first of all; but if, on the other hand, we detected the other three first, that in itself would mean that the object of our search had been discovered. For, then, clearly it could only be the remainder."

"You are right," he said.

"Then since the objects of our present inquiry are four, ought we not to adopt this method?"

"Clearly."

"Now, in the present case, I think that wisdom is the first to be apparent, and here we are confronted with a paradox."

"What?" he asked.

"This city which we have described is, I think, really wise. For it is prudent in deliberation, is it not?"

"Yes."

"And this faculty of prudent deliberation is clearly a kind of knowledge. For obviously it is by reason of knowledge and not of ignorance that their deliberations are prudent."

"Obviously."

"But there are in the city many and various kinds of knowledge?"

"Surely."

"Then does the knowledge of the carpenter make us call the city wise and prudent?"

"Certainly not. Such knowledge makes us call it a city of good carpentry."

"Then the city is not to be called wise because of the knowledge it possesses about wooden vessels and its deliberation on their proper manufacture?"

"No, indeed."

"Then is it knowledge about vessels of brass, or any other knowledge about things of that sort, more relevant?"

"No; no knowledge of that kind at all."

"And its knowledge of the mode of raising crops from the soil is relevant to the question of its being a successful agricultural state, but not to the question of its being wise?"

"I agree."

"Then," I said, "in the city which we have just founded is there any knowledge among any of its citizens in virtue of which it deliberates not over any of the constituents in the city, but over the whole city, considering what is its best policy, both internal and external?"

"Yes, there is."

"What is it," I asked, "and with whom is it found?"

"It is nothing but the knowledge of guarding, and it is found among those rulers whom we have just named perfect guardians."

"Then what do you call the city in virtue of this knowledge?"

"I call it prudent in deliberation and really wise," he said.

"Then do you think," I asked, "that in our city the brass-smiths or these true guardians will be in a majority?"

"The brass-smiths," he said, "easily."

"Then of all the different classes," I said, "whose names indicate the knowledge they possess, will not the guardians be the least numerous of all?"

"Yes, much the least numerous."

"Then a city founded in accordance with nature will be wise as a whole in virtue of the smallest class and part of itself, and of the knowledge possessed by that, the presiding and ruling part. And this class, whose office it is to partake of the one and only kind of knowledge to which belongs the name of wisdom, is, as we see, naturally the least numerous?"

"That is very true," he said.

"Here, then, we have somehow or other discovered one of the four and its seat in the city."

"For my part," he said, "I think it has been made out satisfactorily."

"Well, then, it is not very hard to perceive courage and the part of the city in which it was found and from which the city deserves to be called courageous."

"How is it to be perceived, then?"

"Who," I said, "in calling a city cowardly or courageous would think of considering any except that part which fights and makes war on its behalf?"

"No," he said, "no one would consider any but that."

"Whether the rest in the city are cowardly or brave," I said, "does not, I imagine, determine the character of the city one way or the other."

"No."

"Then a city is courageous in virtue of a part of itself, in that it has in that part power to preserve throughout the belief as to the things to be feared, which they are and what their nature, in accordance with the declaration of the law-giver in the system of education. Is not this what you call courage?"

"I have not quite understood what you said," he answered. "Will you say it again?"

"I mean," I said, "that courage is a kind of safe-keeping."

"Yes; but what kind?"

"The safe-keeping of the belief produced by law.

through education, concerning the number and nature of things to be feared. By preserving throughout I meant preserving it and never losing it in pains and in pleasures, in desires and in fears. I will, if you like, illustrate it by a figure which seems to me to be apt."

"Please do."

"You know, then," I said, "that when dyers want to dye wool purple they first select from wools of different colours one particular kind, namely white; they then prepare the wool, treating it most elaborately in order that it may take the colour as well as possible, and then finally they put it in the dye. Wool that is dyed in this manner takes the dye in a most lasting way; no washing, whether with or without solvents, can take out the colour. But you know what happens when these precautions are neglected, when colours other than white are selected for dyeing, or when the white wool is not treated beforehand."

"I do," he said; "the colour washes out in a ridiculous way."

"Then," I said, "you may conceive that we, too, were following some such method to the best of our power when we selected the soldiers and educated them in 430 music and gymnastic. Our purpose simply was that they should be dyed with the laws as beautifully as possible, so that with their possession of the proper nature and education their belief both concerning things to be feared and other matters should be lasting. Their colour would then be impervious to those terribly effective solvents—pleasure, which works more powerfully than any potash or lye, and pain, and fear, and desire, which are stronger than any solvent in the world. Such a power of preserving throughout the right and lawful belief concerning what is and what is not to be feared I define as courage, and give it that name if you do not object."

"No, certainly not," he said; "for I fancy that mere right opinion on these same matters such is not the result of education but the expression of an animal and slavish nature, you are very far from thinking legitimate or from calling courage."

"You are perfectly right," I said.

"Then I accept this account of courage."

"Accept it, at least," I said, "as an account of the courage of a city, and you will not go wrong. We shall discuss it more satisfactorily later, if you please. As it is, we have been looking, not for courage, but for justice, and therefore, I imagine, we have done enough for our investigation of the former."

"You are right," he said.

"Then we have still two things left to discover in the city—temperance and, finally, the main object of all our inquiry, justice."

"Yes."

"Not to give ourselves further trouble over temperance, how shall we find justice?"

"I certainly have no notion," he said, "and in any case I have no desire to discover it first if we are to have no further inquiry into temperance. What I personally should prefer is that you should first examine that."

"Certainly," I said. "I am very glad to do so. I should be churlish to refuse."

"Go on then with the examination," he said.

"I will," I replied. "At first sight it is more like a harmony or a musical mode than the former virtues."

"In what way?"

"Temperance," I said, "is surely an ordering and a control of certain pleasures and desires, as is declared by the common but mysterious expression that a man is master of himself; and there are other similar expressions which give a clue to its nature. Do you not agree?"

"Most certainly," he said.

"But is not 'master of himself' a ridiculous phrase? For he that is master of himself will surely also be slave of himself, and he that is slave, master; for the same person is mentioned in all these phrases." **481**

"Undoubtedly."

"This expression, however," I said, "seems to me to mean that there is in the man himself, that is, in his soul, a better and a worse, and when the better has by nature control of the worse, then, as we say, the man is master of himself; for the expression is one of approval. When, on the other hand, in consequence of bad training, or the influence of associates, the better is weaker than the worse, and is overcome by its superior numbers, this is condemned as something disgraceful, and the man who is in this condition is called slave to himself, and intemperate."

"Yes, that is a probable explanation," he said.

"Consider then," I said, "our new city, and you will find óne of those conditions realized in it; for you will grant that it may be justly called master of itself if the terms 'temperate' and 'master of itself' are to be applied to that wherein the better rules the worse?"

"I have considered," he said, "and find that you are right."

"We may say further that of desires and pleasures and pains, the many and diverse will be found especially in children and women and slaves, and in the vulgar herd among nominal freemen."

"Yes."

"But the simple and orderly desires which are guided by reason, and which accompany intelligence and right belief, you will find in a small number of men, in those who have the best natures and have received the best education."

"True," he said.

"Then do you not see this latter condition of things in your city, where the desires which reign in the vulgar herd are mastered by the desires and the wisdom residing in the cultivated minority?"

"I do," he said.

"Then if any city ought to be called master of pleasures and desires, and master of itself, it is this one?"

"Most certainly," he said.

"And for all these reasons must it not be called temperate also?"

"Yes, indeed," he said.

"And further, in no other city as in this one are both rulers and ruled inspired with the same belief as to who ought to rule. Do you not think so?"

"Certainly I do."

"Then in whom among such citizens will you say that temperance is to be found? In the rulers, or in the ruled?"

"In both, surely," he said.

"You see, then," I said, "that it was a clever divination of ours to say that temperance is like a harmony?"

"Why, pray?"

432  "Because temperance in its action is not like courage and wisdom. The wisdom and the courage which make the city wise and courageous reside each in a particular part, but temperance is spread through the whole alike, setting in unison of the octave the weakest and the strongest and the middle class—a unison of wisdom, if you would have that; and strength, if you would have that; of numbers also, and wealth, and any other such element. So that we may most justly say that this unanimity is temperance, the concord of the naturally worse and the naturally better as to which should rule in the city or in the individual."

"I entirely agree with you," he said.

"Good," I answered. "Then we have descried in the city three out of the four; at least so it appears. As for the last principle which completes the virtue possessed by the city, what will it be? Obviously it will be justice."

"Obviously."

"Now then, Glaucon, like hunters we must stand round the cover and watch carefully, lest by any chance justice escape us and vanish into obscurity; for it is quite plain that it is there somewhere. Do you look and make a zealous search, and possibly you may see it before I do, and point it out to me."

"I wish I could," he said. "But I shall think you are treating me fairly enough if you let me follow, so that I can see what is pointed out to me."

"Offer prayer with me," I said, "and come on."

"I will do so," he said. "But do you lead."

"Truly," I said, "the ground is difficult and overgrown. It is dark too, and the cover is thick. Nevertheless on we must go."

"Yes, we must," he said.

I looked about me and cried, "Joy, joy, Glaucon, we seem to be on the track, and I don't think the game will altogether escape."

"Good news," he said.

"Well, really," I said, "we are being stupid."

"In what way?"

"Why, my good sir, it appears that the quarry has been rolling before our feet the whole time, and we have never seen it, but have made utter fools of ourselves. Just as people sometimes go about looking for a thing which they are holding in their hands, we have been gazing somewhere miles away instead of looking at the thing before us, and quite probably that is how it has escaped us."

"What do you mean?" he said.

"I mean," I said, "that we seem to have been mentioning it and hearing it mentioned all this time without realizing that we were in a way describing it ourselves."

"A long preface," he said, "for one anxious to hear."

433 "Well," I said, "listen, and hear whether there is anything in what I say. For at the beginning when we were founding our city, the principle which we then stated should rule throughout, or at least a form of it, was, I think, justice. We stated surely, and, if you remember, have often repeated our statement, that each individual should pursue that work in this city for which his nature was naturally most fitted, each one man doing one work."

"Yes, we did."

"But we have often said ourselves, and heard others saying, that to mind one's own business and not be meddlesome is justice."

"Yes, we have."

"Well, then, my friend," I said, "this in some form or other is what justice seems to be, minding one's own business. Do you know how I infer this?"

"Do tell me," he said.

"We have examined," I said, "temperance and courage and wisdom, and I think that the remaining virtue in the city is that which enabled all these to find a place in it, and after they have appeared preserves them so long as it is present in the city. But we said that if we found the first three, the remaining one would be justice."

"Yes, inevitably," he said.

"But," I said, "if we had to decide which of those virtues by its presence does most to make the city good, it would be hard to say whether it is the unanimity of rulers and ruled, or the preservation of lawful belief concerning what is and what is not to be feared, that makes its appearance among the soldiers, or the wisdom and guardianship of the rulers, which most contributes to the city's goodness; or whether, finally, it is not this principle abiding in child and woman, in slave and freeman and artisan, in ruler and ruled, that each minded his own business, one man one work, and was not meddlesome."

"It is, in truth, a hard question," he said.

"Then apparently the principle of each man doing his own business in a city competes in promoting that city's virtue with its wisdom and temperance and courage?"

"Certainly," he said.

"But would you not affirm that the principle which competes with these in promoting a city's virtue is justice?"

"Most assuredly."

"Consider now whether this point of view brings us to the same conclusion. Will you make the rulers in the city judge law-suits?"

"Surely."

"And in their decisions will not their aim be merely to prevent either party having what belongs to others or being deprived of what is their own?"

"Yes, that will be their aim."

"On the assumption that that is just?"

"Yes."

"So from this point of view the possession and prac- **434** tice of what belongs to us and is our own would be acknowledged to be justice?"

"True."

"Consider, now, whether you agree with me. Do you think it will do any notable harm to the city if a builder attempts a shoemaker's work, or a shoemaker a builder's, or if they take one another's tools or pay, or even if the same man try to do both, and there is a general interchange in such professions?"

"No," he said.

"But I fancy when he that is by nature a craftsman or a money-maker of some kind is so elated by his wealth, or his numerous supporters, or his bodily strength, or some such qualities, that he essays to enter the warrior class; or when one of the warriors aspires to the counselling and guardian class when he is unworthy of it, and these take one another's tools and privileges, or when the same man tries to combine all these offices, then, I fancy, you think with me that such change and meddling among those classes is death to the city?"

"Most certainly."

"Our classes are three, and meddling and interchange among them is the greatest of injuries to the city, and might justly be described as the extreme of evil-doing."

"It is exactly as you say."

"Then will you not admit that the worst kind of evil-doing to one's own city is injustice?"

"Surely."

"This then is injustice; and conversely the opposite of this—when each class, money-makers, auxiliaries, and guardians, attends to what belongs to it, each doing its own work in the city—will be justice, and will make the city just."

"I certainly think," he said, "it is as you say."

"Don't let us state it quite positively yet," I said. "If this conception is also admitted by us to be justice, when applied to each individual man, we shall then assent. For what need we say more? But if it is not, then we shall search for something else. Let us now complete the inquiry which we undertook in the belief that if we first managed to perceive justice in some bigger thing which possessed it, it would then be easier to see its nature in an individual. We thought that a city was a thing of this sort, and we therefore founded the best we could, knowing that justice would be found in the good city. Let us now apply to the individual the conception that has been revealed to us there, and if the result is consistent, so much the better. But if something different is revealed in the individual, then we shall go back to the city and test it there. And perhaps 435 by looking at the two side by side, and rubbing them together, we may make justice blaze out, like fire from two sticks, and when it is revealed, we shall set it firmly in our minds."

"Well," he said, "there is method in your proposal, and we must follow it."

"Then," I said, "when to two things, a greater and a smaller, we give the same name, will they, in so far as they are called the same, be unlike or like?"

"Like," he said.

"Then, so far as the mere form of justice is concerned, the just man will in no way differ from the just city, but will be the same?"

"He will," he said.

"But it has been seen that a city is just when the three types of natures in it do each their own work, and that it is also temperate, courageous, and wise through other similar affections and conditions of those three kinds."

"True," he said.

"Then similarly, my friend, we shall expect that the individual has these same forms in his soul, and the same affections of them, if he is rightly called by the same name as the city."

"That is inevitable," he said.

"Then, my good friend," I said, "we have stumbled upon a trifling little inquiry as to whether these three forms of natures exist in the soul or not."

"It certainly does not seem to me to be trifling," he said. "But perhaps, Socrates, the common saying is true, that the beautiful is difficult."

"It appears so," I said. "And if you want to know my opinion, Glaucon, I don't think that we shall ever settle this whole question accurately by our present methods. The road which leads to that result is longer and more toilsome, but perhaps we can manage to come up to the standard of our previous statements and inquiries."

"Shall we not be content with that?" he said. "It will be quite good enough for me at this moment."

"Well, then," I said, "it will be quite sufficient for me also."

"Don't give up, then," he said, "but begin your inquiry."

"Well," I said, "are we not absolutely compelled to admit that there are in each one of us the same kinds and characteristics as there are in the city? For how else could they have got there? It would be ridiculous to imagine that among peoples who bear the reputation for being spirited, like the inhabitants of Thrace, Scythia, and the north generally, the spirited character in their states does not come from the individual citizens, or that it is otherwise with the love of learning which would be chiefly ascribed to this country, or with the 436 love of riches, which people would especially attribute to the Phoenicians and the inhabitants of Egypt."

"Certainly," he said.

"Then we may take this as a fact," I said, "and one not hard to comprehend?"

"No, it is not."

"But this is a hard question, whether in our actions we always use the same element, or whether there are different ones which are used for different purposes. Do we, that is, learn with one and feel anger with another of

the elements within us and with a third desire the
pleasures of food and drink and propagation, and so
on; whenever we have an impulse to action, do we employ the whole soul on each of these different occasions?
These are the questions which are hard to determine
satisfactorily."

"I agree with you," he said.

"Then let us try this method of ascertaining whether
these elements are identical with one another, or different."

"What method?"

"It is obvious that the same thing will not at one and
the same time, in the same part of it, and in the same
relation, do two opposite things or be in two opposite
states; so that if we find such conjunction of opposites
in these elements, we may be sure that they are not
one, but several."

"Good."

"Now consider what I say."

"Speak on," he said.

"Can the same thing," I asked, "at one and the same
time, and in the same part of it, be at rest and in
motion?"

"Certainly not."

"Let us come to a more exact understanding. If we go
too fast we may fall into ambiguities. If someone were
to say of a man who was standing still, but moving his
arms and his head, that the same man was at the same
time at rest and in motion, we should say, I fancy, that
this was not a proper description, but that one part of
him was at rest and another in motion. Is not that the
case?"

"It is."

"Well, if our friend were to become still more subtle,
and make the pretty point that peg-tops are at one and
the same time at rest and in motion throughout, when

they spin with their pegs fixed to the same place, and that the same is true of anything else which revolves in a fixed spot, we should agree, on the ground that the parts in respect of which they are at rest and in motion on these occasions are different. We should say rather that they have an axis and a circumference and in respect of the axis are at rest, inasmuch as they do not lean to one side, but in respect of the circumference they revolve. But if, while they are revolving, they at the same time incline the axis either to the right or the left, or forward or backward, then they are in no sense at rest."

"That is perfectly correct," he said.

"Then none of those objections will frighten us," I said, "nor in any way persuade us that under any circumstances any one and the same thing could at one and the same time, in the same part of it, and in the same relation, be acted upon in two opposite ways, or 437 be two opposite things, or produce two opposite effects?"

"No, I shall certainly not be persuaded," he said.

"In any case," I said, "we don't want to be compelled to examine in detail all difficulties of this kind, and to waste our time in establishing their falsehood; and so we may proceed on the assumption that what we have said is right, agreeing that if at any time we have to change our opinion, all the consequences of our assumption shall be considered invalid?"

"Yes," he said, "that is our best method."

"Now," I said, "would you say that assent and dissent, the seeking after an object and the refusal to take it, attraction and repulsion, and so on, are mutual opposites? Whether they are actions or passions makes no difference?"

"Yes," he said, "they are opposites."

"Then," I said, "would you say thirst and hunger

and the desires generally, including also willing and wishing, may be classed with the former of those general terms just mentioned? For example, would you not admit that the soul of him who desires seeks after that which he desires, whatever it may be, or attracts to himself that which he wishes to have, or, again, so far as he is willing that something should be given him, his soul longing for its accomplishment nods assent to this as though she were asked a question and were replying to herself?"

"I should."

"Again, shall we not class not wishing and not willing and not desiring with repulsion and rejection, and all those opposed general terms?"

"Surely."

"This being so, shall we say that there is a class of desires, and that what we call thirst and hunger are the most marked of those?"

"Yes," he said.

"The first is a desire for drink; the second, for food?"

"Yes."

"Then will thirst so far as it is thirst, be a desire in the soul for anything more than drink? Is thirst, that is to say, thirst of hot drink or of cold, or of much drink or of little, or in a word, of drink of a particular kind? Or is the desire for cold drink the additional result of heat and thirst combined, and for hot drink the result of cold and thirst? And again, does the desire for much drink arise when the thirst is much owing to the presence of muchness, and for little drink when the thirst is little? That is, is the mere state of being thirsty ever a desire for anything besides its natural object, namely, drink, and similarly with hunger and the desire for food?"

"In that way," he said, "each mere desire is a desire only for its mere natural object, while the desires for this or that kind of object are the result of additions."

**438** "Well, then," he said, "let no one take us unaware and vex us with the objection that no man desires drink only but good drink, or food only but good food. For all men, they say, desire things that are good. Therefore, since thirst is a desire, it will be a desire for something good—drink, or whatever it may be—and similarly with other desires?"

"Yes," he said, "there might seem to be something in that objection."

"But surely," I said, "wherever you have terms which imply something else, the qualified terms, I think, imply a qualified, and simple unqualified terms a simple."

"I don't understand," he said.

"Do you not understand," I said, "that the greater implies, that is, is greater than, something?"

"Certainly."

"Implies the less?"

"Yes."

"And the much greater the much less? Does it not?"

"Yes."

"And the sometimes greater the sometimes less, and the future greater the future less?"

"Certainly."

"Then does not 'the more' in this way imply 'the less,' and the 'double' 'the half,' and so on, 'the heavier' 'the lighter,' and 'the swifter' 'the slower,' and also 'the hot' 'the cold,' and similarly with similar epithets?"

"Assuredly."

"Then does the same apply to the various kinds of knowledge? Mere knowledge implies the mere knowable, however we ought to describe the object of knowledge, but knowledge of a particular quality implies an object of a particular quality. For example, when a science of building houses arose, was it not distinguished from the other sciences and called the science of build-ing?"

"Yes."

"And was that not because it was of a particular qual-ity, like none of the others?"

"Yes."

"And did it not get this particular quality from the particular quality of its objects? And does not the same apply to the other trades and sciences?"

"It does."

"Then," I said, "you may take it that this was my meaning, if you now understand, that when you have terms that imply another, the simple imply the simple, the qualified the qualified. I don't in the least mean that the relatives are of the same quality as their cor-relatives, that the science of the healthy and the dis-eased, for example, is healthy and diseased, or the sci-ence of the evil and the good is evil and good, but as soon as you had a science which was not of the mere knowable, but of an object of a particular quality, in this case healthy and diseased, then the science in its turn assumed a particular quality, and the result was that it was no longer called simply science, but the quality was added, and it was called medical science."

"I understand," he said, "and I think you are right."

"Well, then," I said, "will you not agree that thirst, 439 in being what it is, is one of those things which imply another? Thirst, of course, implies—"

"Yes," he said, "it implies drink."

"Then a particular quality of thirst implies a par-ticular quality of drink, but thirst pure and simple does not imply much or little, or good or bad drink, or, in a word, any particular quality of drink, but thirst and nothing more implies drink and nothing more."

"Assuredly."

"Then the soul of the thirsty man, in so far as it is

thirsty, wants only to drink, and longs and strives after this?"

"Obviously."

"Then if there is anything which holds it back when it is thirsty, will it not be something in it distinct from that which thirsts and which drives it like a beast to drink? For surely, as we said, the same thing does not at one and the same time with the same part of itself and in the same relation do opposite things?"

"No, certainly not."

"Just as, I fancy, it is incorrect to say of an archer that his hands are at one and the same time drawing the bow towards him and thrusting it away. We ought rather to say that one hand is thrusting it away, and the other drawing it towards him."

"Assuredly," he said.

"Now, can we say that people are sometimes thirsty and yet decline to drink?"

"Most certainly," he said; "that often happens with many people."

"Then what are we to say about them?" I asked. "Must we not say that there is that in their soul which orders them to drink, and there is that which hinders them from drinking, the latter being distinct from, and master of, the former?"

"I certainly think so," he said.

"May we say then that that which hinders in these cases, whenever it arises in the soul, is produced there by reasoning, while the impulses leading and dragging the soul are engendered by particular conditions and diseases?"

"Apparently."

"Then we shall have reason," I said, "in affirming that these are two and distinct from one another. The first, that with which the soul reasons, we shall call the rational part; the second, that with which it loves, and hungers, and thirsts, and flutters round the other desires, we shall call the irrational and desiring part, the companion of various indulgences and pleasures."

"Yes, we have good cause to think so," he said.

"Let us assume then that we have distinguished these two parts in the soul. Now is spirit, or that by which we feel indignant, a third part, or, if not, with which of these two is it naturally connected?"

"Possibly," he said, "with the second, the desiring element."

"Well," I said, "I rely on a story which I once heard, how Leontius, the son of Aglaion, was coming up from the Peiraeus, close to the outer side of the north wall, when he saw some dead bodies lying near the executioner, and he felt a desire to look at them, and at the same time felt disgust at the thought, and tried to turn aside. For some time he fought with himself and put his hand over his eyes, but in the end the desire got the better of 440 him, and opening his eyes wide with his fingers he ran forward to the bodies, saying, 'There you are, curse you, have your fill of the lovely spectacle.'"

"Yes," he said, "I have heard the story myself."

"But observe," I said, "that the story shows that anger sometimes fights against the desires, which implies that they are distinct principles."

"It does," he said.

"And do we not often notice on other occasions," I said, "when a man is forced by his desires against his reason, that he abuses himself, and is indignant with that within him which is constraining him? In such a case there is strife between two principles, and the spirit appears as an ally of the reason. But I fancy that you will not assert that you have ever noticed either in yourself or in any one else the other phenomenon, the spirit siding with the desires when the reason decides that they are not to interfere with it."

"No, assuredly not," said he.

"Well," I said, "when a man thinks he is in the wrong, what then? Is it not the case that the nobler he is the less is he capable of being angry because he is made to suffer hunger and cold, or anything else, at the hands of him whom he conceives to be inflicting a just punishment; in other words his spirit declines to be roused against his punisher?"

"True," he said.

"But what of a man who thinks he is wronged? Does he not then fume and chafe and fight on the side of what he believes to be just? Though he suffer hunger and cold and every kind of privation, he perseveres till he conquers, and never desists from his noble indignation, until he has either accomplished his purpose or perished, or until reason within him calls him back as a shepherd calls his dog, and he relents."

"Yes," he said, "it is much as you describe it. And indeed in our city we have made the auxiliaries subject to the rulers like sheep-dogs of the city's shepherds."

"You understand beautifully what I mean," I said. "But consider this further point."

"What?"

"Our present view of the spirited element is the opposite of what we held a while ago. For we then thought that it was in some way of the nature of desire, but we now say that it is anything but that. Rather in the war of the soul it ranges itself on the side of the rational part."

"Certainly," he said.

"Then is it distinct from this also, or is it a form of the rational element, so that there are not three kinds in the soul, but two—the rational and the desiring? Or, as 441 the city was composed of three classes—money-making, auxiliary, and counselling—is there likewise in the soul also this third element of spiritedness, which is the natural auxiliary of the rational, so long as it is not corrupted by evil upbringing?"

"It must be a third part," he said.

"Yes," I said, "if it appears to be distinct from the rational, as it has been seen to be from the desiring element."

"But that is easily seen," he said. "You may observe that in children: from their earliest years they are full of spirit, but some of them seem to me never to acquire reason, and most of them only do so quite late."

"On my word, that is well said," I answered; "and the truth of your remarks is confirmed by considering animals. And besides this evidence there is the case which we mentioned some time ago, to which Homer witnesses in the words:

> He chid his angry spirit and beat his breast.

For in this passage Homer clearly distinguishes between two principles, and depicts the one, which reasons concerning the better and the worse, rebuking the other for its unreasoning anger."

"You are perfectly right," he said.

"Well," I said, "after a hard fight for it we have swum to shore, and are pretty well agreed that there are in a city and in the soul of each individual the same three kinds."

"We have."

"Then does it not now follow that the individual will be wise in the same way and by reason of the same element as the city?"

"Surely."

"And the city will be courageous by reason of the same element and in the same way as the individual is courageous and both will have all the other elements of virtue in the same way?"

"Inevitably."

"Then finally, Glaucon, we shall say that a man is just in the manner in which a city was just."

"That, too, follows inevitably."

"But we have surely not forgotten that the city was just by reason of the three classes within it each doing their own work?"

"I think we have not forgotten," he said.

"Then we must bear in mind that each one of us will be just and doing his own work if the parts within him are doing severally their own work?"

"Yes," he said. "Certainly we must bear that in mind."

"Then is it not befitting that the rational part should rule, inasmuch as it is wise and has foresight for the whole soul, and that the spirited part should be its subject and ally?"

"Certainly."

"But is it not the case, as we said, that a blending of music and gymnastic will make these elements harmonious, inciting and nourishing the reason by noble words 442 and instruction, and slackening the other by soothing admonition, taming it by harmony and rhythm?"

"Undoubtedly," he said.

"And these two so nurtured, truly taught and trained in their own offices, will be set over the desiring element, which of a truth makes the greatest part of each man's soul, and is by nature insatiably covetous. Over it they will keep guard lest it fill itself with the false pleasures of the body, and becoming great and strong no longer attend to its own work, but try to get the rule and mastery over those matters that do not belong to it, and so quite overturn the life of the whole."

"Certainly," he said.

"And would not these two," I said, "also be the best guards of the whole soul and of the body against external enemies, the rational element giving counsel and the other fighting its battles, following its ruler, and bravely executing its purposes?"

"Yes."

"And I fancy that we call the individual courageous in this part of him, when the spirited element preserves, in spite of pains and pleasures, the precepts of reason concerning what is and what is not to be feared?"

"That is right," he said.

"And we call him wise by reason of that other small part, that in him which rules and issues these precepts, that which possesses in itself knowledge of what is advantageous to each and all of those three principles?"

"Certainly."

"Further, do we not call him temperate by reason of the friendship and harmony of these elements, when the ruler and the two subjects are agreed that the rational element must rule, and there is no rebellion against it?"

"Certainly," he said; "temperance in a city or in an individual is nothing else than this."

"Well, then, the individual will be just in virtue of our oft-repeated principle, and in that way?"

"Inevitably."

"What then?" I said. "Do we find justice at all dimmer to our eyes or different from what it was seen to be in the city?"

"I certainly do not think so," he said.

"Well, we can make perfectly sure," I said, "if there be any doubt lingering in our souls, by comparing our result with common notions."

"To which do you refer?"

"For example, if we were discussing this city, and the man who by nature and training is like to it, and had to decide whether such an one would appropriate gold or silver which had been left in his trust, do you think that any one would believe that he would do it more readily than men of another nature?"

"No one," he said.

"And would he not also keep himself clear of sacrilege, and theft, and of being false to his friends or a traitor to his city?"

"He would."

"And of course he will never be in any way guilty of bad faith in oaths or in any other compact?"

"Surely not."

"And he is the last man who would be capable of adultery and neglect of parents and want of observance to the gods?"

"Yes, assuredly," he said.

"And is not the reason for all this that each of the elements within him keeps to its own work in regard to ruling and being ruled?"

"That and nothing else."

"Then do you still seek justice elsewhere than in this power which produces men and cities of such a character?"

"No," he said, "not I."

"Then that of which we dreamed has now its perfect fulfilment; I mean, the suspicion we expressed that at the very beginning of our construction of the city we stumbled by some divine providence upon a principle and type of justice?"

"Yes; certainly."

"For in point of fact, Glaucon, there was an image of justice in the principle that he whom nature intended for a shoemaker should attend to shoemaking and nothing else, and that the carpenter should do carpentry, and so on; and that is why it helped us."

"Apparently."

"And in truth, justice, as it appears, is something of this kind. But it does not concern a man's management of his own external affairs, but his internal management of his soul, his truest self and his truest possessions. The just man does not allow the different principles within him to do other work than their own, nor the distinct classes in his soul to interfere with one another; but in the truest sense he sets his house in order, gaining the mastery over himself; and becoming on good terms with himself through discipline, he joins in harmony those different elements, like three terms in a musical scale—lowest and highest and intermediate, and any others that may lie between those—and binding together all these elements he moulds the many within him into one, temperate and harmonious. In this spirit he lives; whether he is money-making or attending to the wants of his body, whether he is engaged in politics or on business transactions of his own, throughout he considers and calls just and beautiful all conduct which pursues and helps to create this attitude of mind. The knowledge which superintends these actions is for him wisdom, while any conduct which tends to destroy this 444 attitude is for him unjust, and the belief which inspires it ignorance."

"That is most certainly true, Socrates," he said.

"Good," I said. "Then if we declare that we have discovered the just man and the just city, and justice which rules in them, I fancy that we shall not be thought to be speaking altogether falsely."

"No, by heaven!" he said.

"Then shall we make this declaration?"

"Yes."

"Let it be done then," I said. "And now I think we have to inquire into injustice?"

"Clearly."

"Must not it be a kind of quarrel between those three— a meddlesomeness and interference and rebellion of one part of the soul against the whole that it may gain a rule over it to which it has no right; while the whole is such by nature that that part ought to be a slave, and the other part, which is of the royal class, ought not? Such a state of affairs, I fancy, and the disturbance and confusion of these principles, we shall declare to constitute injustice and incontinence, and cowardice and ignorance, and, in a word, all wickedness."

"Yes, precisely so."

"Then," I said, "since injustice and justice are now revealed to us, is it not quite clear what it is to act unjustly and to be unjust, and what it is also to act justly?"

"In what way?"

"Clearly," I said, "they do not differ from healthy and diseased conditions. As those are to the body, so are acting justly and acting unjustly to the soul."

"How?" he asked.

"Surely healthy conditions produce health, and diseased conditions disease?"

"Yes."

"Well, does not just action likewise produce justice, and unjust action injustice?"

"Necessarily."

"Now to produce health is to put the various parts of the body in their natural relations of authority or subservience to one another, while to produce disease is to disturb this natural relation."

"Yes."

"Then to produce justice," I said, "is to put the parts of the soul in their natural relations of authority or subservience, while to produce injustice is to disturb this natural relation, is it not?"

"Surely," he said.

"Then virtue, seemingly, will be a kind of health and beauty and good condition of the soul, vice a disease and ugliness and weakness."

"That is true."

"Then do not fair practices conduce to the acquisition of virtue, ugly practices to the acquisition of vice?"

"Necessarily."

"There now apparently remains for us to inquire whether it is profitable to act justly and follow fair practices and be just, and that whether the just man is recognized as such or not, or whether acting unjustly and being unjust is profitable, even if the unjust man is not punished, or reformed by correction." 445

"But, Socrates," he said, "this inquiry seems to me ridiculous at this stage, now that we have reached those respective conclusions about justice and injustice. People think that when the constitution of the body is ruined life is not worth living, not with all the foods and drinks and wealth and dominion in the world; and are we to believe that, when the constitution of the very principle of our life is in confusion and ruin, life is then worth living, though a man do whatever he please—unless only he find some means of escaping from vice and injustice, and of acquiring justice and virtue?"

"Yes, it is ridiculous," I said. "Still, since we have got to a position where we can perceive the truth of this most clearly, we must not give up."

"No, most certainly not," he said.

"Come here, then," I said, "and look with me on the different forms of vice as I conceive them, or as many of them as are worth observing."

"Say on," he said, "I follow."

"Well," I said, "I look out from the mountain top to which we have climbed in our argument, and see that there is one form of virtue but innumerable forms of vice, and among them four that are specially worthy of mention."

"What do you mean?" he said.

"There will probably be," I said, "as many varieties of souls forming specific kinds as there are similar varieties of political constitutions."

"And how many are there?"

"Five varieties of constitution," I said, "and five of souls."

"Tell us which they are," he said.

"I will," I answered. "One variety of constitution will be that which we have described, though it may have two names. It will be called a monarchy when there is one man of surpassing excellence among the rulers; when there are more than one, it will be called an aristocracy."

"True," he said.

"This, then," I said, "I designate as one form; for whether there are several rulers or only one will not make them disturb any fundamental law of the city, so long as they observe the nurture and education which we have described."

"No, naturally not," he said.

# BOOK V

"Good and right, then, do I call such a city and constitution, and such a man; and the others, since this is right, I call bad and mistaken, whether they deal with the government of cities or the organization of the character of the individual, and they may be arranged in four varieties of vice."

"What are they?" he asked.

I was going on to deal with them in order as they appeared to me to develop from one to the other, when Polemarchus, who was sitting some little way from Adeimantus, stretched out his hand, and taking hold of him by the garment high up near the shoulder, drew him to him, and leaning forward whispered something in his ear of which we only heard the following: "Shall we let be," he said, "or what shall we do?" "Certainly not," said Adeimantus, quite loud.

"What in particular," I asked, "are you not going to let be?"

"You," he said.

"Because of what particular remark of mine?" I asked.

"We think," he said, "that you are shirking and are cheating us out of a whole division of the subject, and a most important one, which you don't want to go through. You thought that we should not notice that trifling remark of yours, that it would be obvious to every one that as concerns women and children friends have things in common."

"Well, was I not right, Adeimantus?" I said.

"Yes," he said. "But like the rest, this 'right' needs explanation. We must know by what method this com-

munity is to be carried out. For there are many possibilities. Do not, therefore, pass over the plan which
you propose. We have been waiting all this time expecting that you would certainly tell us of the conditions
of begetting children, and how they will be reared after
they are born, and would explain all this community of
wives and children of which you talk. For we conceived
that it would make a great or rather the whole difference
to the constitution whether it was rightly or wrongly
managed. But now that you are taking up another constitution without handling these questions satisfactorily,
450 we came to the resolve which you heard, that we should
not let you be till you had discussed these questions as
you did the rest."

"You may put me down," said Glaucon, "as voting
for that resolution."

"It's all right," said Thrasymachus. "You may consider, Socrates, that we have passed it unanimously."

"What a deed you have done," I said, "in fastening
upon me! What a long discussion about the constitution
you are starting again from the very beginning! I was
rejoicing in the thought that I had finished with it by
this time, and quite content that what I said then should
be accepted and allowed to pass. You don't know what
a swarm of discussions you are rousing by reviving these
topics now. I saw them and let them alone before, to save
you endless trouble."

"Why," said Thrasymachus, "do you imagine that we
have come here to find an El Dorado, and not precisely
to listen to discussions?"

"No doubt," I said; "but of a reasonable length."

"Yes, but, Socrates," said Glaucon, "to men of understanding their whole life is a reasonable time to listen
to such discussions. But never mind about us. For yourself, do not weary of answering our questions on these
subjects, and choose whatever method you think best to

explain what kind of community our guardians will observe concerning the children and the women, and the nurture of the children while they are young in the period between their birth and their education. That, indeed, is considered the most troublesome business of all. Try, then, to tell us in what manner it must be arranged."

"It is no easy matter to discuss, my sanguine friend," I said. "There are many more points in it which will tax your confidence than in the subjects of our previous discussions. In the first place, the practical possibility of my proposals will not be believed, and, secondly, it will also be doubted whether on the assumption of their being completely carried out they are actually the most desirable. And for these reasons I have some hesitation in having anything to do with them, for fear, my dear friend, that the argument may seem to be an idle dream."

"Have no hesitation," he said, "for your audience are neither without understanding nor incredulous nor unfriendly."

"My good sir," I replied, "are you really seeking to encourage me by those words?"

"I am," he said.

"Well," I answered, "their effect is precisely the opposite. If I were confident that I was speaking with knowledge, your encouragement would be excellent. For to speak with knowledge of the truth about matters dear to us and of the highest importance among men of understanding who are our friends is a thing that may be done with assurance and safety. But to bring forward proposals when one is still incredulous and inquiring, as I am doing now, that is a dangerous and alarming task. Not that I am afraid of making myself ridiculous. To be so 451 were childish. But I am afraid of slipping from the truth, and being overthrown just where a false step is most to be dreaded, and not only falling myself, but dragging my friends after me. And I bow to Nemesis, Glaucon, touching what I am about to say. For I do believe that to be an involuntary homicide is a less crime than to be a deceiver concerning noble and good and just laws. This venture, therefore, is better made among enemies than among friends. So you see how well you encourage me."

Glaucon smiled and said, "Well, Socrates, if we suffer anything amiss from the discussion, we acquit you and pronounce you guiltless of our blood and not our deceiver. So take courage and say on."

"Well," I said, "in cases of homicide he that is acquitted is free from guilt, according to the law. And if in that case, it is likely that he will be in this."

"For these reasons," he said, "say on."

"We must go back, then," I said, "and say what perhaps should have been said in its proper place. However, it may be right after the men have played their part that the women should come on in their turn, especially when you demand it in this way. For men who are, by nature and education, such as we have described, there is, in my opinion, no right possession or use of children and women except along the lines on which we originally started them. We tried in our argument, if you remember, to make our men like guardians of a flock."

"Yes."

"Then let us follow this up and give corresponding rules for birth and nurture, and see whether we approve the result or not."

"How?" he asked.

"In this way. Do we think that the females of watchdogs ought to watch as well as the males, ought to hunt with them, and generally share their occupations, or should they be kept indoors in the kennels, on the ground that breeding and rearing the puppies disables them for anything else, while the hard work and all the care of the flocks is reserved for the males?"

"They should share in everything," he said. "Only we treat the females as the weaker and the males as the stronger."

"Can you," I said, "use any living creature for the same work as another unless you rear and train it in the same way?"

"No," he said.

"Then if we employ women at the same tasks as men, we must give them the same instruction?"

"Yes."

"The men were given music and gymnastic."

"Yes."

"Then we must assign to the women also these two arts, and the art of war in addition, and treat them in the same way."

"That follows from what you say," he said.

"Possibly," I said, "if our words are translated into action, these proposals may seem to involve many ridiculous breaches of etiquette."

"They certainly will," he said.

"Which of them do you find most ridiculous?" I asked. "Is it not obviously the notion of women exercising in the palaestra naked along with men, and not only young women, but positively the older also, just like those old men in the gymnasia who keep up their devotion to gymnastic though they are wrinkled and ugly?"

"Yes, most certainly," he said. "It would appear ridiculous, at least under present conditions."

"Well," I said, "as we have started the subject we must not be afraid of the gibes of fine gentlemen, of all the different things they will say against such a change taking place in the gymnasia, in music, and not least, in the bearing of arms, and horse-riding."

"You are right," he said.

"But since we have begun the subject we must go on

over the rougher ground of this law of ours, and request these jesters to stop minding their own business and to be serious. We shall remind them that it is not long since the Greeks thought it ugly and ridiculous to see men naked, as most barbarian races do now, and that when gymnastics were introduced first by the Cretans, and later by the Lacedaemonians, the witty men of the day had the opportunity of making fun of all these things. Do you agree with me?"

"I do."

"But I fancy when they found from experience that it was better to strip than to cover up the body, then too what had seemed ridiculous to the eye disappeared before the face of the arguments showing what was best; and this proved that he is a fool who thinks that anything but the bad is ridiculous, and tries to raise a laugh by regarding any spectacle, except that of folly and evil, as ludicrous, or indeed he who aims seriously at any standard of beauty which he may set up for himself, except the good."

"Most certainly," he said.

"But must we not first come to an agreement as to whether these proposals are practical or not, and allow any one, whether he is a jester or a serious person, to 453 raise the question whether female human nature is capable of sharing with the male in all his occupations, or in none of them, or whether it is capable of some and not of others, and to ask in the last case to which of these classes warfare belongs? Would not this naturally be the best beginning, and lead to the best conclusion?"

"Much the best," he said.

"Then," I said, "shall we on behalf of these other people put the question to ourselves, that the other side may not be besieged without having defenders?"

"There is nothing to hinder us," he said.

"Then shall we say on their behalf: 'Socrates and

Glaucon, there is no need for others to raise an objection against you. For in the beginning of your settlement of the city, you yourselves admitted that each should, as nature provides, do his own work, one person one work.' "

"I think we did. How could we do otherwise?"

" 'But is not a woman by nature very different from a man?' "

"Certainly she is different."

" 'And ought not different tasks to be assigned to different individuals in accordance with the nature of each?' "

"Yes."

" 'Then are you not mistaken and inconsistent now in maintaining, as you do, that men and women should do the same things, seeing that they have widely different natures?' Will you be able to offer any defence to that, my wonderful friend?"

"It is certainly not easy just at the moment," he said. "But I shall have to ask you, as I do now, to interpret our argument also, whatever it is."

"This, Glaucon," I said, "with many other similar difficulties, is what I have foreseen all this time. For that was why I was afraid, and hesitated to touch on the law concerning the possession and nurture of women and children."

"I don't wonder," he said. "By Zeus, no, it is not an easy task."

"It is not," I said. "But the truth is, whether a man falls into a small swimming-bath or into the middle of the mighty ocean, he has to swim all the same."

"Certainly."

"Well, then, we must strike out and try to get safe out of the argument, in the hope of a dolphin taking us up, or of some other impossible means of salvation."

"It looks like it," he said.

"Come, then," I said, "let us see whether we can possibly find a way out. We admit that different natures ought to do different things, and that the natures of a man and of a woman are different, but now we say that these different natures should do the same things. Is that the accusation against us?"

"It is."

454    "A noble thing, Glaucon," I said, "is the power of the art of controversy."

"Why do you say so?"

"Because," I said, "many people seem to me to fall into it quite against their will, and to think that discussion which is really contention, because they cannot examine the subject of their argument by analysing its various forms, but will urge their contradiction of what has been said in reliance on the mere sound of the word, dealing with one another by contention, and not by scientific argument."

"Yes," he said, "that happens with very many people. But does it touch us at this moment?"

"Most certainly it does," I said, "for we seem, quite against our will, to be dealing with controversial arguments."

"In what way?"

"When we insist that what are not the same natures ought not to have the same pursuits, we cling to the verbal point most bravely and contentiously, but we have never inquired at all of what kind were the sameness and the difference and with reference to what we were then distinguishing them, when we proposed to give different pursuits to different natures, and the same pursuits to the same natures."

"No," he said, "we did not inquire."

"In the same way," I said, "we might evidently ask ourselves whether bald and hairy men had the same or opposite natures; and, agreeing that they have opposite natures, might forbid hairy men to be shoemakers if bald men are, or forbid bald men if hairy men are."

"Well, that would be ridiculous," he said.

"But would it not be ridiculous," I said, "simply because, in that proposition, we did not mean same and different in general? Our rule was only directed against that particular form of likeness and difference which concerns those particular pursuits. We meant, for example, that the soul possessed of medical capacity and a doctor have the same nature. Do you agree with me?"

"I do."

"But a doctor and a carpenter have different natures."

"Of course."

"Then," I said, "if we find either the male or the female sex excelling the other in any art or other pursuit, then we shall say that this particular pursuit must be assigned to one and not to the other; but if we find that the difference simply consists in this, that the female conceives and the male begets, we shall not allow that that goes any way to prove that a woman differs from a man with reference to the subject of which we are speaking, and we shall still consider that our guardians and their wives ought to follow the same pursuits."

"And quite rightly," he said.

"Is not our next step to invite the supporters of the contrary opinion to show us in reference to what art or 455 what pursuit among all those required for the service of the city, the nature of men and women is not the same, but different?"

"That is certainly just."

"Perhaps others might make the same reply as was made by you a little while ago, that it is not easy to give a satisfactory answer at the moment, but that it would not be difficult after consideration."

"They might."

"Then shall we request our objector to follow us, in

the hope that we may prove to him that there is no occupation in the organization of the city which is peculiar to women?"

"Certainly."

" 'Come, then,' we shall say to him, 'answer this. When you say that one man has a natural talent for anything, and another is naturally unfitted for it, do you mean that the first learns it easily, while the second learns it with difficulty? that the first, after a little study, would find out much for himself in the subject which he has studied; but the second, in spite of much study and practice, would not even keep what he had learned? that in the one the mind would be well served by the bodily powers, in the other it would be thwarted? Are not these the only signs by which you meant to determine in any case natural talent or the want of it?' "

"No one," he said, "will name any others."

"Then, do you know any human occupation in which the male sex does not in all these particulars surpass the female? Need I bore you by referring to weaving and the making of pastry and preserves, in which, indeed, the female sex is considered to excel, and where their discomfiture is most laughed at?"

"What you say is true," he said. "Speaking generally, the one sex is easily beaten by the other all round. There are indeed many cases of women being better than men in many different employments, but, as a general rule, it is as you say."

"Then, my friend, there is not one of those pursuits by which the city is ordered which belongs to women as women, or to men as men; but natural aptitudes are equally distributed in both kinds of creatures. Women naturally participate in all occupations, and so do men; but in all women are weaker than men."

"Certainly."

"Shall we, then, assign all occupations to men and none to women?"

"Of course not."

"But we shall say, I fancy, that one woman is by nature fit for medicine, and another not; one musical, and another unmusical?"

"Surely."

"And is not one woman a lover of gymnastic and of war, and another unwarlike and no lover of gymnastic?" 456

"I should think so."

"And one a lover and another a hater of wisdom; one spirited, another spiritless?"

"Yes."

"Then one woman will be capable of being a guardian and another not. For did we not select just this nature for our men guardians?"

"We did."

"Then for the purposes of guarding the city the nature of men and women is the same, except that women are naturally weaker, men naturally stronger?"

"Apparently."

"Then we must select women of the necessary character to share the life of men of like character and guard the city along with them, inasmuch as they are capable and of a kindred nature?"

"Certainly."

"Then must we not assign the same occupations to the same natures?"

"Yes."

"So we are come round to what we said before, and allow that there is nothing unnatural in assigning music and gymnastic to the wives of the guardians?"

"Most certainly."

"Then our legislation has not been an impracticable dream, seeing that we have made our law in accordance with nature? Present conditions which depart from this are evidently much more a departure from nature."

"Evidently."

"Now were we not inquiring whether our proposals are practicable and desirable?"

"We were."

"And we are agreed that they are practicable?"

"Yes."

"Then we must next come to an agreement on their desirability?"

"Obviously."

"Then surely if women are to become fit to be guardians, we shall not have one education to make guardians of the men and another for the women, especially when education will have the same nature to work upon?"

"No."

"What is your opinion in a question like this?"

"Like what?"

"How do you conceive to yourself one man as better and another as worse? or do you think that all are alike?"

"Certainly not."

"Then, in this city which we were founding, do you think that our guardians, who have received the education we have described, will be better men than the shoemakers who have been trained in shoemaking?"

"The question is ridiculous," he said.

"I understand," I said. "Then are not these the best of all the citizens?"

'Much the best."

"Further, will not these women be the best of the women?"

"Yes, much the best also."

"Then is anything better for a city than that it should contain the best possible men and women?"

"Nothing."

"But will not music and gymnastic, employed as we 451
have described, bring about this result?"

"Surely."

"Then we have laid down laws for the city which are
not only practicable, but also desirable?"

"Yes."

"Then we must make the wives of our guardians strip,
for they will clothe themselves with excellence instead of
garments, and we must make them take their share in
war and the other duties of guarding the city, and let
them do nothing else. Only of these we must assign the
lighter to the women, because of the weakness of the sex.
And the man who laughs at naked women, when their
exercise has the best as its aim, plucks from his wisdom
the unripe fruit of laughter, and has no notion apparently at what he laughs or what he does. For in truth the
common saying will ever be the fairest saying, that the
useful is beautiful and the harmful ugly."

"Most certainly."

"This, then, is one wave which, we may say, has been
surmounted in our discussion of the law for women. We
have, without being swamped, managed to reach the conclusion that our men and women guardians must follow
all pursuits in common: rather the argument somehow
comes to an agreement with itself that its proposals are
practical and advantageous."

"Certainly," he said; "it is a small wave that you are
surmounting."

"You will say that it is no great one," I said "when you
see the next."

"Say on, and let me see it," he answered.

"This new law," I said, "follows, I fancy, the one we
have just had, and all those that went before."

"What is it?"

"That these women should be all of them wives in
common of all these men, and that no woman should live

with any man privately, and that their children too should be common, and the parent should not know his own offspring nor the child its parent."

"This," he said, "is much more formidable than the other. It is much harder to believe in its being practicable or advantageous."

"I don't think," I said, "so far as the question of advantage is concerned, there could be much dispute as to its being the greatest blessing to have both wives and children common, if it were possible. But I fancy that there might be keen controversy as to whether the proposal is practicable or not."

"Both points might very easily be disputed," he said.

"Then we shall have to face an alliance of arguments," I said. "I was expecting that I should run away from one if you agreed as to the advantage of the proposal, and then I should be left with the question whether it was practicable or not."

"Well, you have not managed to run away," he said, "but have been caught; prepare, therefore, to defend both points."

"I must pay the penalty," I said. "But grant me this 458 favour. Let me keep holiday, like those lazy-minded men who are wont to feast themselves on their own thoughts when they are travelling alone. Such men, you know, do not wait to discover the means of attaining the object of their desires. They let that question alone to save themselves the weariness of deliberating about what is practicable and what is not. They suppose that they have what they desire, and then proceed to arrange the remainder of the business, and amuse themselves by enumerating all that they will do when their desire is realized, so making their already lazy minds even lazier. I, too, now am yielding to laziness, and I wish to defer the first question as to the practicability, of these proposals and consider it later. In the meantime, if you will allow me, I shall assume their practicability, and examine what arrangements the rulers will make when these proposals are put into practice, and show that their realization will be of the greatest possible benefit to both city and guardians. I shall try thoroughly to discuss these points with you first, and leave the others till later, if you will allow me."

"I will," he said, "so begin your discussion."

"I imagine," I said, "that if our rulers are worthy of the name, and if their auxiliaries are the same, that the latter will be willing to carry out their orders, and the former in giving their orders will themselves obey the laws, or where we leave them discretion, will be faithful to their spirit."

"Naturally," he said.

"Then you, the lawgiver, as you have selected the men, will select the women, choosing as far as possible those of a similar nature, and place them together. Both sexes will live together, with common houses and common meals, no one possessing any private property; and associating with one another in the gymnasia and in the rest of their daily life, they will be led, I imagine, by an inherent necessity to form alliances. Do you not think that this will be inevitable?"

"Yes," he said; "not by geometric but by lovers' necessity, which, perhaps, is stronger than the other in its power to persuade and constrain the mass of men."

"You are right," I replied. "But next, Glaucon, promiscuous unions or anything of that kind would be a profanation in a state of happy citizens, and the guardians will not allow it."

"No, it would not be just," he said.

"Then clearly we shall next see to making the marriages as sacred as possible, and this sanctity will attach to those which are most advantageous."

"Most certainly."

459 "How then will they be most advantageous? Tell me this, Glaucon. I see that you have in your house hunting dogs and a great many game birds. Tell me, I conjure you, have you paid any attention to their unions and breeding?"

"In what respect?" he said.

"Firstly, though they are all well bred, are there not some which are, or prove themselves to be, the best?"

"There are."

"Then do you breed from all alike, or are you anxious to breed as far as possible from the best of them?"

"From the best of them."

"Then do you breed from those that are very young or very old, or as far as possible from those that are in their prime?"

"From those in their prime."

"And if you did not breed in this way, are you of opinion that the stock of birds and dogs would greatly deteriorate?"

"I am," he said.

"What is your opinion in regard to horses and other living creatures?" I said. "Would it be different with them?"

"The idea is absurd," he said.

"Good heavens, my dear friend," I said, "what surpassing excellence we need in our rulers, if the same principles apply to the human race!"

"They certainly do," he said. "What then?"

"Because," I said, "they will have to administer a great deal of medicine. You know that for cases where medicine is not needed, and the constitution will respond to a diet, we think a quite ordinary doctor good enough; but when medicine has to be administered, we know that a much more courageous doctor is needed."

"True. But what is your point?"

"This," I answered. "It seems that our rulers will have to administer a great quantity of falsehood and deceit for the benefit of the ruled. For we said, if you remember, that all such practices were useful in the form of medicine."

"Yes, and we were right," he said.

"And the rightness of it seems to find special application in marriages and the begetting of children."

"In what way?"

"From our admissions," I said, "it follows that the best of both sexes ought to be brought together as often as possible, the worst as seldom as possible, and that we should rear the offspring of the first, but not the offspring of the second, if our herd is to reach the highest perfection, and all these arrangements must be secret from all save the rulers if the herd of guardians is to be as free as possible from dissension."

"You are perfectly right," he said.

"We must then have statutory festivals, at which we shall bring together the brides and bridegrooms. There should be accompanying sacrifices, and our poets must 460 compose strains in honour of the marriages which take place. But the number of marriages we shall place under the control of the rulers, that they may as far as possible keep the population at the same level, having regard to wars and disease and all such ravages, and also taking care to the best of their power that our city become neither great nor small."

"You are right," he said.

"They must invent, I fancy, some ingenious system of lots, so that those less worthy persons who are rejected when the couples are brought together may on each occasion blame their luck, and not the rulers."

"Certainly," he said.

"And surely to our young men who acquit themselves well in war or other duties we may give, along with other rewards and prizes, a more unrestricted right of cohabitation in order that there may be a colourable excuse for such fathers having as many children as possible."

'You are right."

"Then the children as they are born will be taken in charge by the officers appointed for the purpose, whether these are men or women, or both. For of course offices also are common to men and women."

"Yes."

"The children of good parents, I suppose, they will put into the rearing pen, handing them over to nurses who will live apart in a particular portion of the city; but the children of inferior parents and all defective children that are born to the others, they will put out of sight in secrecy and mystery, as is befitting."

"Yes, they must," he said, "if the race of guardians is to be pure."

"And will not these officers also superintend the rearing of the children, bringing the mothers to the nursery when their breasts are full, and taking every precaution to prevent any woman knowing her own child, and providing wet-nurses if the mothers are not enough; and will they not take care that the mothers do not give too much time to suckling the children, and assign night watches and all troublesome duties to nurses and attendants?"

"As you describe it," he said, "child-bearing will be a very easy matter for the wives of the guardians."

"So it ought to be," I said. "Let us now discuss the next point in our proposals. We said that children must be born from parents in their prime."

"True."

"Then do you agree with me that on an average a woman is in her prime for twenty years, and a man for thirty?"

"Which twenty, and which thirty?" he said.

"For a woman," I said, "the proper time is to begin at

twenty years and bear children for the city until she is forty; for a man the proper time to begin is when he has seen 'the swiftest prime of his running' go by, and to beget children for the state until fifty-five."

"Yes," he said, "in both cases that is the period of their 461 prime both in body and mind."

"Therefore if a man above or below these ages meddles with the begetting of children for the commonwealth, we shall declare this to be a transgression both impious and unjust; he is raising up a son for the state who, though his birth be secret, will not be born the child of the sacrifices and prayers which the priests and priestesses and the whole city will offer, when on each occasion of marriage they pray that the children may be ever better and more useful than their good and useful parents; but he will be born in darkness, the child of dire incontinence."

"You are right," he said.

"And the same law will apply," I said, "if a man who is still of an age to be a father meddles with a woman of marriageable age when the ruler has not joined them. We shall say that he is giving to the city a child that is a bastard, unauthorized and unholy."

"You are perfectly right," he said.

"Then I fancy that when the men and women have passed the age of having children we shall, of course, leave them at liberty to associate with whomsoever they please; except that a man must not associate with his daughter or his mother, or his granddaughter or grandmother; and the women we shall allow to associate with any one but a son or a father, or grandson or grandfather; and all this only after we have exhorted them to be very careful that no child, if one should be so conceived, should see the light; but if one should by any chance force its way to the light, they must dispose of it on the understanding that such an offspring is not to be reared."

"These are certainly reasonable proposals," he said. "But how will they distinguish one another's fathers and daughters, and the relations you have just mentioned?"

"They will not do so," I said. "But all the children that are born in the tenth month, and also in the seventh, after a man's bridal day, will be called by him, if male his sons, and if female his daughters, and they will call him father, and similarly he will call the offspring of his generation grandchildren, and they again will call him and his fellow-bridegrooms and brides grandfathers and grandmothers; and, lastly, those born in the time when their fathers and mothers were having children will be called brothers and sisters, so that in accordance with what we said a moment ago, they will not associate with one another; but the law may allow the union of brothers and sisters if the lot falls in that way, and the priestess of Apollo approves."

"Quite right," he said.

"Such, then, Glaucon, is the community of wives and children for the guardians of your city. Its consistency with the rest of the constitution and its pre-eminent desirability we must go on to establish from the argument. Do you agree?"

462 "Yes, by all means," he said.

"Then is not the first step in our search for agreement that we should ask ourselves what is the greatest good that we can mention for the equipment of our city, at which the lawgiver must aim in his legislation, and what the greatest evil; and then we may inquire whether the institutions we have described fit into our outline of the good and are contrary to our outline of the evil?"

"Most certainly."

"Can we mention any greater evil to a city than that which rends it asunder and makes it not one city but many? or any greater good than which binds it together and makes it one?"

"We cannot."

"Then does not communion in pleasure and pain bind the city together, when, as far as may be, all the citizens rejoice and grieve alike over the same births and the same deaths?"

"Certainly," he said.

"On the other hand, is not individuality in these feelings a dissolving force, when one part of the citizens are smitten with grief and the other transported with joy over the same experiences of the city or its inhabitants?"

"Surely."

"And does not this state of things result when such words as 'mine' and 'not mine,' 'another's' and 'not another's,' are not pronounced in the city in concert?"

"Yes, indeed."

"Then that city is best governed, whichever it may be, in which the largest number of men agree in applying these words, 'mine' or 'not mine,' to the same thing?"

"Very much so."

"And is it not this that is nearest the condition of a single individual? For consider, when any one of us hurts his finger, the whole fellowship of body and soul which is bound into a single organization, namely, that of the ruling power within it, feels the hurt, and is all in pain at once, whole and hurt part together. And so we say that the man has a pain in his finger. And in regard to any part of the human body whatever, may not the same account be given of the pain felt when a part is hurt, and of the pleasure felt when it is at ease?"

"Yes," he said. "And to return to your question, the life of the best governed city comes very near to this condition."

"Then I fancy that when an individual citizen has any experience, whether good or bad, such a city will most certainly declare that experience its own, and the whole city will share his joy or his sorrow."

"That must certainly be the case if the city has good laws," he said.

"It will now be time for us," I said, "to return to our own city and examine whether in it we shall find the conclusions of our argument most strikingly realized, or whether in this point some other city surpasses it."

"Yes, we must do so," he said.

463 "Well, then, in this city, as in the rest, there are rulers and people, are there not?"

"Yes."

"And do not these all call each other citizens?"

"Surely."

"But in other cities, what do the people call the rulers besides citizens?"

"In many cities they call them masters, but in democratic cities simply rulers."

"What of the people in our city? What do they call the rulers besides citizens?"

"Saviours and helpers," he said.

"And what do these call the people?"

"Wage payers and supporters."

"But what do the rulers in other cities call the people?"

"Slaves," he said.

"And what do the rulers call each other?"

"Fellow-rulers," he said.

"And in our city?"

"Fellow-guardians."

"Then can we say of a ruler in other cities that he may address one of his fellow-rulers as a kinsman and another as a stranger?"

"Yes, many might."

"Then does he not think and speak of the kinsman as belonging to him, and of the stranger as not belonging?"

"Yes."

"But what of your guardians? Could any of them think of or address one of his fellow-guardians as a stranger?"

"Certainly not," he said, "for in every one he meets he will think he has a brother or sister, or father or mother, or son or daughter, or grandchild or grandparent."

"Excellent," I said. "But answer me this also. Will your law prescribe for them only names of kinship, or must all their actions be in accordance with these names? In their behaviour towards their fathers must they not observe all that the law prescribes for this relation— reverence, filial care, and the proper obedience to parents—or else suffer at the hands of God and man? For he who acts otherwise profanes heaven and wrongs man. Will not those sayings be sung by all the citizens, and sound in their ears from their earliest childhood with reference to those who are pointed out to them as fathers and other relatives?"

"They will," he said. "It would be ridiculous if with their lips alone they uttered the names whilst they neglected the acts of friendship."

"Then in this city above all others, when any one meets with good fortune or with bad they will join in uttering the words of which I have just spoken, saying 'It is well with mine' or 'It is ill with mine.'"

"Very true," he said.

"Did we not say that upon this belief and its expression followed a community in pleasures and pains?"

464

"We did, and we were right."

"Then will not our citizens most truly have community in the same thing, that to which they will apply the name 'mine,' and having such community, will they not most truly have community of pleasure and pain?"

"Certainly."

"And besides the general arrangements of the state, is not the guardians' community of wives and children a cause of this?"

"Most certainly it is," he said.

"But you remember that when we likened a well established city to the relation of a body and its members in its feelings of pleasure and pain, we agreed that this was the greatest good that could come to it."

"And we were right," he said.

"Then we have proved the auxiliaries' community of wives and children to be a cause of the greatest good that a city can have?"

"Certainly we have," he said.

"Then in this we are also consistent with our former remarks. For we said, did we not, that if they were to be guardians in reality they must not have houses or land or any other possession of their own, but must receive what they need for sustenance from the other citizens as wages for their guardianship, and lay it out in common?"

"We were right," he said.

"Then am I correct in saying that these regulations, together with our former statements, will do still more to make them true guardians, and prevent the disruption of the city which would result if each man gave the name of 'mine' not to the same but to different things; if all took what they could get for themselves, and dragged it off to different private houses; if each called a different wife and different children his own, and thus implanted in the city the individual pleasures and griefs of individuals: rather they will have one single belief concerning what is their own and be all concerned in the same purpose, and so will all be, as far as is possible, simultaneously affected by pleasure and pain?"

"That is perfectly true," he said.

"Further, will not lawsuits and prosecutions almost have disappeared if their own persons are their only private property and everything else is common? Will they not, therefore, be free from all those quarrels that arise among men from the possession of money, or children, or kinsmen?"

"It is quite inevitable that they should," he said.

"Further, no actions for forcible seizure or for assault will rightly arise among them; for we shall declare, I suppose, that it is honourable and just for equals to defend themselves against equals, so compelling them to keep themselves in condition."

"That is right," he said.

"Yes, and here is further reason why this law is right. 465 When any man is angry with another, if he may vent his anger in this way he is less likely to make a serious quarrel of it."

"Certainly."

"Further, we shall authorize the elder to rule over and chastise all the younger."

"Clearly."

"Also a younger man will never dare to strike or in any other way do violence to an older unless at the command of the guardians. That we may reasonably expect. And I fancy that he will not do him dishonour in any other way. For two guardians will be strong enough to prevent him—fear and shame—the shame that forbids him to lay hands on his parents, and the fear that the others will come to the rescue of the injured man, whose sons and brothers and fathers they are."

"Yes, that will be the result," he said.

"Then in every way our laws will make these men dwell at peace with one another?"

"Yes, to a large extent."

"Then if they are free from dissension, there is no fear of the rest of the city quarelling either with them or with one another?"

"No, certainly not."

"I am almost ashamed to go on and mention the petty evils which they will escape. The poor will no longer need to flatter the rich; they will be free from all the perplexities and worries of bringing up children and making an income which are entailed in the upkeep of a household—the borrowing and repudiation, the scraping together of money to give to their wives and servants to manage for them. The nature and extent of men's sufferings over these matters are obvious, and ignoble too, not deserving mention."

"Yes, they are obvious even to the blind," he said.

"Then they will be rid of all those troubles, and their life will be more blessed than the blissful life of Olympian victors."

"How?"

"Well, the happiness of Olympian victors consists in but a small portion of the blessings of our guardians. For the guardians' victory is nobler and their public maintenance more complete. For the victory they win is the salvation of the whole city, and sustenance and all that life requires is the crown given to them and to their children. Their own city gives them privileges in their lifetime, and after death a fitting burial."

"Yes, these are noble gifts," he said.

"But do you remember," I said, "that a little while 466 ago we were troubled by someone's objecting that we were not making our guardians happy, who with power to have all the wealth of the citizens had actually nothing? We replied, did we not, that we should examine this question later if it came in our way, but that at the moment we were making our guardians real guardians and making the city as happy as we could, not confining ourselves to one class in the city and making that happy?"

"I remember," he said.

"Then, since the life of the auxiliaries is seen to be far nobler and better than that of Olympian victors, can we possibly think it on a level with the life of shoemakers or any other craftsmen, or with the life of farmers?"

"I think not," he said.

"No, but we may justly say now, what I said then,

that if our guardians try to be happy in such a way that they cease to be guardians, if they will not be satisfied with a life so moderate and secure, a life which, as we say, is the best, if an insensate and childish notion about happiness possesses their souls and impels them, because of the power they possess, to make everything in the city their own, then they will know how truly wise Hesiod was when he said 'the half is greater than the whole.' "

"Yes," he said, "if they take my advice they will remain true to the life we have described."

"Then do you agree," I asked, "to this community of women with men in education, in the care of the children and guardianship of the other citizens, and that they must both remain in the city and go out to war, guard and hunt with the men like dogs, and as far as possible take their full share in everything, and that by so doing their actions will be most desirable and not contrary to the natural relations of male and female or their natural community?"

"I agree," he said.

"Then," I said, "have we now only left for consideration whether the establishment of this community is as possible among men as it is among other living creatures, and in what way it is possible?"

"That is the question with which I was going to interrupt you," he said. "You have forestalled me."

"We need not speak about war," I said, "for it is obvious, I fancy, what will be the manner of their wars."

"What?" he asked.

"Both sexes will go to war together, and will take with them such of the children as are strong enough, that, like the children of other craftsmen, they may have a sight of what they will have to do when they are grown up. Besides looking on, they will have to give the general help and service required in war, and assist their fathers 467 and mothers. Have you not noticed this in the various ʃrafts, that the children of potters, for example, have to spend a long time in looking on and helping before they start making pots?"

"Certainly."

"And ought they to be more careful in training their children in experience of, and acquaintance with, their duties than are the guardians?"

"No, that would be ridiculous," he said.

"And, besides, every creature fights more bravely in the presence of its offspring?"

"That is so. But, Socrates, there will be considerable danger in the case of those defeats which are common in war, that both they and their children will fall, and the rest of the city be unable to recover."

"That is true," I said. "But, in the first place, do you think that we should always try to avoid the possibilities of danger?"

"Certainly not."

"Then if we must have danger, had we not better have it when success will mean improvement?"

"Obviously."

"But do you think it unimportant whether the men who are to be warriors should, or should not, see warfare when they are children, and not worth some risk?"

"No, it certainly is important for the purpose you mention."

"We must arrange, then, that the children should see war, and contrive that they shall do so safely. In that way all will be right, will it not?"

"Yes."

"Well, in the first place," I said, "will not their fathers know and understand, as far as men may, which expeditions are dangerous, and which are not?"

"That is probable," he said.

"And they will take the children to the latter, but be careful not to take them to the former kind?"

"Rightly so."

"And, no doubt," I said, "they will set rulers over them, and those not the meanest of the citizens; men of experience and mature age shall be their guides and tutors?"

"That is only proper."

"Still we may object that many things fall out quite contrary to expectation."

"Certainly."

"Then in view of such contingencies, my friend, our children must from the first be given wings, in order that, in case of necessity, they may fly away and escape."

"What do you mean?" he said.

"We must set them on horseback," I said, "in their earliest years, and when we have had them taught to ride, must take them to view the fighting mounted not on spirited chargers, but on the fleetest and most docile horses we can find. For in this way they will get the best view of the work for which they are destined, and, in case of necessity, will most securely make their escape, following in the train of their grown-up tutors."

"I think you are right," he said.

468

"To come now to war regulations," I said, "how should you have your soldiers disposed to one another and to their enemies? Am I right in my ideas?"

"Tell me what they are," he said.

"If any of them deserts his rank," I said, "throws away his arms, or does any cowardly action of that sort, must he not be degraded to a craftsman or a farmer?

"Certainly."

"And him who is taken alive by the enemy, shall we not present to his captors to use their catch as they please?"

"Yes."

"But when a man has done bravely and distinguished himself, do you not think that, in the first place, he ought to be crowned on the field by each in turn of the youths and children who are serving with the army?"

"Certainly I do."

"And shaken by the hand."

"Yes, that also."

"But I fancy that in this you will no longer agree with me."

"In what?"

"In the suggestion that he should kiss and be kissed by each in turn."

"I am for that, most strongly of everything," he said. "And I make this addition to the law, that, as long as the campaign lasts, no one whom he wishes to kiss may say him nay, in order that if any soldier be in love, whether with male or female, he may be more eager to carry off the prize of valour."

"Excellent," I said. "And we have already mentioned that there are more marriages arranged for a brave man than for the others, and more frequent selections of such men than of the others, in order that as many children as possible may be obtained from such a father."

"Yes, we have," he said.

"For that matter, we have it on Homer's authority that it is just to honour brave youths in this way. For Homer says that Ajax when he had distinguished himself in battle received as a reward 'whole chines of beef,' implying that this was a proper way of honouring a brave man in the prime of his manhood, a reward which was a mark of honour, and at the same time would increase his physical strength."

"You are perfectly right," he said.

"Then on this point we shall follow Homer," I said. "At sacrifices, and on all similar occasions, we shall honour the brave according to their degree of merit, not only with hymns and the rewards we have just mentioned, but also with 'special seat and special meat and fuller goblets,' that we may while honouring our brave men and women, also discipline them."

"Your remarks are excellent," he said.

"Good. And when men are killed in a campaign, shall we not say, in the first place, that he who has made a glorious end belongs to the golden race?"

"Most certainly we shall."

"And on the death of men of this race shall we not say With Hesiod that

469

> As holy spirits they dwell on earth and guard
> Humanity, kind warders off of evil?

"Yes, we shall."

"And shall we not inquire of the god how to order the sepulture of sacred and divine persons, and with what special ceremonies, and bury them with the rites the god advises?"

"Surely we shall."

"And for all time to come shall we not render service and worship at their tombs, as at the tombs of demigods? And shall we ordain the same rites for any of those who have been judged of surpassing excellence of life when they die of old age, or from any other cause?"

"That is but just," he said.

"Further, how will our soldiers deal with their enemies?"

"To what does your question refer?"

"Well, in the first place, take the practice of ɛnslavement. Do you think it just that Greek cities should enslave Greeks? or should they make it their rule, and enforce the same in other cities, to spare all of the Greek race, fearing their own enslavement by the barbarians?"

"That is beyond all comparison the better course," he said.

"And do you agree that they must not hold Greeks in

slavery, and must advise the rest of Greece to follow their example?"

"Certainly," he said. "Their energies would thus be directed more against the barbarians and less against their countrymen."

"Further, is it well after victory to strip the slain of anything except their arms? Does not this give cowards a pretext for keeping out of the fighting line on the excuse that, when they are stooping over the dead, they are engaged in necessary work; and have not many armies been lost by this practice of spoiling?"

"Yes."

"Do you not think it mean and avaricious to spoil a dead body, and the sign of a small feminine mind, when your foe is dead and flown away, leaving only that with which he has fought, to think that his body is your enemy? Are men who do so any better, in your opinion, than dogs who worry the stones that are thrown at them and do not touch him who throws them?"

"Not a bit better," he said.

"Then we must let alone the spoiling of the dead or prevention of the removal of the fallen?"

"Yes, assuredly we must let that well alone," he said.

"Nor, of course, must we carry the arms to the temples to dedicate them there—certainly not the arms of Greeks, 470 if we have any thought for the goodwill of the rest of Greece. Rather we shall be afraid of polluting the temples by bringing to them the spoils of our kinsmen, unless, indeed, the god instructs us otherwise."

"That is very right," he said.

"Consider now the practices of ravaging Greek territory or burning homesteads. What attitude will your soldiers adopt to those practices in warfare?"

"I should like to hear your opinion on the subject," he said.

"I think," I said, "that they would refrain from both

these practices, and would be content with taking the yearly harvest. Shall I give you my reasons?"

"Please do."

"It appears to me that war and sedition, as they are two in name, are also two in reality. For the words are applied to differences arising in two things—namely, in what is akin or related, and what is foreign or alien. Sedition is the name given to the enmity of what is akin; war that given to the enmity of what is alien."

"That is a very just mode of speaking," he said.

"Then see if this is also justly spoken. I declare the Greek race to be akin and related to themselves, but foreign and alien to the barbarians."

"And you say well," he said.

"Then when Greeks and barbarians fight, we shall say that they are natural enemies, warring against one another, and this enmity is to be called war; but when Greeks fight with Greeks, we shall declare that naturally they are friends, and that when anything of this kind occurs, Greece is sick and attacked by sedition, and this kind of enmity is to be called sedition."

"Yes," he said, "I agree to view the matter in this way."

"Now observe," I said, "what happens in the case of what is ordinarily called sedition. When anything of this kind occurs and a city is divided against itself, if one faction ravages the territory or burns the homesteads of the other, the sedition is thought to be sinful, and both parties are looked upon as unpatriotic. If they were not they would never have dared to mangle the land which is their nurse and mother. But it is considered reasonable that the victors should carry off the crops from their adversaries, but that they should feel that they are not always going to be at war, but will some day be reconciled."

"Yes, this feeling betokens a far more civilized condition than the other," he said.

"Well, then," I said, "will not the city of which you are founder be Greek?"

"It must be," he said.

"Then its citizens will be good and civilized?"

"Very much so."

"And patriotic Greeks, too, will they not, who will consider all Greece as their own country, and share in the common festivals with the rest of Greece?"

"Most certainly."

471 "Then will they consider a difference with Greeks to be a difference with kinsmen, and therefore sedition? They will certainly not call it a war."

"No."

"And will they not prosecute their quarrel in the hope of being eventually reconciled?"

"Certainly."

"They will therefore correct them in a friendly spirit, and chastise them without any intention of enslaving or destroying them, since they are their correctors, not their enemies?"

"Yes," he said.

"Then none who are Greeks will ravage Greece or burn homesteads. They will never consider all the inhabitants of a city, men, women, and children, to be their foes, but only those few who are responsible for the quarrel. And for all those reasons, since the majority in any city are their friends, they will not consent to ravage their land or destroy their houses. They will prosecute their quarrel only until the guilty parties are compelled by the sufferings of the innocent to give satisfaction for their offence."

"I agree," he said, "that our citizens should adopt this behaviour towards their opponents, and they should behave to barbarians as Greeks now behave to one another."

"Then shall we prescribe this law to the guardians,

that they must neither ravage territory nor burn home-steads?"

"Yes, we will; and we will assume that this and the former enactments are excellent. But really, Socrates, if we allow you to go on in this way, I think you will never come to the question which you postponed some time ago before you entered on all these topics—the question whether this constitution is realizable, and if so, in what way it could ever come into being. For, as far as your contention is concerned—that if it could, nothing but advantage would result to the city where it was found—I not only agree with you, but can offer some additional arguments which you omit. They would fight most valiantly against their enemies, as they would be very unlikely to desert one another, acknowledging each other as brothers, fathers, or sons, and calling each other by these names. And if their womankind fought with them—whether in the same ranks or posted behind as a reserve to strike terror into their enemies, and to give assistance wherever it might be wanted—then I know that they would be absolutely invincible. Also, I see all the advantages which they would enjoy at home, which you have omitted. Now, since I acknowledge that they would have all those advantages, and thousands more, were this constitution realized, you need not go on describing it in fuller detail, but let us now try to persuade ourselves on this point: Is the city realizable? If so, how? And we may leave the other question alone."

"What a sudden attack you have made upon my argument," I said, "and what little mercy you have on my hesitation! Perhaps you are not aware that, after I have just managed to escape those two waves, you are bringing down on me the greatest and the most formidable of the three. When you see and hear what it is, you will certainly forgive me for my natural hesitation and my fear of 472 stating or trying to inquire into an argument so paradoxical."

"The more you talk like that," he said, "the less we shall excuse you from stating how this constitution can be realized. So begin without delay."

"Well, first of all," I said, "we must remember that it is a search after the nature of justice that has brought us to this point."

"We must. What about it?" he said.

"Nothing. Only if we discover what justice is like, shall we expect that the just man must in no way differ from this conception, but be in every respect the same as justice is? or shall we be content if he comes very close to it, and partakes of it more than any one else?"

"Yes," he said, "we shall be content with that."

"It was in order to have a standard," I said, "that we were inquiring what justice itself is like, and what the perfectly just man would be like, if he should come into existence, and were inquiring similarly as to injustice and the perfectly unjust man. We wanted to be able to see how those two men appeared to us to enjoy happiness or its opposite, so that we might be compelled to acknowledge concerning ourselves that he who resembles them most closely will also have a lot most closely resembling theirs. We had no desire to prove that these standards could be realized."

"Yes," he said, "that is true."

"Now, do you think any less well of an artist who has painted a pattern of what the most beautiful man would be like, with everything correct in the composition, because he cannot prove that such a man might possibly exist?"

"No, certainly I do not," he said.

"Well, then," I said, "were not we two fashioning in argument a pattern of a good city?"

"Certainly."

"Then do you think any less of our words because we cannot prove that is possible to found a city of the manner we have described?"

"Surely not," he said.

"That is the truth of the matter," I said. "But if to please you I must exert myself and show in what especial way and under what conditions it can be most nearly realized, you must make me these same admissions with a view to this demonstration."

"What admissions?"

"Can anything be done as it is spoken, or is it nature 473 that action should lay less hold of truth than speech, though not every one thinks so? Do you agree or not?"

"I do," he said.

"Then in that case do not compel me to show that what we have decided in our argument could in all respects be reproduced in experience. If we manage to discover how a city could be organized in any close correspondence to our description, then you must allow that we have discovered that your commands could be realized. Will you not be content with that? I certainly should be."

"Yes, I will," he said.

"Then, next, apparently we must try to discover and demonstrate what evil practice in the cities of to-day prevents them from being organized in this way, and what is the smallest change by which a city might arrive at this manner of constitution. We shall hope to confine ourselves to a single change, or, if that is impossible, to two, or if that will not suffice, to changes as few in number, and small in their effect, as is possible."

"Most certainly," he said.

"Well, there is one change," I said, "which I think we could prove would bring about the revolution. It is certainly neither a small nor an easy change, but it is possible."

"What is it?" he said.

"Now," I said, "I am at the very topic which we likened to the greatest wave. Spoken, however, it shall be, even though it is likely to deluge me with laughter and ridicule, like a wave breaking in merriment. Consider then what I am about to say."

"Say on," he said.

"Unless," I said, "philosophers bear kingly rule in cities, or those who are now called kings and princes become genuine and adequate philosophers, and political power and philosophy are brought together, and unless the numerous natures who at present pursue either politics or philosophy, the one to the exclusion of the other, are forcibly debarred from this behaviour, there will be no respite from evil, my dear Glaucon, for cities, nor, I fancy, for humanity; nor will this constitution, which we have just described in our argument, come to that realization which is possible for it and see the light of day. It is this which has for so long made me hesitate to speak. I saw how paradoxical it would sound. For it is given to few to perceive that no other constitution could ever bring happiness either to states or individuals."

"After venturing on a statement like that, Socrates," he said, "you may expect that many most redoubtable assailants will wait for no more, but will pull off their coats and, snatching the first weapon that comes to hand, rush at you in tremendous eagerness, ready to do all kinds of extraordinary deeds. Unless you can keep them off by your argument and escape them, you will learn to your cost what flouting means."

"Have you not brought all this upon me?" I asked.

"I have," he said, "and I was right to do so. Still I shall not betray you, but defend you by what means I can. I can give you sympathy and encouragement, and perhaps answer you a little more carefully than another might. That is the sort of assistance you will get, so you must endeavour on those terms to prove to the sceptics that what you say is true."

"I must," I said, "especially when you offer me such a valuable alliance. Now I think that if we are in any way to escape the opponents you mention, it is essential that we should define to them what we mean by 'philosophers' when we venture to say that they ought to rule, because, when the distinction is made, a defence will be possible if it is shown that some persons are by nature fitted to embrace philosophy and take the lead in a city, while the others are not fitted to embrace it, but only to follow their leader."

"Definition would be opportune," he said.

"Come, then, follow after me in the hope that in some way or other we may expound our notion satisfactorily."

"Lead on," he said.

"Must I remind you," I said, "or do you remember that if we say that a man is a lover of anything, if the expression is rightly used, it must be shown, not that he loves one part of it and not another, but that he cares for the whole of it?"

"I need to be reminded apparently," he said, "for I do not exactly remember."

"Now, Glaucon," I said, "you are the last person who should say that. An amorous man ought not to forget that a boy-loving amorous person is in some way or other stirred and attracted by all who are in their bloom. He thinks they all deserve his attention and caresses. Is not that the way of you gentlemen with the fair? A snub-nosed boy you praise and call charming, another's hooked beak you call kingly, a third, who is between the two extremes, you describe as beautifully proportioned; dark boys are manly to look upon, fair are the children of the gods. Where do you think the name of "honey-pale" comes from, if not from the excuses of a lover who could put

up with paleness when he found it in the cheek of youth?
175  In a word, you make every kind of excuse and invent
every conceivable name sooner than reject any that are
in the flower and bloom of life."

"You choose to cite me as an example of how amorous
persons behave," he said; "but I agree for the argument's
sake."

"Further," I asked, "do you not observe lovers of wine
behaving in the same way, gladly accepting any wine on
any excuse?"

"Certainly."

"And you find the same, I imagine, in lovers of honour
or ambitious men. If they can't be generals, they are glad
to be subalterns. If they cannot win the honour of the
great and good, they are content to be honoured by the
mean and contemptible, since they have an indiscriminate
appetite for honour."

"That is perfectly true."

"Then is this true, or not? If we say that a man has an
appetite for anything, shall we assert that he has an appetite for the whole class that the term includes, not for
one part of it to the exclusion of another?"

"Yes, for the whole class," he said.

"Then shall we not also say that the lover of wisdom
or the philosopher has an appetite for wisdom, not for
some to the exclusion of other wisdom, but for all?"

"True."

"Then the man who grumbles at his lessons, especially
when he is young and cannot yet distinguish between
what is profitable and what is not, we shall not call fond
of learning or a philosopher, any more than we say that a
man who is nice about his food is hungry or has an appetite for food; him we call, not a lover of food, but a
bad feeder."

"Yes, and we shall be right."

"But the man who tastes eagerly every kind of learning,

who sets himself readily to his lessons and can never have enough, him we shall justly call a lover of wisdom and a philosopher, shall we not?"

To this Glaucon remarked: "Of such people you will have many and strange examples. For all lovers of sights seem to me to be included because of their joy in learning; and lovers of sounds, too, are the most astonishing people to class as philosophers. They would not willingly attend philosophic discussions or any such occasions, but as though they had hired out their ears to listen to any and every chorus they run about at the Dionysia, not missing a single performance in town or country. Shall we give the name of philosophers to all these, and to others who have a similar taste for learning, and to the masters of the petty crafts?"

"By no means," I said. "We shall say that they are counterfeit philosophers."

"Then whom do you mean by the term true philosophers?"

"Those," I said, "who love to see the truth."

"Yes, that is certainly right," he said. "But what do you mean by that?"

"It is not easy to explain to any one else," I said, "but I fancy that you will agree with me in this."

"In what?"

"Since beautiful is opposite to ugly, these are two." **476**

"Surely."

"Then since they are two, each is one?"

"Yes."

"And the same holds of just and unjust, good and bad, and all forms. Each in itself is one, but by reason of their community with actions and bodies, and with each other, they appear everywhere, and each seems many."

"You are right," he said.

"In this way, then, I make my distinction," I said. "On one side put those we have just mentioned, lovers of sights and lovers of crafts and men of action, and then on the other those with whom the argument is concerned, who alone are rightly called philosophers."

"What do you mean?" he said.

"Well," I said, "the lovers of sounds and of sights admire beautiful sounds and colours and figures and all things fashioned out of such, but their understanding is incapable of seeing or admiring the nature of real beauty."

"That is certainly the case," he said.

"Then will not those who are capable of approaching the real beauty, and of seeing it as itself, be few in number?"

"Yes, indeed."

"But if a man recognizes that there are beautiful things, but disbelieves in real beauty, and cannot follow should another lead him to the knowledge of it, do you think that such a one leads a waking or a dreaming life? For, consider, is not a man dreaming, whether he is asleep or awake, when he thinks a likeness of anything to be not a likeness, but the reality which it resembles?"

"I certainly," he said, "should say that such a man was dreaming."

"But what of him who, contrariwise, recognizes a certain real beauty, and is able to discern both it and the objects which participate in it, and does not take the participating objects for it or it for them, do you think he leads a waking or a dreaming life?"

"A waking life, most certainly," he said.

"Then may we not justly say that his understanding is knowledge because he knows, while the other's is belief because he only believes?"

"Certainly."

"Then what shall we do if this person is angry with us because we say that he believes but does not know and if he disputes the truth of our statement? Shall we be able to appease him and gently persuade him, without letting him know that he is barely sane?"

"Yes, we must," he said.

"Come, then, consider what we shall say to him. Shall we make inquiries of him in this way, and say that we do not grudge any knowledge he may have, but shall be very glad to see that he knows something? 'But tell me this,' we shall say, 'does he that knows, know something or nothing?' Do you answer me for him."

"I shall answer," he said, "that he knows something."

"Something which is, or something which is not?"

"Something which is. For how could that which is not 477 be known?"

"Then are we sure of this, in however many ways we look at it, that what is completely, is completely knowable, and what in no way is, is in every way unknowable?"

"Perfectly sure."

"Good. Then if there be something so constituted as both to be and not to be, will it not lie between what absolutely is and what in all ways is not?"

"It will."

"Then knowledge is set over that which is, and ignorance of necessity over that which is not; and over this that is between, must we not now seek for something between ignorance and knowledge, if there is such a thing?"

"Certainly."

"But do we say that belief is anything?"

"Surely."

"A power distinct from knowledge, or identical with it?"

"Distinct."

"Then belief is set over one thing and knowledge over another, each according to its own power?"

"Yes."

"Then is it not the nature of knowledge, being set

over that which is, to know how it is? But first, I think we had better make this distinction."

"What?"

"We shall say that powers are a certain general class of existences, by means of which, indeed, we and every other thing can do what we can. Sight and hearing, for example, I call powers. Perhaps you understand what I have in mind."

"Yes, I understand."

"Then listen to my opinion about them. In a power I see no colour or figure, or any such attributes as many other things have and in reference to which I distinguish them to myself as differing from one another. In a power I look only to that over which it is, and to what it effects, and on this principle I used the term power in each case; and any powers which are set over the same thing, and have the same effect, I call the same; if they are over different things and have different effects, I call them different. What is your practice? Do you do the same?"

"Yes," he said.

"Then come back to this point, my excellent friend," I said. "Do you call knowledge a power, or, if not, in what class do you place it?"

"It is a power, and the strongest of all powers," he said.

"Further, shall we call belief a power, or place it in some other class?"

"Certainly not the latter," he said. "For that by which we are able to believe, is nothing else than belief."

"But a little time ago you admitted that knowledge and belief are not the same."

"How could any sensible man identify the infallible with the fallible?" he said.

"Good," I said. "Then clearly we have agreed that belief is distinct from knowledge?"

"We have."

"Then each of them has by nature a distinct power over distinct things?"

"Inevitably."

"But knowledge surely is set over that which is, to know how it is?"

"Yes."

"While the part of belief, we assert, is to believe?"

"Yes."

"Does it believe the same thing as knowledge knows; and can what is known and what is believed be the same; or is that impossible?"

"Its impossibility follows from our admissions," he said. "If different powers are by nature set over different objects, and if belief and knowledge are both powers, each, as we assert, distinct from the other, it is incompatible with this that what is known and what is believed should be the same."

"Then if that which is, is known, what is believed will be something different from that which is?"

"It will."

"Then will belief believe that which is not? Or is it impossible even to believe that which is not? Consider. Does not he who believes fix his belief on something? or is it possible to believe and yet to believe nothing?"

"That is impossible."

"Then will he who believes, believe some one thing?"

"Yes."

"But that which is not, would be most accurately described not as one thing, but as nothing, would it not?"

"Certainly."

"Then do we not necessarily assign ignorance to not being and knowledge to being?"

"That is right," he said.

"Then belief will believe neither being nor not being?"

"No."

"And neither ignorance nor knowledge can be belief?"

"Naturally not."

"Then is belief something beyond these, surpassing knowledge in certainty or ignorance in uncertainty?"

"No."

"Rather," I said, "do you think belief darker than knowledge and brighter than ignorance?"

"Yes, very much so."

"Then does it lie within the limits of the two?"

"Yes."

"Then belief is between these two?"

"Just so."

"Then did we not say a little while ago that if we found anything which was and was not at the same time, it would lie between what absolutely is and what thoroughly is not, and that set over it would be neither knowledge nor ignorance, but that which was found to be between ignorance and knowledge?"

"Yes, and we were right."

"But have we not now found something between these two, which we call belief?"

"We have."

"Then apparently we have still left to find that which partakes of both being and not being and which could not rightly be described as either absolutely, and if we find it, we shall with justice be able to say that this is what is believed, so assigning extremes to extremes and mean to mean. Is not that the case?"

"It is."

479        "Then this having been established. I shall say, That worthy who thinks that there is no real beauty and no Form of real beauty eternal and invariable, but recognizes many beautifuls, let him speak and answer—this lover of sights who will let no one say that the beautiful, and the just, and so on are one. 'Of all these many beautifuls, O most excellent sir,' we shall say, 'is there any that will not appear ugly? or of the justs any that will

not appear unjust? or of the holies any that will not appear unholy?' "

"No," he said, "they must appear somehow both beautiful and ugly, just and unjust, and so on with them all."

"What of the many doubles? May they not appear halves just as much as doubles?"

"They may."

"And so with the things which we call great and small, and light and heavy, can one of those opposites be attributed to them any more than the other?"

"No, at any moment every one of them may have both attributed to it."

"Then is each of those many more really that which one may assert it to be than it is not?"

"This is like the puzzles one hears at dinner," he said, "and the children's riddle about the eunuch and his throw at the bat, where there is a catch about the eunuch and the bat, and what he threw at it, and what it was sitting on. For there is a puzzle here too, and none of the many can be fixedly conceived as either being or as not being, or as both being and not being, or as neither."

"Then do you know what to do with them," I said, "or have you any better place to put them than between being and not being? For they will not appear in greater darkness than that which is not, by exceeding it in not being, nor in greater light than that which is, by exceeding it in being."

"Perfectly true," he said.

"Then we have apparently discovered that the multitude's multitudinous formulae concerning the beautiful and so on tumble about somewhere between what is not and what absolutely is?"

"We have."

"But we agreed, if any such thing should be discovered, that we should have to call it the object of belief, not the object of knowledge, this shifting intermediate world being apprehended by the intermediate faculty."

"We did."

"Then we shall say that those who look at many beautifuls, but do not see real beauty, and are unable to follow another's guidance to it, and who see many justs but not real justice, and so on, these throughout believe but know nothing of what they believe?"

"The conclusion is inevitable," he said.

"But what are we to say of those who look at all the invariable unchanging realities? Do they not know rather than believe?"

"That conclusion too is inevitable."

480 "Then may we not also say that they will admire and love the objects of knowledge, while the others love the objects of belief? For do you not remember that we said that these loved and admired beautiful sounds and colours and the like, but real beauty they will not tolerate as being anything?"

"I remember."

"Then we shall not be wrong in calling them lovers of belief rather than lovers of wisdom or philosophers? Will they be very angry with us if we say that?"

"No, not if they take my advice," he said; "for it is not right to be angry at the truth."

"But shall we call those who admire in each case the reality that is, not lovers of belief, but philosophers?"

"Most assuredly."

# BOOK VI

"THE philosophers and the non-philosophers, Glaucon," I said, "have gone through a somewhat lengthy argument, and have after some difficulty at last revealed their respective natures."

"Yes," he said, "in a short argument it would not perhaps have been easy."

"I think not," I said, "and I still think that it could be better set forth if we had only to speak on this one point and had not to discuss all the many remaining questions which are before us in our inquiry as to the difference between the just and the unjust life."

"What, then," he said, "have we to discuss after this?"

"What but what comes next in order?" I said. "As those are philosophers who are able to grasp that which is always invariable and unchanging, while those are not who cannot do this but are all abroad among all sorts of aspects of many objects, which of these ought to be leaders of the city?"

"What would be a reasonable answer to that question?" he said.

"We must make guardians whichever of the two appear able to guard the laws and institutions of the city," I said.

"Rightly so," he said.

"But can there be any question whether a blind or a sharp-sighted watchman should guard a thing?"

"There cannot," he said.

"Then are they any better than blind who are always and in every case without the knowledge of that which really is, who have no distinct pattern in their soul, and cannot look away, like painters, to the perfect truth, and contemplate the standard which they have yonder with the greatest care, before they prescribe the earthly notions concerning things beautiful and just and good, when such prescription is necessary, and who cannot guard and preserve them when once prescribed?"

"No," he said, "assuredly they are not much better than blind."

"Then shall we appoint them guardians rather than those who have come to know every reality, and who are at the same time no whit behind the others in experience or any other part of virtue?"

"It would be ridiculous," he said, "to choose any one else if they do not fall behind in other ways. For this very thing in which they excel is about the most important of all."

485    "Then shall we discuss in what manner the same persons will be able to fulfil both requirements?"

"Certainly."

"That is, as we said at the beginning of this argument, we must first of all have a thorough knowledge of their nature, and I fancy that if we agree satisfactorily on that point, we shall agree also that the same persons may fulfil these requirements, and that they and they alone ought to be leaders of our city."

"In what way?"

"Concerning philosophic natures we may surely agree to this, that they are lovers of whatever learning will reveal to them anything of that reality which always is, and is not driven to and fro by generation and decay."

"We may."

"And to this also," I said, "that they are lovers of all that reality, and willingly resign no part of it, whether great or small, esteemed or slighted, like the lovers of honour or the amorous whom we described a little while ago."

"You are right," he said.

"Consider, now, whether those who are to be such as we described must have in their nature this further quality."

"What is that?"

"Truthfulness; that is, a determination never voluntarily to receive what is false, but to hate it and to love the truth."

"That is probable."

"It is not only probable, my friend, but absolutely inevitable that he who is naturally amorous of anything should look with affection on all that is akin and related to the beloved object."

"You are right," he said.

"And can you find anything more akin to wisdom than truth?"

"Surely not," he said.

"Then is it possible that the same nature should be a lover of wisdom and a lover of falsehood?"

"Certainly not."

"Then he that is really a lover of learning must from his earliest years strive with all his heart after all truth?"

"I quite agree."

"But we know that whenever any man's desires flow in full current towards any one object, like a stream that has had a channel dug for it, towards all other objects they flow the more feebly?"

"Certainly."

"Then when the current of a man's desires has set towards the sciences and all learning, I fancy they will be concerned with the pleasure of the mind itself in itself, and will desert the pleasures that come through the body, if he is not feignedly but truly a philosopher?"

"That is certainly inevitable."

"Such a man, moreover, will be temperate and in no way covetous; for he is the last man in the world to pursue with eagerness those aims for the sake of which men love wealth and lavish expenditure."

"Yes."

486 "Further, when you would decide between the philosophic and the non-philosophic nature, you must consider this point also."

"What is that?"

"You must look out for any secret inclination to meanness. For surely smallness is the most inapt quality for a mind destined ever to reach out after the divine and the human in its wholeness and its totality."

"Very true," he said.

"And do you fancy that an understanding endowed with loftiness and the power of looking out over all time and all being can attach any great importance to our human life?"

"That is impossible," he said.

"Then will such a one regard death as anything to be feared?"

"Certainly not."

"But a cowardly and mean nature will probably have no participation in true philosophy?"

"No, I think not."

"Further, can a man of well-balanced mind, who is neither covetous nor mean, nor a coward, nor a boaster, be by any possibility hard to deal with or unjust?"

"No."

"Then in looking for the philosophic and the non-philosophic soul you will examine in early youth whether the mind is just and gentle, or unsociable and savage?"

"Certainly."

"And this again you will not neglect, I fancy."

"What?"

"Whether the mind is ready or slow to learn. Do you expect that any one will have a proper affection for that which he practises with pain and in which he makes small progress with great exertions?"

"No, that would be impossible."

"What if he could retain nothing that he had learned, being full of forgetfulness? Could he be other than empty of knowledge?"

"No."

"And if he labours to no profit, do you not think that in the end he will be compelled to hate himself and his unprofitable practice?"

"Surely."

"Then let us not include a forgetful soul among those that are really philosophical, but demand rather that the philosophical soul shall be of retentive memory."

"Most certainly."

"Further, we shall say that the unmusical and the ungracious nature tends only to excess?"

"Yes."

"But do you think truth akin to excess or to measure?"

"To measure."

"Then let us seek for an understanding endowed also with natural measure and grace, whose innate disposition will bear it easily to the Form of every reality."

"Yes, let us."

"Now, then, do you think that the qualities we have enumerated are in any way unnecessary for the soul or inconsistent if it is to participate sufficiently and perfectly in that which is?"

"No, they are absolutely necessary," he said.          487

"Then can you find any fault in a profession which cannot be adequately practised by any who are not naturally of retentive memory, ready learners, lofty-minded, and gracious, lovers and kinsmen of truth, justice, courage, and temperance?"

"Momus himself," he said, "could find no fault with it."

"Then," I said, "when such characters are perfected by education and mature years, would you not entrust the city to their sole charge?"

Here Adeimantus remarked: "No one, Socrates, could possibly object to what you say. But here is more or less the experience of those who from time to time hear what you now say: they think that through their want of skill in asking and answering questions the argument leads them a little astray at every question, and when all those littles are added together at the end of the discussion they become aware that the lapse is immense and quite subversive of their original position. Just as a clever draught player will in the end of the game shut up an unskilful player in a corner so that he can't move, so they feel that by the end of the argument they are shut in a corner and can't speak at this other kind of draughts which is played with arguments for counters. For they are not in the least more inclined to think that the truth is with you. I speak with reference to our present condition. Any one would agree that at each question you ask he cannot oppose you with words, but as a matter of fact he sees that of those who devote themselves to philosophy—not those who study it in youth as a means to general culture and then give it up, but those who spend a considerable time on it—the most are very queer creatures if not rascally knaves, and the best of them seem from this profession which you praise to have achieved the result that they are useless to their country."

When I heard his remarks I replied, "Then do you consider these accusations false?"

"I don't know," he said, "but I should like to hear your opinion."

"You may hear that I think them true."

"Well," he said, "how can it be right to say that states will have no respite from evil till philosophers rule in them, when we admit that they are useless to their cities?"

"Your question," I said, "must be answered by a simili-
tude."

"And I suppose that you are not accustomed to speak
in similitudes?"

"Never mind that," I said. "Would you mock me after
getting me into an argument so hard of demonstration? 488
But hear my simile that you may see the more how greedy
I am of making them. The best of these men suffer in
relation to their cities a fate so hard that there is no one
thing that can be compared with it. We must defend
them and describe their fate by a simile compounded
from many sources, as painters paint goat-stags and the
like by fusing creatures together. Conceive something of
this kind happening on board ship, on one ship or on
several. The master is bigger and stronger than all the
crew, but rather deaf and shortsighted. His seamanship
is as deficient as his hearing. The sailors are quarrelling
about the navigation. Each man thinks that he ought
to navigate, though up to that time he has never studied
the art, and cannot name his instructor or the time of
his apprenticeship. They go further and say that navigation cannot be taught, and are ready to cut in pieces
him who says that it can. They crowd round the solitary
master, entreating him and offering him every induce-
ment to entrust them with the helm. Occasionally when
they fail to persuade him and others succeed, they kill
those others and throw them overboard, overpower the
noble master by mandragora or drink or in some other
way, and bind him hand and foot. Then they rule the ship
and make free with the cargo, and so drinking and feasting make just such a voyage as might be expected of men
like them. Further, they compliment any one who has
the skill to contrive how they may persuade or compel
the master to set them over the ship, and call him a good
seaman, a navigator, and a master of seamanship; any
other kind of man they despise as useless. They have

no notion that the true navigator must attend to the year and the seasons, to the sky and the stars and the winds, and all that concerns his craft, if he is really going to be fit to rule a ship. They do not believe that it is possible for any one to acquire by skill or practice the art of getting control of the helm, whether there is opposition or not, and at the same time to master the art of steering. If ships were managed in that way, do you not think that the true navigator would certainly be called a star-gazer and a useless babbler by the crews of ships of that description?"

489

"Yes, certainly," said Adeimantus.

"Now, I fancy," I said, "that if you examine the simile you will not fail to see the resemblances to cities in their attitude towards true philosophers, and you will understand what I mean."

"Yes, certainly," he said.

"Then propound this parable to your friend, who is astonished that philosophers are not honoured in cities, and try to persuade him that it would be much more astonishing if they were."

"Yes, I will," he said.

"Show him that you are right in saying that the best of the students of philosophy are useless to the world; but bid him blame for this uselessness not the good philosophers, but those who do not use them. For it is not natural that the navigator should entreat the sailors to be ruled by him, or that the wise should wait at rich men's doors. The author of that sneer spoke false. The truth established by nature is that he who is ill, whether he be rich or poor, ought to wait at the doctor's door, and every man who needs to be ruled at the door of him who can rule. The ruler, if he is really good for anything, ought not to request his subjects to be ruled. But under present political conditions you will not be wrong in likening the rulers to the sailors we have just described, and those whom they call useless talkers in the air to the true navigators."

"You are right," he said.

"For these reasons and under these conditions it is difficult for the best of professions to win esteem from those who follow contrary courses. But far the greatest and most serious scandal to philosophy arises from its professed followers, whom the accuser of philosophy describes when, as you say, he declares that most of those who woo philosophy are rascally knaves, and the best of them are useless; which statement of yours I admitted to be true. Did I not?"

"Yes."

"Then have we explained the uselessness of the good philosophers?"

"Certainly."

"Then shall we next explain why the majority are necessarily rascals, and try to show, if we can, that this is not the fault of philosophy either?"

"Certainly."

"Then let us listen and speak in turn, first reminding ourselves of our description of the natural character essential to him who is to turn out a noble, good man. Truth, if you remember, was first of all his leader. He has 490 to follow her at all times and in all ways, or be a braggart and have no part in true philosophy."

"Yes, that was what we said."

"But is not this one point we have mentioned very inconsistent with our present ideas about him?"

"Yes," he said.

"Then shall we not make a reasonable defence when we say that the true lover of learning naturally strove toward what is, and would not abide by the many particulars that are believed to be, but went forward undiscouraged, and did not cease from his passion until he grasped the nature of each reality that is, with that part of his soul which is fitted to lay hold of such by reason of its affinity with it; whereby being come near to and married with true being, and begetting reason and truth, he came to knowledge and true life and nourishment, and then, and only then, ceased from the travail of his soul?"

"That defence is as reasonable as possible," he said.

"Well, will this man have any love of falsehood, or will he on the contrary hate it?"

"He will hate it," he said.

"Yes, I fancy we shall never declare that when truth was leader an evil chorus followed in her train."

"Surely not."

"No, a sound and just disposition attended her, and after went temperance."

"You are right," he said.

"Then why need I begin again and marshall all the attendant train of the philosophic nature, insisting on their necessity? For you remember that, akin to those, came courage, loftiness of spirit, readiness of learning, and memory. Then you interposed and said that every one would be forced to agree to what we were saying, but that if he left the argument and cast his eyes on the men to whom it referred, he could say that of those he saw some were useless, and most were thorough villains. We are examining the reasons for this misrepresentation, and are now considering why the majority are villains, and for that reason we have again referred to and been forced to define the nature of the true philosophers."

"That is so," he said.

"Then," I said, "we must observe the corruptions of this nature, and see how in many men it is destroyed; only a small number escape; these are they who are described not as rascals, but as useless. Next we must ob-
491 serve the natures that imitate the philosophic and establish themselves in its profession, and see what manner

of souls these are who presume to a pursuit too high
and too good for them, who by their varied blunders have
brought on philosophy everywhere and all the world over
the reputation you describe."

"What are the corruptions to which you refer?" he said.

"I shall try to describe them to you if I can," I said.
"But I fancy that any one will grant us this, that natures
such as we have described, endowed with all the qualities
which we have just prescribed for him who is to be a
complete philosopher, are few and far between among
mankind. Do you agree with me?"

"Most certainly."

"Then consider how many and how great are the causes
of destruction to those rare souls."

"What are they?"

"One you will be extremely surprised to hear. Each of
those very qualities which we praised as belonging to the
philosophic nature destroys the soul possessing them and
draws it away from philosophy—I mean courage, temperance, and the rest."

"That certainly sounds strange," he said.

"Not only those," I said, "but all things which are
called good destroy and pervert the soul—beauty, riches,
strength of body, powerful connections in a city, and all
similar things. You understand the general type of the
things I mean?"

"I do," he said, "but I should like to grasp your meaning more precisely."

"Well," I said, "grasp the notion of them as a whole,
and what has been said about them will become perfectly
clear and not seem paradoxical."

"What do you mean me to do?" he said.

"In the case of all seeds or growing things, whether
plants or animals, we know," I said, " that any one which
does not receive its proper nutriment, climate, or habitat.
fails in its proper virtues the more strikingly the stronger

it is; for evil is of course more contrary to good than to what is not good."

"Surely."

"Then I fancy it is according to reason that the best of natures deteriorates more seriously from uncongenial nutriment than an inferior nature?"

"It is."

"Then, Adeimantus," I said, "shall we not also say that similarly the most richly endowed natures, if they receive a bad upbringing, become surpassingly evil? Or do you fancy that great crimes and unmixed wickedness come from a feeble nature and not rather from a noble nature ruined by education, while a weak nature will never be the author of great good or great evil?"

"Yes, it is as you say," he said.

492 "Then I think that this nature which we have ascribed to the philosopher, if it receives proper instruction, must of necessity develop and attain to all virtue; but if it is not sown and planted in proper soil and does not get its nutriment therefrom, its course will be the very opposite, unless one of the gods comes to the rescue. Or do you hold the opinion of the public that there are any appreciable number of young men corrupted by sophists, or that it is individual sophists who corrupt them? Are not those who say this themselves the greatest sophists, who most carefully educate and fashion to the character they want both young and old, men and women?"

"When, pray?" he said.

"When," I answered, "they sit down together in large numbers in the assemblies or the law courts, or the theatres or camps, or any other place where crowds come together, and proceed with great noise and confusion to find fault with some of the things that are being said or done and to praise others, their fault-finding and their praise being equally extravagant, shouting and clapping their hands till the rocks and the place in which they are

join with them and echo back redoubled the uproar of
their condemnation and their praise. Amid such a scene
where, think you, is a young man's heart? What private
education will hold out and not be swamped by such a
volume of condemnation and praise, and swept down
stream wherever such a current takes it, till he calls beautiful and ugly what they do, acts as they do, and becomes
like them?"

"It is quite inevitable, Socrates," he said.

"Yes, and we have not yet mentioned the mightiest
compulsion," I said.

"What is that?" he said.

"The practical inducements offered by these educators
and sophists when their words have no effect. Do you not
know that they punish the disobedient with dishonour,
fines, and death?"

"Yes, assuredly they do," he said.

"And do you think that any other sophist could prevail,
or any individual's arguments which had a contrary
tendency?"

"No," he answered.

"No," I said, "the very attempt would be utter folly.
For there is not, and never has been, nor ever will be, a
character produced by education whose virtue has pre-
vailed and stood out against the instruction of the
many—not humanly speaking, my friend, for with God,
as they say, all things are possible. For you must certainly
know that while the constitution of states is what it is, ⁴⁹³
if anything is preserved and made what it ought to be,
you will not be wrong in ascribing that salvation to divine
providence."

"I am quite of that opinion," he said.

"Then go on to be of this opinion also," I said.

"What?"

"That each of those salaried individuals whom the
public call sophists and regard as their rivals, teaches

nothing but those beliefs which the multitude express in their assemblies, and this they call wisdom. It is as though a man who is keeper of a huge and powerful beast had got to know its tempers and its desires, how best to approach and how best to handle it, when it has its sulkiest and when its mildest moods and what causes them, on what occasions it is in the habit of uttering its various cries, and what sounds will soothe or provoke it. Now, suppose him, after he had got to know all these things from long experience of the animal, to call this knowledge wisdom, and systematizing it into an art to take to teaching. He has no true knowledge as to which of these beliefs and desires is beautiful or ugly, good or bad, just or unjust. He employs all these terms in accordance with the opinions of the mighty beast, calling things that please it good, things that displease it bad. Other reason for his use of these terms he has none, but calls what is compulsory just and good. He has never perceived, nor could he teach another, the vast difference which really exists between the nature of the compulsory and the good. In heaven's name, do you not think that a man like that would make a strange instructor?"

"I do," he said.

"Well, do you think he differs at all from one who thinks that careful attention to the whims and pleasures of great promiscuous crowds is wisdom, whether in painting or music, or finally in politics? This is certain, that if a man mixes with the many and offers for their approval a poem or other work of art, or a public service, and makes them his arbiters of taste more than is absolutely necessary, the fatal necessity is laid upon him of doing whatever they approve. But have you ever heard any of them offering any evidence that is not ridiculous to show that what they approve is really good and beautiful?"

"No," he said, "and I don't expect to hear any."

"Then having observed so much, remember this. Is it

possible that the multitude will endure, or believe in, the existence of beauty itself, or of any reality itself? They only admit the existence of many beautifuls, and many particulars." 494

"It is certainly impossible," he said.

"Then a multitude cannot be philosophical?" I said.

"No."

"And it is inevitable that the philosophers should incur their censure?"

"It is."

"And the censure of those individuals who mix with the mob and try to please it?"

"Clearly."

"Then considering this, do you see any chance of salvation for a philosophic nature, by which it may abide in its profession and reach its goal? Consider our previous admissions. We agreed that readiness to learn and a good memory and courage and loftiness of soul were marks of this nature."

"Yes."

"But will not such a one from his earliest years be first in everything, especially if he has a body to match his mind?"

"Surely," he said.

"Then, I fancy, his kinsmen and his fellow-citizens will wish to employ him, when he grows older, in their own affairs?"

"Yes."

"Then they will lay at his feet their supplications and honours, making sure of securing his future power by timely flattery?"

"That is certainly what ordinarily happens," he said.

"Then what do you think he will do in such circumstances, especially if he happens to belong to a great city, and is one of her rich and noble citizens, and is also beautiful to look upon and tall? Will he not be filled with impossible ambitions, and think that he will be capable of ruling both Greeks and foreigners, and so highly exalt himself, and be full of self-importance and conceit without sense?"

"Yes, certainly," he said.

"And if, when he is sinking into this condition, someone comes to him and quietly tells him the truth, that there is no mind in him, and that he needs it, but cannot get it without serving for it, do you think that amid such evil influences it will be easy for him to listen?"

"Far from it," he answered.

"But if," I said, "by reason of his natural goodness, and the affinity of what is said with his nature, he does somehow understand and let himself be turned round and drawn to philosophy, how do you imagine those others will behave when they think that they are losing his help and companionship? Will they not do anything, leaving nothing unsaid and nothing undone, from private intrigue to public prosecution, to prevent him from being persuaded, and to disable his adviser from persuading him?"

495 "That is quite inevitable," he said.

"Then is it possible that he will become a philosopher?"

"Certainly not."

"You see, then," I said, "that I was not wrong in saying that the very elements of the philosophic nature become, as a result of bad training, in a certain sense a cause of the desertion of the pursuit of philosophy, as do such so-called good things as riches and all outward pomp and state?"

"No," he said, "you were quite right."

"This, then, my fine fellow," I said, "is the course of destruction. It is in this way that the best of natures is so often spoiled for the best of vocations. And, as we say, this appears seldom enough. From these men come those who commit the greatest crimes against cities and individuals, as from them come benefactors also when the current sets that way. But a little nature never does anything great either to city or to individual man."

"Very true," he said.

"So those to whom philosophy most belongs have deserted her, and lead a false and alien life, leaving her desolate and unwed, and other unworthy suitors have swooped down upon this defenceless ward, and disgraced and brought reproach upon her—the reproach of which you speak when you say that of her associates some are worthless, but most are deserving of heavy punishment."

"Yes, certainly," he said, "that is what is said."

"And quite naturally too," I said. "For other feeble creatures see this territory bare of inhabitants, but rich with noble names and titles, and as escaped prisoners betake themselves to the temples, so they eagerly escape from their handicrafts and betake themselves to philosophy whenever they show themselves particularly smart at their own little trade. For though philosophy is in this plight, nevertheless there is still left to her a reputation outshining that of the other arts. And this many covet whose natures are imperfect, and whose trades and handicrafts, as they have disfigured their bodies, so, too, have battered and mutilated their souls, by reason of their sordidness. That is what must happen, is it not?"

"Certainly," he said.

"Then do you think," I said, "that they are different to look upon from a little bald tinker who has come into money, and has just had his chains knocked off, had a bath, put a new coat on his back, and has got himself up as a bridegroom, who means to take advantage of the poverty and loneliness of his master's daughter to marry her?"

"No, not very different," he said.

496

"And what children can we expect of such parents? They will be bastards and weaklings, will they not?"

"Inevitably."

"Then when those who are unworthy of instruction unworthily approach and associate with her, what thoughts and beliefs will be their children? Will they not be such as really deserve to be called sophisms—nothing that is genuine or has part in true thought?"

"Most certainly," he said.

"Then, Adeimantus," I said, "a very small band is left of those who worthily associate with philosophy: possibly a noble and well-nurtured character saved by exile, which in the absence of corrupting influences has been true to its own nature and stayed by philosophy, or a great soul born in a small city, and so despising and looking beyond politics; and possibly one or two noble natures might come to philosophy from some other art which they rightly despised. Then, again, the bridle of our comrade Theages might have constraining power. For Theages has all the endowments that might have induced him to desert philosophy except bodily health, and his feebleness of body keeps him from a political life. Of my own safeguard, the heavenly sign, we need not speak. For few, if any, before my time have had that. Now those who have become members of this small band, and have tasted the sweetness and blessedness of their prize, can all discern the madness of the many and the almost universal rottenness of all political actions. The philosopher sees that he has no ally with whose aid he might go and defend the right with a chance of safety. He is like a man in a den of wild beasts. Share their injustice he will not. He is not strong enough to hold out alone where all are savages. He would lose his life before he could do any benefit to the city or his friends, and so be equally useless to himself and to the world. Weighing all these considerations he holds his peace and does his own work, like a man in a storm sheltering behind a wall from the driving wind of dust and hail. He sees other men filled with lawlessness, and is content if by any means he may live his life here unspotted by injustice and evil deeds till with fair hope he take his departure in peace and good-will."

"Well," he said, "he will certainly have accomplished 497 not the least of things when he takes his departure."

"Yes," I said, "but not the greatest unless he finds a constitution suited to him. For in a suitable constitution he will grow more himself, and succour both his own and the public fortunes. I think, then, that we have sufficiently discussed the reasons why philosophy is slandered, and shown their injustice. Have you anything to add?"

"Not on that point," he said. "But which of our present-day constitutions do you call suited to philosophy?"

"None," I said. "That is my complaint—that no present day constitution is worthy of the philosophic nature, which is therefore warped and changed. As a seed from abroad sown in a foreign soil loses its type under the new influence and passes into the native species, even so this nature cannot now preserve its own powers, but degenerates into an alien character. But if it should find the constitution that is best, even as it is best, then it will show that it is truly divine, while all else, natures and institutions alike, are human. You will now, of course, ask what this constitution is?"

"You are wrong," he said. "I was not going to ask that question, but whether it is the city which we have just been founding, or another?"

"It is the same in all points but one," I said. "But even at the time we said that there would also have to be in the city some power possessing the same understanding of the constitution as you, the legislator, had when you prescribed its laws."

"We did," he said.

"Yes, but not distinctly enough," I said, "in fear of these topics and the long and difficult demonstration of them which your insistence has realized, since even what remains is by no means our easiest subject."

"What is that?"

"In what way a city may handle philosophy without being destroyed by it; for all great things are perilous, and it is true, as the proverb says, that beautiful things are hard."

"Nevertheless," he said, "let this be made clear and the demonstration so completed."

"Not want of will," I said, "but want of ability may hinder me. You will see my zeal with your own eyes. Consider now the zeal and hardihood of my words when I say that a city must deal with this pursuit in just the opposite way from that now followed."

"How?"

498 "At present," I said, "those who engage in philosophy at all are mere striplings just past their boyhood; before they enter upon housekeeping and business they dally with the hardest part of the subject (by the hardest part I mean dialectic), and then take themselves off. And they, forsooth, are regarded as accomplished in philosophy, and in later years, if they do consent on invitation to listen to others who study philosophy, they esteem it a great condescension, thinking that it ought to be regarded as an occasional pastime. Towards old age all but a very few of them give out altogether even more effectually than the sun of Heraclitus, for they never take fire again."

"Then what is the proper course?" he said.

"Just the opposite. When they are striplings and children they should partake in culture and training which is fit for striplings, and give good heed to their bodies while they are growing up to manhood, so preparing them to serve philosophy. When the years advance in which the soul begins to reach maturity, their mental exercise must be keener. But when their physical strength begins to wane, and is past political and military duties, then, and not till then, should they range the sacred fields at will and do nothing else unless casually, if they are to live happily and after death to crown the life they have lived with a fitting destiny in the world below."

"Truly, Socrates," he said, "I think you speak with enthusiasm. But I fancy that many of your hearers oppose you with even more enthusiasm, and are not in the least likely to agree, Thrasymachus among the first of them."

"Don't try to make bad blood between Thrasymachus and me," I said, "when we have so lately become friends— not that we were enemies before; for we shall in no way relax our endeavours until we persuade Thrasymachus, and the rest with him, or do them some good for that life when they shall be born again and enjoy similar discourses to these."

"That will not be long," he said.

"No," I said, "no time at all compared to eternity. But that most people should not agree to what we are saying need not surprise us, for they have never yet seen our proposals in practice. Phrases they have seen somewhat resembling these patched and pieced into consistency, not falling into spontaneous harmony like ours. But a man fashioned into the most perfect possible conformity and likeness to virtue in word and in deed, ruling in a city like to himself, that they have never seen, neither once nor many times. Do you think so?" 499

"No, certainly not."

"Nor, my wonderful friend, have they listened enough to noble and free discourses, where truth is sought after intently in every way for the sake of knowledge, and a wide berth is given to smart controversial arguments which seek only after seeming and controversy, whether in public trials or private gatherings."

"No, to the first they have not listened," he said.

"It was for these reasons," I said, "and because we foresaw these results, that on that former occasion, though we were afraid, yet truth constrained us and we said that neither city nor constitution, no, nor yet an individual man, will ever be perfect, until fortune grants that some necessity encompass the philosophers, those few who are not evil but who are now called useless, so that whether they will or not they take charge of the city, and find the city obedient to them, or until upon those who now hold dominions and kingdoms or upon their sons some breath of heaven sends a true love of true philosophy. To suppose that either or both of these alternatives is impossible I maintain to be quite unreasonable. If they are, then we may be justly ridiculed as speaking what are merely idle dreams. Is it so?"

"It is."

"But if some compulsion to take charge of a city has ever, in the infinite time that is past, descended upon those who are pre-eminent in philosophy, or if it exists now in some barbarian region far removed from our vision, or if it ever arises in the future, then we are ready to contend in argument that the constitution we have described has arisen, exists, and will arise when the Muse of philosophy becomes mistress of a city. That she should do so is not impossible, nor are the things we describe impossible. But we admit that they are hard."

"Yes," he said, "I agree with you."

"But the many, you will say, do not agree?"

"Perhaps."

"My good friend," I said, "do not condemn the many so severely. They will change their opinion if you are kind to them, and do not quarrel with them, but wipe away the reproach of philosophy by showing them whom 500 you mean by philosophers, and by defining, as we did lately, their nature and practice. Then they will not think that you mean what they now imagine. Do you think that any one who is considerate and gentle can be angry with one who will not quarrel, or feel malicious towards one who will not bear malice? I will anticipate your answer, and say that a few may be as rude as that, but not most people."

"Yes, I entirely agree with you," he said.

"Then agree with me in this also, that the unkind disposition of the many towards philosophy is the fault of those outsiders who have burst in like drunken revellers where they have no right, who abuse and wrangle with one another, and spend their whole time in personalities and in behaviour that is entirely unfitting to philosophy."

"It certainly is," he said.

"For, Adeimantus, he that truly keeps his understanding bent on the realities has no time to look down at the affairs of men, to fight and become full of malice and hate. Such men rather look upon and behold a world of the definite and uniform, where doing or suffering injustice is unknown, and all is governed by order and reason. This they imitate, and become as far as possible like to it. Or do you think it in any way possible that a man should not imitate that with which he lovingly associates?"

"No, it is impossible," he said.

"Then the philosopher associating with what is divine and ordered becomes ordered and divine as far as mortal may, though there will always be someone to pick holes?"

"Most certainly."

"Then," I said, "if some necessity comes upon him, not only to mould himself, but to put into practice in men's characters, and to realize in individual and city his heavenly vision, do you think that he will be a bad craftsman of temperance and justice and the whole virtue of the people?"

"No, certainly not," he said.

"Then if the many come to understand that our words concerning him are true, will they still quarrel with the philosophers, and still be incredulous when we say that a city will never know happiness unless its draughtsmen are artists who have as their pattern the divine?"

"They will not be angry if they understand. But what is the manner of this draughtsmanship?"

501 "They will take as their canvas," I said, "a city and human character, and first they will make their canvas clean—not at all an easy matter. But you know that it is just here that they will be different from all others. They will not consent to lay a finger on city or individual, or draft laws, until they are given, or can make for themselves, a clean canvas."

"And they will be right," he said.

"Then after this, do you think they would sketch the outline of the city?"

"Surely."

"Then I fancy in their work their eyes will turn from model to picture, and from picture to model. They will look at natural justice and beauty and temperance and all the other virtues, and produce the human copy after their likeness, so combining and mixing from various institutions the colour and likeness of true manhood, taking hints from that realization of it in men which Homer has called godly and godlike?"

"You are right," he said.

"Sometimes I fancy they will rub out, sometimes they will make their drawing again, until they have made human character as dear to God as human character can be."

"Certainly," he said, "it will be the fairest of drawings."

"Then," I said, "are we now beginning to persuade those who you said were rushing furiously upon us that such a painter of constitutions is to be found in the man whom we were then praising to them. They were angry when we proposed to hand over cities to him; when they hear our present explanation, will they be any milder?"

"Much milder," he said, "if they are sensible."

"But what ground for objection can they have? Can they say that philosophers are not lovers of what is and of truth?"

"That would be too ridiculous," he said.

"Or that their nature, as we have described it, is not akin to that which is best?"

"No."

"Then can they say that such a nature, set among appropriate institutions, will not become more perfectly good and philosophical than any other? Will they prefer those whom we have discarded?"

"No, surely not."

"Then will they still be furious when we say that until the race of philosophers become masters of a city there will be no cessation of evils for city or citizens, nor will the constitution which we are picturing in word receive fulfilment in deed?"

"Perhaps," he said, "they will be less so."

"If you please," I said, "let us not only say 'less,' but that they are perfectly pacified and convinced, that we 502 may at least shame them into agreement."

"Certainly," he said.

"Well," I said, "let us suppose that they are so far convinced. Will any one further object that kings or rulers would not by any chance have sons whose natures are philosophical?"

"No one," he said.

"But can it be said that though they are born philosophical their corruption is quite inevitable? That their salvation is difficult, we ourselves agree. But can any one contend that in all time no one of them all will ever be saved?"

"No."

"But," I said, "though only one arises and has a city obedient to him, that is enough to perfect all those things of which we now despair?"

"It is," he said.

"For if he is ruler," I said, "and lays down the laws and institutions which we have described, it is surely not impossible that the citizens should consent to carry them out?"

"By no means."

"Then is it anything extraordinary and impossible that others should approve?"

"I think not," he said.

"And I fancy that we have already sufficiently shown that these proposals, if they are practicable, are certainly desirable?"

"We have."

"Then this seems to be our position in regard to this legislation. Our proposals are desirable if they could be realized, and their realization is difficult but not impossible."

"That is our position," he said.

"Then since we have with difficulty brought this question to a conclusion, we must discuss what remains, namely, in what manner and by means of what studies and institutions the saviours of the constitution will come to exist in our city; and, further, at what ages they are to enter upon their various studies and duties?"

"Yes, we must," he said.

"I got nothing," I said, "out of my wisdom in leaving aside some time ago the troublesome question of the possession of wives, and the birth of children, and the establishment of the rulers, because I know that the perfectly true arrangement is unpopular and difficult of realization. For none the less the necessity of discussing these questions has now come upon me. The question of the wives and children we have finished, but we must now pursue from the beginning the question of the rulers. We said, if you remember, that they must show themselves lovers of their city. They were to be tested in pleasures and pains, and were to show that no toils or fears or any other change made them unfaithful. He that failed was to be rejected, but he that always emerged unsullied, like gold tried in the fire, was to be made ruler, and privileges and rewards were to be his in life and after death. That was more or less what we said, though the argument (for fear of raising the question now before us) kept turning aside and veiling its face."

"That is perfectly true," he said. "I remember."

"I hesitated, my friend," I said, "to speak what I have now already ventured. But let me venture to say this also, that we must make our most perfect guardians philosophers."

"Yes, let that be said," he answered.

"Consider now how few you will naturally have; for of that nature which we describe as necessary to them, the elements very seldom choose to appear together. In most cases the philosophic nature is torn asunder."

"In what way?"

"Readiness to learn, memory, sagacity, quickness, and such qualities, together with spirit and high-mindedness, are, as you know, not often found along with the disposition to live soberly a quiet and steadfast life. Men with these gifts are carried by their sharpness hither and thither, and all steadiness goes from them."

"That is true," he said.

"Then, on the other hand, those steadfast characters who do not lightly change, who are trusted and employed with confidence, and who in war are not easily moved to fear, retain their immobility in their studies. They are as slow to move and slow to learn as though they were torpid, and are full of sleep and yawns whenever they have to toil at anything of the kind."

"That is so," he said.

"But we declare that the guardians must partake of both these sets of qualities in full and fair degree, or else have no portion in the special education, nor in honour nor office."

"You are right," he said.

"Then do you think that this will happen very rarely?"

"Surely."

"We must test this nature in the toils and fears and pleasures we have described, and we may now say also what we then omitted; we must exercise it in many 504 studies, and observe whether it is able to endure even the greatest studies, or whether it will flinch as others flinch in other trials."

"Yes," he said, "it is good that we should make such observations. But what do you mean by 'the greatest studies'?"

"You surely remember," I said, "that we drew conclusions concerning the respective definitions of justice and temperance, and courage and wisdom, by distinguishing three elements in the soul?"

"If I did not remember that," he said, "I should not deserve to hear what remains."

"Well, do you remember what had preceded that?"

"What?"

"We said that if we were to perceive them in the best possible way, there was another longer route to be taken by which we should find them revealed to us, but that it was possible to give a demonstration on a level with our previous arguments. You said this would do; and so we said then what, in my opinion, was not quite accurate— whether it was accurate enough for you is for you to say."

"Well," he said, "I certainly thought that you gave us good measure, and so did the others."

"But, my friend," I said, "short measure in such cases or in any case is never good measure; for there can be no imperfect measure of anything. But occasionally some people fancy that enough has been done, and that there is no need for further inquiry."

"Yes, people often take that attitude from laziness."

"But, surely," I said, "that is an attitude not at all wanted for a guardian of a city and its laws?"

"That is likely enough," he said.

"Then, my friend," I said, "our guardian must go round by the longer route, and work as hard at study as at gymnastic; otherwise, as we were saying, he will never reach the completion of the study which is the greatest of all and which concerns him most closely."

"Then are not these the greatest?" he said. "Is there any still greater than justice and the virtues we have discussed?"

"Certainly there is," I said, "and further, we must not be content with a sketch of these virtues, which is all we have seen as yet. We should not neglect their most perfect elaboration. Is it not ridiculous to make every effort after preciseness and accuracy in other matters of little importance, and yet not to demand the greatest accuracy in subjects of the greatest importance?"

"Yes, indeed," he said. "But as to what you call the greatest study, and what you conceive to be its subject, do you suppose that any one will let you off without asking what they are?"

"Certainly not," I said; "please ask. As a matter of fact, you have heard it quite often, but now you either don't understand, or want to bother me again by your per- 50  sistency. I expect that that is the explanation. For you have often heard that the Form of the good is the greatest study, and is that by whose use just things and the rest become helpful and useful. Now you certainly know that I was going to say this, and also that we have no proper knowledge of the Form of the good. And if we don't know it, though we should have the fullest knowledge possible of all else, you know that that would be of no use to us, any more than is the possession of anything without the good. Or do you think there is any advantage in universal possession if it is not good, or in understanding the whole world except the good, and understanding nothing that is good and beautiful?"

"By heaven, not I," he said.

"Then this, too, you know, that the many think the good is pleasure, and the more enlightened think it is intelligence?"

"Surely."

"Also, my friend, that those latter can't reply when we ask 'what intelligence?' and are forced in the end to say 'intelligence of the good'?"

"Yes, it is a ridiculous answer," he said.

"Surely it is," I said, "if they reproach us for not knowing the good, and then repeat the word 'good' as though we did know it. For they say that it is intelligence of good, as though we understood what they mean when they solemnly utter the word 'good.' "

"That is perfectly true," he said.

"Then what of those who make pleasure the good? Are they any less astray than the others? Are not they, too, compelled to acknowledge that there are bad pleasures?"

"Most certainly."

"Then the result is that they acknowledge the same thing to be both good and bad. Is not that the case?"

"Certainly."

"Then is it not evident that there are many and formidable difficulties in the subject?"

"Surely."

"Further, is it not evident that many people will choose what seems just and beautiful, and will be content to do and have and express what so seems, even though it

actually is not, just and beautiful? But seeming good
never yet contented any man. Here all seek the reality
and semblance is treated by every one with contempt."

"Certainly," he said.

"This, then, is that which every soul pursues, the
motive of all its actions. That it is something, the soul
divines, but what it is, she can never in her perplexity
fully comprehend. She has no steady confidence concerning it, as she has about other things, and therefore she
loses any advantage she might have got from these. Concerning a subject so great and so important, can we say
that the best men in our city, those to whom we shall   506
entrust everything, ought to be unenlightened?"

"Certainly not," he said.

"I think, in any case," I said, "that if a man does not
know how particular instances of justice and beauty
are also good, these just and beautiful things will find
in him a worthless guardian. For I divine that no man
will know them thoroughly until he has acquired this
knowledge."

"You divine excellently," he said.

"Then will our constitution be set in proper order if
such a guardian, one who has this knowledge, directs it?"

"Inevitably," he said. "But for yourself, Socrates, do
you say that the good is knowledge, or pleasure, or something else?"

"Yes, that is like you," I said. "You have made it perfectly clear all this while that you wouldn't be content
with other people's opinions on these matters."

"Well, Socrates," he said, "it does not seem to me right
to be ready to repeat other people's opinions and never
your own when you have given so much time to these
subjects."

"Well," I said, "do you think it right to make pretensions to knowledge where one has none?"

"No," he said, "certainly not to make pretensions to

knowledge; but it is right that you should be prepared to state what you think, as being what you think."

"But have you not observed," I said, "that beliefs which are not founded on knowledge are all ill-favoured? The best of them are blind. Do you think that men who unintelligently believe what is true are any better than blind men going the right road?"

"No better," he said.

"Then do you want us to look at ill-favoured, blind, and crooked things when we might hear shining and beautiful things from others?"

"Now, by heavens, Socrates," said Glaucon, "don't stop as if you were at the end. We shall be quite content if you discuss the good in the same way as you have discussed justice, and temperance, and the other virtues."

"Well, yes, my friend," I said, "I shall be quite content myself. But I am afraid that I shall not manage it, and if I have the courage to try, my awkwardness will be laughed at. But, my very good friends, let us leave for the moment the question of what the good actually is. To reach what is now in my mind seems too ambitious for our present attempt. But I am ready to state what seems to me to be an offspring of the good, and extremely like it, if the proposal pleases you; if not, I will leave it alone."

"Please state it," he said, "and you will render your account of the parent another time."

507 "I wish," I said, "I could pay and you could collect the parent sum, and I did not have to put you off with the increase like this. Still, take this increase and offspring of the good itself. But be careful that I do not unwittingly deceive you by giving you a false account of the increase."

"We shall take as good care as we can," he said. "Will you only state it?"

"Yes," I said. "But we must first come to an agreement

by my reminding you of what we said before and have often stated elsewhere."

"What?" he said.

"We say," I said, "and make the distinction in our thought, that there are many beautifuls and many goods, and so on."

"Yes."

"And on the other hand, we set up also a real beauty and a real good, and so on with all the things we before set up as many, and we put each now under one Form, holding that there is but one Form of each, and we call that 'that which each is.' "

"That is so."

"The first we say are seen but are not thought, while the Forms are thought but are not seen."

"Most certainly."

"With what in ourselves do we see what is seen?"

"With sight," he said.

"And do we not also," I said, "hear what is heard with hearing, and perceive with the other senses all sensible objects?"

"Surely."

"Now, have you noticed," I said, "how the fashioner of the senses has made the power of seeing and being seen in much the most marvellous way?"

"I don't know that I have," he said.

"Well, look at it like this. Is there anything of another kind which is required for hearing and sound if the one is to hear and the other to be heard, so that in the absence of this third thing, hearing will not hear and sound not be heard?"

"Nothing," he said.

"And I fancy," I said, "that there are not many other faculties, if there are any, which require anything of this sort. Can you name any?"

"No," he said.

"But do you not observe that the power of sight and being seen requires this?"

"In what way?"

"Surely when there is sight in the eyes, and the man who has sight tries to use it, and there is colour in the visible objects, still you know that unless a quite different third thing which exists just for this end is also present, sight will see nothing, and colour will be invisible."

"To what do you refer?" he asked.

"It is what you call light," I said.

"You are right," he said.

"Then the sense of sight and the power of being seen are joined together by a yoke nobler in no small degree than the bond which unites other yoke-fellows, inasmuch as light is not ignoble."

"It is very far from being that," he said.

"Then whom of the gods in heaven can you name as the author of this, whose light makes our sight see in the fairest manner, and makes what is seen be seen?"

"Him whom you and all others would name," he said. "For your question clearly refers to the sun."

"Then is not sight by its nature in this relation towards this god?"

"In what relation?"

"Neither sight itself, nor that in which it arises, which we call the eye, is the sun."

"No, of course not."

"But I fancy that of all the organs of the senses it is most like the sun."

"Very much so."

"And does it not possess the power which it has, by the sun's dispensation, as an effluence from it?"

"Certainly."

"Then the sun is not sight, is it; but, being the cause of sight, it is seen by the same?"

"That is so," he said.

"Then you may say," I said, "that this is my statement concerning the offspring of the good, that which the good has produced analogous to itself, which in the visible world bears the same relation to sight and what is seen, as in the intelligible the good bears to mind and what is thought."

"How?" he said. "Explain to me still further."

"You know," I said, "that when a man turns his eyes not to those objects on whose colours the light of day is shining, but to those where the lights of night shine, his eyes grow dim and appear almost blind, as though pure sight were not in them?"

"Yes, certainly," he said.

"But when they look at objects on which the sun is shining, I fancy that these same eyes see distinctly, and it becomes manifest that sight is in them?"

"Surely."

"Now consider the soul in this same manner. When it is stayed upon that on which truth and being are shining, it understands and knows and is seen to have reason. But when it is stayed on that which is mingled with darkness, that which is coming into being and passing away, then it believes and grows confused as its beliefs waver up and down, and has the appearance of being without reason."

"Yes, it has."

"This, then, which imparts truth to the things that are known and the power of knowing to the knower, you may affirm to be the Form of the good. It is the cause of knowledge and truth, and you may conceive it as being known, but while knowledge and truth are both beautiful, you will be right in thinking it other and fairer than these. And as in the other world it is right to think light and sights unlike, but not right to think them the sun, so here it is right to think both knowledge and truth like the good, but not right to think either of them the

509

good. The state or nature of the good must be honoured still more highly."

"You speak of an incalculable beauty," he said, "if it gives knowledge and truth, and itself excels them in beauty. Surely you do not mean that this is pleasure?"

"Do not blaspheme," I said. "Rather consider its image in this further aspect."

"How?"

"I fancy that you will say that the sun gives to visible objects not only the power of being seen, but also their generation and growth and nourishment, not being itself generation."

"Of course not."

"Then you may say of the objects of knowledge that not only their being known comes from the good, but their existence and being also come from it, though the good is not itself being but transcends even being in dignity and power?"

Glaucon said very comically, "By Apollo, a miraculous transcendence."

"Well," I said, "it is your fault, you compelled me to say what I think about it."

"Don't stop, please," he said, "or at any rate complete the simile of the sun if you have still anything to say."

"Yes," I said, "I still have many things to say."

"Well, don't omit the smallest thing," he said.

"I fancy," I said, "that I shall omit much. But nevertheless I shall not, if I can help it, omit anything which can be brought forward now."

"Do not," he said.

"Consider, then," I said, "that, as we say, the Sun and the Good are two; the one is king of the intelligible class and sphere, the other of the visible. I do not say king of heaven, lest you should think I was playing with words. Now, have you those two classes, visible and intelligible?"

"I have."

"Now, take a line divided into two unequal segments, and divide each segment in the same proportion, and suppose the first segment to belong to the visible, and the second to the intelligible. The different segments will represent in their comparative clearness and obscurity— in the visible sphere, the first segment images. By images I mean, firstly shadows, secondly, reflections in water, and in things that are close-grained, smooth, and bright, and all similar things, if you understand." 510

"Yes, I understand."

"Make the second segment that whereof this first is an image, ordinary living creatures, everything that grows and everything that is made."

"I have done so," he said.

"Then will you also," I asked, "consent to say that, in respect of truth and falsehood, the section has been made so that the copy stands in the same relation to that of which it is a copy, as that which is believed to that which is known?"

"Yes, certainly I will," he said.

"Then consider further how the intelligible segment must be divided."

"How?"

"Thus. In the one subdivision the soul is forced to conduct her search from hypotheses, using as images the things which were in the first segment the objects of imitation, proceeding not to a beginning but to an end; while in the other, that which leads to a beginning that has no hypothesis, she starts from a hypothesis, without using the images used in the first, and conducts her inquiry simply and solely by the Forms themselves."

"I have not quite understood what you say," he said.

"Then have it again," I said. "You will understand the more easily for what has been already said. I fancy that you know that those who study geometry and calculation and similar subjects, take as hypotheses the odd and the even, and figures, and three kinds of angles, and other similar things in each different inquiry. They make them into hypotheses as though they knew them, and will give no further account of them either to themselves or to others on the ground that they are plain to every one. Starting from these, they go on till they arrive by agreement at the original object of their inquiry."

"Yes, that I know," he said.

"Then you know that they use the visible squares and figures, and make their arguments about them, though they are not thinking about them, but about those things of which the visible are images. Their arguments concern the real square and a real diagonal, not the diagonal which they draw, and so with everything. The actual things which they model and draw, which again have their shadows and images in the water, these they now use as images in their turn, seeking to see those very 511 realities which cannot be seen except by the understanding."

"That is true," he said.

"Therefore I described this class as intelligible; but I said that the soul is compelled to use hypotheses in its investigation of it, and does not go to a beginning, since it is unable to step out of and beyond hypotheses, but uses as images those originals from which images were made by the objects lower down, and which in comparison with those remoter objects are esteemed and honoured as distinct and clear."

"I understand," he said, "that you speak of the subject of geometrical investigations and the kindred arts."

"Then by the other segment of the intelligible you may understand me to mean that which the mere reasoning process grasps by the power of dialectic, treating its hypotheses not as first principles, but as literally hypotheses, that is, as stepping-stones and starting-points, until it comes as far as that which is not hypothesis, to the first principle of everything. This it grasps, and then reversing its procedure takes hold of that which takes hold of this first principle, until it so completes its ·descent. It never uses the help of any sensible object at all, but using only the Forms themselves it descends to them, and with Forms it ends."

"I understand," he said. "Not quite satisfactorily, for I think you are describing an arduous task; but I see that you wish to distinguish that part of the real and the intelligible which is considered by the science of dialectic, as truer than that which is the object of what are called the arts. These have their hypotheses as first principles, and though their students are obliged to study them with the understanding, not with the senses, still, inasmuch as they do not make their inquiries with reference to a first principle, but by starting from hypotheses, you think that they do not exercise intelligence on these subjects, although with a first principle they are intelligible. This faculty in geometricians and such people you seem to call understanding and not intelligence, on the ground that understanding lies somewhere between belief and intelligence."

"Your demonstration is quite satisfactory," I said. "Now assume with me that corresponding to these four segments there are four states which arise in the soul. To the highest segment assign intelligence, to the second understanding, to the third faith, and to the last imagining. Then arrange these proportionately, and consider them to have such a degree of clearness as their objects have of truth."

"I understand," he said, "and agree and arrange them as you propose."

# BOOK VII

<sup>514</sup> "THEN after this," I said, "liken our nature in its education and want of education to a condition which I may thus describe. Picture men in an underground cavedwelling, with a long entrance reaching up towards the light along the whole width of the cave; in this they lie from their childhood, their legs and necks in chains, so that they stay where they are and look only in front of them, as the chain prevents their turning their heads round. Some way off, and higher up, a fire is burning behind them, and between the fire and the prisoners is a road on higher ground. Imagine a wall built along this road, like the screen which showmen have in front of the audience, over which they show the puppets."

"I have it," he said.

"Then picture also men carrying along this wall all <sup>515</sup> kinds of articles which overtop it, statues of men and other creatures in stone and wood and other materials; naturally some of the carriers are speaking, others are silent."

"A strange image and strange prisoners," he said.

"They are like ourselves," I answered. "For in the first place do you think that such men would have seen anything of themselves or of each other except the shadows thrown by the fire on the wall of the cave opposite to them?"

"How could they," he said, 'if all their life they had been forced to keep their heads motionless?"

"What would they have seen of the things carried along the wall? Would it not be the same?"

"Surely."

"Then if they were able to talk with one another, do you not think that they would suppose what they saw to be the real things?"

"Necessarily."

"Then what if there were in their prison an echo from the opposite wall? When any one of those passing by spoke, do you imagine that they could help thinking that the voice came from the shadow passing before them?"

"No, certainly not," he said.

"Then most assuredly," I said, "the only truth that such men would conceive would be the shadows of those manufactured articles?"

"That is quite inevitable," he said.

"Then consider," I said, "the manner of their release from their bonds and the cure of their folly, supposing that they attained their natural destiny in some such way as this. Let us suppose one of them released, and forced suddenly to stand up and turn his head, and walk and look towards the light. Let us suppose also that all these actions gave him pain, and that he was too dazed to see the objects whose shadows he had been watching before. What do you think he would say if he were told by someone that before he had been seeing mere foolish phantoms, while now he was nearer to being, and was turned to what in a higher degree is, and was looking more directly at it? And further, if each of the several figures passing by were pointed out to him, and he were asked to say what each was, do you not think that he would be perplexed, and would imagine that the things he had seen before were truer than those now pointed out to him?"

"Yes, much truer," he said.

"Then if he were forced to look at the light itself, would not his eyes ache, and would he not try to escape, and turn back to things which he could look at, and think that they were really more distinct than the things shown him?"

"Yes," he said.

"But," I said, "if someone were to drag him out up the steep and rugged ascent, and did not let go till he had been dragged up to the light of the sun, would not 516 his forced journey be one of pain and annoyance; and when he came to the light, would not his eyes be so full of the glare that he would not be able to see a single one of the objects we now call true?"

"Certainly, not all at once," he said.

"Yes, I fancy that he would need time before he could see things in the world above. At first he would most easily see shadows, then the reflections in water of men and everything else, and, finally, the things themselves. After that he could look at the heavenly bodies and the sky itself by night, turning his eyes to the light of the stars and the moon more easily than to the sun or to the sun's light by day?"

"Surely."

"Then, last of all, I fancy he would be able to look at the sun and observe its nature, not its appearances in water or on alien material, but the very sun itself in its own place?"

"Inevitably," he said.

"And that done, he would then come to infer concerning it that it is the sun which produces the seasons and years, and controls everything in the sphere of the visible, and is in a manner the author of all those things which he and his fellow-prisoners used to see?"

"It is clear that this will be his next conclusion," he said.

"Well, then, if he is reminded of his original abode and its wisdom, and those who were then his fellow-prisoners, do you not think he will pity them and count himself happy in the change?"

"Certainly."

"Now suppose that those prisoners had had among themselves a system of honours and commendations, that prizes were granted to the man who had the keenest eye for passing objects and the best memory for which usually came first, and which second, and which came together, and who could most cleverly conjecture from this what was likely to come in the future, do you think that our friend would think longingly of those prizes and envy the men whom the prisoners honour and set in authority? Would he not rather feel what Homer describes, and wish earnestly

> To live on earth a swain,
> Or serve a swain for hire,

or suffer anything rather than be so the victim of seeming and live in their way?"

"Yes," he said, "I certainly think that he would endure anything rather than that."

"Then consider this point," I said. "If this man were to descend again and take his seat in his old place, would not his eyes be full of darkness because he had just come out of the sunlight?"

"Most certainly," he said.

"And suppose that he had again to take part with the prisoners there in the old contest of distinguishing between the shadows, while his sight was confused and 517 before his eyes had got steady (and it might take them quite a considerable time to get used to the darkness), would not men laugh at him, and say that having gone up above he had come back with his sight ruined, so that it was not worth while even to try to go up? And do you not think that they would kill him who tried to release them and bear them up, if they could lay hands on him, and slay him?"

"Certainly," he said.

"Now this simile, my dear Glaucon, must be applied in all its parts to what we said before; the sphere revealed by sight being contrasted with the prison dwelling, and the light of the fire therein with the power of the sun. If you will set the upward ascent and the seeing of the things in the upper world with the upward journey of the soul to the intelligible sphere, you will have my surmise; and that is what you are anxious to have. Whether it be actually true, God knows. But this is how it appears to me. In the world of knowledge the Form of the good is perceived last and with difficulty, but when it is seen it must be inferred that it is the cause of all that is right and beautiful in all things, producing in the visible world light and the lord of light, and being itself lord in the intelligible world and the giver of truth and reason, and this Form of the good must be seen by whosoever would act wisely in public or in private."

"I agree with you," he said, "so far as I am capable."

"Come, then," I said, "and agree with me in this also; and don't be surprised that they who have come thus far are unwilling to trouble themselves with mortal affairs, and that their souls are ever eager to dwell above. For this is but natural if the image we have related is true."

"It is," he said.

"Then do you think it at all surprising," I said, "if one who has come from divine visions to human miseries plays a sorry part and appears very ridiculous when, with eyes still confused and before he has got properly used to the darkness that is round him, he is compelled to contend in laws courts or elsewhere concerning the shadows of the just or the images which throw those shadows, or to dispute concerning the manner in which those images are conceived by men who have never seen real justice?"

"No, it is anything but surprising," he said.

"Yes," I said, "a sensible man would remember that the eyes may be confused in two ways, and for two reasons—by a change from light to darkness, or from darkness to light. He will consider that the same may happen with the soul, and when he sees a soul in trouble and unable to perceive, he will not laugh without thinking; rather he will examine whether it has come from a brighter light and is dim because it is not accustomed to the darkness, or whether it is on its way from ignorance to greater brightness and is dazzled with the greater brilliance; and so he will count the first happy in its condition and its life, but the second he will pity, and if he please to laugh at it, his laughter will be less ridiculous than that of him who laughs at the soul that has come from the light above."

"You speak with great fairness," he said.

"Then," he said, "if these things be true, we must think thus on the subject before us—that education is not what certain of its professors declare it to be. They say, if you remember, that they put knowledge in the soul where no knowledge has been, as men put sight into blind eyes."

"Yes, they do," he said.

"But our present argument," I said, "shows that there resides in each man's soul this faculty and the instrument wherewith he learns, and that it is just as if the eye could not turn from darkness to light unless the whole body turned with it; so this faculty and instrument must be wheeled round together with the whole soul away from that which is becoming, until it is able to look upon and to endure being and the brightest blaze of being; and that we declare to be the good. Do we not?"

"Yes."

"Education, then," "I said, "will be an art of doing this, an art of conversion, and will consider in what manner the soul will be turned round most easily and effectively. Its aim will not be to implant vision in the instrument of sight. It will regard it as already possessing that, but as being turned in a wrong direction, and not looking where it ought, and it will try to set this right."

"That seems probable," he said.

"Now most of the virtues which are commonly said to belong to the soul seem to resemble the bodily virtues. They seem to be really implanted by habit and exercise where they have not previously existed. But the virtue of wisdom evidently does in reality belong to something much more divine, which never loses its 519 power, but which from conversion becomes useful and advantageous, or again useless and harmful. Or have you never noticed how shrewd are the little eyes of the souls of those men who are reputed vicious but clever, and how sharply they see through the things to which they are directed? Their soul's vision is not feeble, but is forced to serve evil, and therefore the more sharply it sees the more evil things it does."

"Certainly," he said.

"Now suppose," I said, "that from their earliest years such natures had been under the knife and had had cut off from them those growths, heavy as lead, which partake of the nature of becoming, which gluttony with its greeds and pleasures has fastened upon them and which drag downwards their soul's vision; if they had been released from those encumbrances and turned round to the things that are true, the very same souls in those very same men would see them as sharply and keenly as they see the things towards which they are now directed."

"That would be but natural," he said.

"And is this not also natural and inevitable from our previous remarks," I said, "that the city would never be properly governed either by men who are uneducated and without experience in truth, or by men who are allowed to spend all their lives in the process of education? The first have no single mark in their lives at which they should aim in all that they do for themselves or for the state; the second will not act without compulsion, imagining that they have been transplanted to the islands of the blest without waiting for death."

"True," he said.

"Then it will be our task as founders," I said, "to compel the best natures to proceed to that study which we declared a little while ago to be the highest, to perceive the good, and to make that ascent we spoke of and when they have done so, and looked long enough, then we must not allow them the liberty which they now enjoy."

"What is that?"

"The liberty," I said, "of staying there, and refusing to descend again to the prisoners and to share with them in toils and honours, whether they be mean or exalted."

"What!" he said; "are we to do them an injustice, and force on them a worse life when a better is possible for them?"

"You have forgotten again, my friend," I said, "that it is not the law's concern that any one class in a state should live surpassingly well. Rather it contrives a good life for the whole state, harmonizing the citizens by persuasion and compulsion, and making them share with one another the advantage which each class can contribute to the community. It is the law which produces such men in the city; not in order to leave each man free to turn where he will, but that it may itself use them to bind the city together."

"True," he said, "I had forgotten."

"Consider further, Glaucon," I said, "that we shall not really do an injustice to the philosophers who arise in our city, but can speak justly when we proceed to compel them to watch over and care for the others. 'It is quite reasonable,' we shall say, 'that the philosophers who arise in other cities should not share in their toils. For there they are spontaneous growths, and their city's constitution has only hampered them, and it seems fair that the self-sown plant which is debtor to no man for its culture should not be eager to pay the price of its culture to anybody. But you we have begotten for the city as well as for yourselves to be like leaders and kings in a hive. You have received a better and more thorough education than those other philosophers, and are more capable of participating in both public life and philosophy. You must, therefore, descend by turns to dwell with the rest of the city, and must be accustomed to see the dark objects; for when you are accustomed, you will be able to see a thousand times better than those who dwell there, and you will know what each of the images is, and of what it is an image, because you have seen the truth of what is beautiful and just and good. And so your and our city will become a waking reality, and not a dream like most existing cities, which are peopled by men fighting about shadows and quarrelling for office as though that were a notable good. Whereas the truth surely is this, that that city wherein those who are to rule are least anxious for office must have the best and most stable constitution, and where you have the contrary disposition in your rulers you will have the contrary results.' "

"Certainly," he said.

"Then do you fancy that our nurselings when they hear this will disobey us, and will refuse to take their turn in sharing in the labours of the city, while for the most of their time they dwell with one another in the world of light?"

"Impossible," he said. "It is a just demand, and they are just. And assuredly each of them will take up office as a compulsory duty, reversing the attitude of those who now rule in cities."

"Yes, that is so, my friend," I said. "If you can discover a life for those who are to rule, better than ruling, 521 then for you a well-governed city is possible. For there alone the rulers will be those who are truly rich, not in money, but in the proper wealth of the happy man, a good and wise life. But this is impossible where men who are poor and hungry for goods of their own undertake public affairs, imagining that it is from these that their good is to be snatched; for then office becomes a thing to be fought for, and such a civil and intestine war destroys the combatants, and the whole state with them."

"Most true," he said.

"Then, do you know," I said, "any life where political office is despised except the life of true philosophy?"

"No, certainly not," he said.

"Office must not be wooed by those who love her, or you will have rival lovers fighting?"

"Surely."

"Then are there any whom you can compel to undertake the guardianship of the state except those who are wisest in what pertains to the best government of the city, and who also possess honours of a different kind and a nobler life than that of the statesmen?"

"None," he said.

"And now, do you wish us to consider the manner in

which such men will arise in the state, and how they
will be brought up to the light, just as certain heroes
are said to have ascended from Hades to the gods
above?"

"Of course I do," he said.

"And this would seem to be not the mere spinning of
a coin, but the conversion of a soul from a day as dark
as night to the true ascent which leads towards being,
which we shall declare to be true philosophy."

"Certainly."

"Then must we not consider what study has this
effect?"

"Surely."

"Then what study, Glaucon, will draw the soul away
from becoming to being? As I ask, this occurs to me.
Did we not say that these rulers when young had to be
warrior athletes?"

"We did."

"Then the study of which we are in search must have
this further quality?"

"What?"

"It must be not without use to warriors."

"Certainly, if possible," he said.

"Now in our former plan they were trained in music
and gymnastic?"

"Yes," he said.

"But gymnastic surely has to do with the becoming
and perishing, for it presides over the increase and decay
of the body?"

"Evidently."

"Then this will not be the study we seek?"

522    "No."

"Then will it be music as we formerly described it?"

"But that, if you remember," he said, "was the counterpart of gymnastic. It trained the guardians by the
influence of habit, and gave them not knowledge but

a kind of harmoniousness by means of harmony, and rhythmical grace by means of rhythm. On its literary side it had another set of similar characteristics, both in its fables and in those of its tales which were true. There was in it no study leading to anything of the kind which you are seeking."

"You remind me most accurately," I said. "It had, in truth, nothing of the kind. But, my wonderful Glaucon, what will fulfil our requirements? For the crafts, we surely agreed, are mechanical?"

"Surely. But is there any kind of study left, outside of music and gymnastic and the crafts?"

"If we have nothing left to choose outside of those," I said, "see if we can choose something of universal application."

"What?"

"Well, this common study, for example, which is used by all crafts, all modes of thought and sciences, and which every one must begin by learning."

"What is it?" he said.

"This trifling study," I said, "of distinguishing the one and the two and the three. I give it the general name of arithmetic and calculation. Is it not the case that every art and science is compelled to take some share in this?"

"Most certainly," he said.

"The art of war along with them?" I asked.

"Inevitably," he said.

"Yes," I said. "Palamedes, whenever he occurs in tragedy, is always exposing Agamemnon as a most ridiculous general. He says that he, Palamedes, invented number and then marshalled the ranks of the army at Ilium and counted the ships and everything else as though they had been uncounted before, and as though apparently Agamemnon didn't know how many feet he had,

since he could not count. So what sort of a general do
you think he could have been?"

"A strange one," he said, 'if that was true."

"Then shall we not decide," I said, "that the ability
to calculate and count is a study essential for a man in
war?"

"Most essential," he said, "if he is to understand anything about drill, or even if he is to be a man at all."

"Are you struck with the same feature in this study
as I am?" I asked.

"What?" he said.

523     "It seems to be one of those studies we are seeking,
which naturally lead to knowing, though nobody uses
it rightly, a study which wholly draws us towards being."

"What do you mean?" he said.

"I shall try," I said, "to make plain my opinion on
the matter. I distinguish to myself certain things as
leading and others as not leading in the direction of
which we are speaking. You must consider them along
with me and agree or disagree. Then we shall see more
clearly whether it is as I divine."

"Explain, then," he said.

"I will explain," I said, "that there are some things
in sensation which do not stimulate the intelligence to
inquiry because the judgment of sensation upon them
is satisfactory, and others which positively insist upon
the intelligence inquiring into them, because sensation
gives no satisfactory result."

"Obviously," he said, "you mean objects seen at a
distance and painting in perspective."

"You have not quite taken my meaning," I said.

"What then do you mean?" he said.

"The not stimulating," I said, "are those which do
not at once pass over into a contrary perception. I class
as stimulating those which do so pass, where the perception, whether it be of a near or distant object, indi-

cates no one thing more than its contrary. You will
understand more clearly what I mean in this way. Here,
say, are three fingers, the little finger, the middle finger,
and the third."

"Yes," he said.

"You may conceive that I am speaking of them as
seen from close at hand. Now, will you please consider
this question about them?"

"What?"

"Each of these surely appears equally a finger, and so
far as that is concerned, it makes no difference whether
the one we are looking at is the middle or one of the
extremes, whether it is black or white, thick or thin,
and so on. For in all these points the ordinary mind is
not compelled to ask of the intelligence. 'Then what is
a finger?' For sight has not at any stage suddenly in-
formed the mind that the finger is the opposite of a
finger."

"No, certainly not," he said.

"Then," I said, "such an experience naturally does
not stimulate or arouse the intelligence."

"Naturally not."

"But, on the other hand, does sight see adequately
the bigness or the smallness of the fingers, and does
it make no difference whether any one of them is in the
middle or on the outside? The same question may be
asked of the perception of thickness and thinness or
softness and hardness in the sensation of touch. And
are not the communications of the other senses similarly
defective? Is not this the procedure with each of them?
In the first place, is not the perception which deals with E24
the hard also compelled to deal with the soft, so that it
announces to the soul that it perceives the same thing
to be hard and soft?"

"Yes," he said.

"Then in such cases," I said, "must not the soul be

at a loss as to what information the perception is conveying by 'hard,' since it calls the same thing also soft, and what the perception of light and heavy by 'light' and 'heavy,' if it tells of the heavy as light and of the light as heavy?"

"Yes," he said, "these are strange communications for the mind to receive, and call for inquiry."

"Then naturally in such cases," I said, "the mind summons calculation and intelligence to its aid, and tries to consider whether each of the matters announced is one or two?"

"Surely."

"And if two, does not each of these two appear distinct from the other, and one?"

"Yes."

"Then if each is one and both together are two, the mind will understand the two as separate; for if they were not separate, it would not have understood them as two, but as one?"

"True."

"Now, sight also, we say, saw big and little, only not separate, but as a confused something. Is that not so?"

"Yes."

"But in order to make this clear the intelligence was compelled in its turn to see big and little, but in the opposite way from sight, not confused, but distinct."

"True."

"Then is it not from some such reason that it first occurs to us to ask, 'Then what is "the big" and "the little"? ' "

"Assuredly."

"And thus we distinguish on the one hand what is thought, and on the other what is seen?"

"Most true," he said.

"Then this is what I was trying to express a moment ago when I said that some things stimulate the understanding and some do not, and defined as stimulating those things which strike upon the senses along with their opposites; those which do not, as not rousing the intelligence."

"I now understand," he said, "and I agree."

"Well, then, to which of those do number and the one seem to belong?"

"I cannot make up my mind."

"Come!" I said, "draw an inference from our previous remarks. If the one, itself and by itself, is seen or apprehended by any other of the senses adequately, then like the finger we spoke of, it will not have the quality of drawing towards being. But if some contradiction is always seen along with it, so that it seems no more one than the opposite of one, then this will necessitate the critic, and the soul will necessarily in this case be at a loss, and will have to make search, setting the intelligence within it in motion, and to ask, 'What then is the one itself?' and so the studying of the one will be of those things which lead on and turn us round to the sight of that which is." 525

"Yes," he said, "and the seeing of the one has this quality in a marked degree, for we see the same thing at the same time as one and infinite in number."

"Then if this is the case with the one," I said, "is it not the same with all number?"

"Surely."

"But calculation and arithmetic are throughout concerned with number?"

"Certainly."

"Then they are seen to lead towards truth?"

"Yes, in a pre-eminent degree."

"Then here apparently we have one of the studies which we are seeking. For this study is essential to a warrior for his drill, and to a philosopher, because he must rise above becoming and lay hold on being if he is ever to become a reasonable arithmetician."

"That is so," he said.

"But our guardian is both warrior and philosopher?"

"Surely."

"Then it will be fitting, Glaucon, to prescribe this study by law, and to persuade those who are to share in the highest affairs of the city to take to calculation, and embrace it in no amateur spirit. They must go on until they arrive by the help of sheer intelligence at a vision of the nature of numbers, practising it not like merchants and peddlers for the sake of buying and selling, but for the purposes of war, and of an easier conversion of the soul itself from becoming to truth and being."

"Most excellent words," he said.

"Further it strikes me," I said, "now that we have mentioned the study of calculation, how elegant it is and in what manifold ways it helps our desires if it is pursued not for commercial ends but for the sake of knowledge."

"In what way?" he said.

"In this way which we have just been mentioning. It powerfully draws the soul above, and forces it to reason concerning the numbers themselves, not allowing any discussion which presents to the soul numbers with bodies that can be seen or touched. You know how it is with skilled mathematicians? If any one in an argument attempts to dissect the one, they laugh at him, and will not allow it. If you cut it up, they multiply it, taking good care that the one shall never appear not as one but as many parts."

"That is perfectly true."

526 "Then what, Glaucon, if you were to say to them, 'My wonderful friend, what sort of numbers are you discussing in which the one answers your claims, in

which each "one" is equal to every other "one" without the smallest difference and contains within itself no parts?' How do you think they would reply?"

"I fancy by saying that they are talking about those numbers which can be apprehended by the understanding alone, but in no other way."

"Do you see, then, my friend," I said, "that this study may fairly be thought necessary for us, since we find that it necessitates that the soul shall apply intelligence itself to truth itself?"

"Yes, indeed," he said; "it does that in a very marked degree."

. "Further, have you ever noticed that those who have a natural capacity for calculation are, generally speaking, naturally quick at all kinds of study; while men of slow intellect, if they are trained and exercised in arithmetic, if they get nothing else from it, at least all improve and become sharper than they were before?"

"That is so," he said.

"And I fancy you will not easily find many studies which are more trouble to learn and practise than this one?"

"No."

"Then for all these reasons we must not neglect the study, but those who have the best natures must be trained in it?"

"I agree," he said.

"Then let that be one point settled," I said. "Secondly, let us examine whether the study which borders on arithmetic suits us."

"What is that?" he said. "Do you mean geometry?"

"Just that," I said.

"Obviously," he said, "so much of it as applies to warlike operations is suitable. In pitching camp, occupying positions, closing up or deploying an army, and generally in executing other manœuvres on the field of battle or on the march, it will make a difference whether a man is a geometrician or not."

"Yes," I said, "but for such purposes quite a little geometry and calculation is sufficient. For the greater and the more advanced portion we must consider whether it tends to the other result, to making it easier to perceive the Form of the good. All things have this tendency, we say, if they compel the soul to turn towards that region which contains that most blissful sphere of being which it is most necessary for the soul to see."

"You are right," he said.

"Then if it compels us to behold being, it is suitable; if to behold becoming, it is unsuitable?"

"That is our statement."

527 "But none who have even a slight acquaintance with geometry," I said, "will deny that the nature of this science is in exact contradiction to the arguments used in it by its professors."

"In what way?" he asked.

"Well, they talk in most ridiculous and beggarly fashion; for they speak like men of business, and as though all their demonstrations have a practical aim, with their talk of squaring and applying and adding, and so on. But surely the whole study is carried on for the sake of knowledge."

"Most certainly," he said.

"Then must we not admit this further point?"

"What?"

"That it is for the knowledge of that which always is, not of that which at some particular place and time is becoming and perishing."

"That may well be agreed," he said. "For geometrical knowledge is of that which always is."

"Then, my fine fellow, it will draw the souls towards truth and complete the philosophic understanding, mak-

ing us raise upwards what now we wrongly direct downwards?"

"Yes, it will do that as far as may be," he said.

"Then you must prescribe," I said, "as far as may be,
that those in your City Beautiful shall in no way neglect
geometry. Its accidental advantages also are by no means
unimportant."

"Which?" he said.

"Those you mentioned," I said, "which concern war.
And, for that matter, in all forms of study where we
wish to ensure ready understanding, we know perfectly
well that there is all the difference in the world between
one who has studied geometry and one who has not."

"Yes, certainly, all the difference," he said.

"Then shall we decide upon this as a second study
for our young men?"

"Yes," he said.

"Then shall we put astronomy third? Do you agree?"

"Certainly I do," he said. "An attentive observation
of the times of months and years is suitable not only
for agriculture and navigation, but also for generalship
no less."

"You are a charming fellow," I said. "You seem to be
afraid that the multitude will think you are prescribing useless studies. And indeed it is no simple matter,
but quite difficult, to believe that in these studies some
instrument in each man's soul, which was being destroyed and blinded by other pursuits, is here purged
and rekindled—a salvation more precious than that of
thousands of eyes. For with this instrument alone is
truth perceived. Now those who agree with us in this
will most vehemently approve of your proposals, but
those who have never perceived this truth will naturally
think that you are talking nonsense. For they cannot
see any other advantage in those studies worth mentioning. So make up your mind with which party you

528 are arguing, or whether you are not concerned with one or the other of them but will carry on the argument chiefly for your own satisfaction, though you have no objection if any one else gets any advantage from it."

"I choose the latter alternative," he said, "to speak and ask and answer chiefly for my own satisfaction."

"Fall back, then," I said, "for we made a mistake a moment ago in deciding what came next to geometry."

"In what way?" he said.

"After plane geometry," I said, "we took solids already in revolution before solids by themselves. But it is right after the second increase to take the third, and that is surely concerned with cubic increase and bodies with depth?"

"It is," he said. "But those problems, Socrates, seem to be still unsolved."

"There are two reasons for that," I said. "They are difficult, and are only feebly investigated, because no city holds them in honour; and, besides, their investigators need a superintendent; without him they will come to no solutions. To find such a man is hard enough; but when you have found him, as things are at present the investigators in the science would be too conceited to obey him. But if the whole city should co-operate with the superintendent and pay honour to the study, then they would obey, and the real nature of those problems would be brought to light as the result of steady and vigorous investigation. For even now, though the public despise and discourage the subject, and its investigators do not understand its usefulness, nevertheless in spite of all these obstacles it makes progress, such is the charm of the study; and it would be in no way surprising if its problems were explained."

"Yes," he said, "there is an extraordinary charm about the subject. But tell me more clearly what you meant a moment ago. You defined geometry, I think, as the investigation of the plane?"

"Yes," I said.

"Then at first," he said, "you put astronomy next to it, but afterwards you drew back?"

"Yes," I said; "in my hurry to get through everything quickly I only go more slowly. The inquiry into the dimension of depth comes next; but I left it out because it is so ridiculously investigated, and after geometry named astronomy, which is the motion of solids."

"You are right," he said.

"Then," I said, "let us put astronomy fourth, on the supposition that the study that is now neglected will exist if the city takes it up."

"That is reasonable," he said. "You rebuked me a moment ago, Socrates, for my inept praise of astronomy. But now I can praise it from the point of view from which you pursue it. For it seems perfectly obvious to me that astronomy, at any rate, compels the soul to look on high, and from things here leads it yonder." 529

"Possibly," I said, "it is obvious to every one but myself. For I don't think as you do."

"But how then?" he said.

"In the way in which those who would lead us to philosophy now pursue the study, it seems to me simply to make men look downwards."

"What do you mean?" he said.

"You seem to me," I said, "to display a fine assurance in your conception of the nature of the study which deals with things above. Apparently you would think that a man was using his reason and not his eyes, if he learnt something by gazing at a carved ceiling with his head bent back. Possibly you are right to think so, and I am a simple fool. But I cannot think of any other study as one that makes the soul look on high except that which is concerned with being and the unseen. If any one attempts to learn anything which is perceivable—his open mouth may yawn upwards or his closed mouth purse downwards, it makes no difference. He, I declare, will never learn. For such things do not admit of knowledge, and his soul is looking downwards and not up, though you may stretch him in his back on the ground or float him in the sea for his studies."

"I am justly punished," he said. "You were right to rebuke me. But what then did you mean by saying that astronomy ought to be studied on a system very different from the present one, if its students were to learn anything of value for our purposes?"

"This," I said. "These ornaments of the heavens, since they adorn a visible sky, should be thought to be the most beautiful and to have the most perfect nature amongst visible things, but to fall far short of those true adornments, those movements wherewith pure velocity and pure retardation, in true number and in all true figures, are moved in relation to each other, and wherewith they also move that which is within them, which matters are to be apprehended by reason and understanding, but not by sight. Do you disagree?"

"Certainly not," he said.

"Then," I said, "we must use the adornments of heaven as models in our study of those true ornaments, as though we had come across diagrams drawn and elaborated with surpassing skill by Daedalus or some other artist or draughtsman. For surely any competent geometrician on seeing such diagrams would think that they were most beautifully executed, but would consider it ridiculous to examine them seriously with any hope of finding in them the truths of equality or duplicity or any other ratio."

530 "How could it help being ridiculous?" he said.

"Then," I said, "do you fancy that he who is really an astronomer will not feel the same when he contem-

plates the motions of the stars? He will think that
heaven and what it contains have been composed by
heaven's creator with the utmost beauty that the composition of such things allows; but in respect to the relations of night and day, of days and months, and
months and years, and of the other stars to sun and
moon and to each other, do you not think that he will
regard with astonishment the man who considers that
these objects, bodily and visible as they are, are ever invariable and never decline from their courses, and will
think it absurd to make enormous efforts to apprehend
the truth of these matters?"

"Well," he said, "I certainly think so now, as I listen
to your words."

"Astronomy, then," I said, "like geometry, we shall
pursue by the help of problems, and leave the starry
heavens alone; if we hope truly to apprehend it, and
turn natural intelligence of the soul from uselessness to
use."

"The task you prescribe," he said, "is far beyond the
present methods of astronomical study."

"Well, I fancy," I said, "that our other prescriptions
will be in the same manner if we are of any use as legis-
lators. Now, have you any suitable study to suggest?"

"No," he said, "not at this moment."

"Motion presents," I said, "not one, but several
forms, I imagine. The wise will perhaps be able to
name the full list. But even I can distinguish two."

"What are they?"

"One we have had," I said, "the other is its counterpart."

"What is it?"

"Apparently," I said, "as the eyes are fixed on astronomy, so are the ears on harmonics, and these are sister
sciences as the Pythagoreans say, and we, Glaucon, agree
with them. Do we not?"

"Yes," he said.

"Then," I said, "since the subject is complicated, let us inquire of them what they say on these matters, and whether they have any other information to give us. And throughout we shall look after our special interests."

"What is that?"

"That those, whom we are to bring up, shall not attempt to study anything in those sciences which is imperfect and which does not always reach to that point at which all things ought to arrive, as we have just been 531 saying about astronomy. Do you not know that the same sort of thing happens in harmonics? Men expend fruitless labour, just as they do in astronomy, in measuring audible tones and chords."

"Yes, by heaven," he said, "and what fools they make of themselves, talking of 'densities' and what not, and straining their ears as if they were trying to catch a sound which was somewhere in the neighbourhood; and some declare that they can hear another note between two already distinguished, and this is the smallest interval, and should be made the unit of measurement; and others disagree and say that it is not a new note, and both parties put their ears before their reason."

"You are talking of those fine fellows," I said, "who persecute and torture the strings, racking them upon pegs. But I shall not weary you with my simile by telling you of the blows they inflict with the plectrum and the accusations they bring, and of the strings' denials and blusterings. I leave that, and declare that I don't mean these people, but the Pythagoreans, whom we have just said we should question about harmonics. For they behave like astronomers; they try to find the numbers in audible consonances, and do not rise to problems, to examining what numbers are and what numbers are not consonant, and for what reasons."

"That would be a more than human inquiry," he said.

"In any case," I said, "it is useful in the search for the beautiful and the good, but if it is pursued in any other way, it is useless."

"That is likely enough," he said.

"Now I imagine," I said, "that if the inquiry into all those studies which we have described comes to the consideration of their community with and relations to one another, and considers how these different sciences are akin, then our labours will contribute to the purposes we have in view, and we shall not toil in vain; but on any other assumption we shall."

"I venture to prophesy the same," he said. "But you describe a very long task, Socrates."

"Do you say that of the prelude," I said, "or of what? Do we not know that all these studies are but the prelude of the real melody which is to be studied? You surely don't think that men who are clever in these sciences are dialecticians?"

"By heavens, no," he said; "at least only a very few of those I have met."

"But," I said, "do you think that men who are unable to give and receive reasons ever know anything of what we say they ought to know?"

"There again I answer no," he said.

"Then, Glaucon," I said, "is this not at last the real 532 melody played by dialectic? It is intelligible, and its copy is the power of sight which we described as at length endeavouring to look at the real animals, then at the real stars, and finally at the real sun. So too when any one tries by dialectic through the discourse of reason unaided by any of the senses to attain to what each reality is, and desists not until by sheer intelligence he apprehends the reality of good, then he stands at the real goal of the intelligible world, as the man in our simile stood at the goal of the visible."

"Assuredly," he said.

"Then do you not call this progress dialectic?"

"Yes."

"Then," I said, "the release of the prisoners from bondage, the turning round from the shadows to the images and the light, the ascent from the cave to the sunlight, and that stage in the world above when they are still unable to look at animals and plants and the light of the sun, but can look at the divine reflections in water and the shadows of real things, instead of the shadows of images thrown by a light which is itself but an image compared with the sun—this is accomplished by all that pursuit of those arts which we have mentioned. It leads what is best in the soul up to the vision of what is best in things that are, just as in our simile the clearest organ of the body was led up to the vision of the brightest object in the bodily and visible world."

"I accept your statements," he said. "All the same, they certainly seem to me hard to accept, though in another sense it is hard not to accept them. Nevertheless let us assume that the truth is as you state it; we need not be content with what we hear now, but must return to the subject often in the future. And now let us proceed to the real melody, and describe it as we have described the prelude. Tell us, therefore, what is the character of the power of dialectic, into what forms is it divided, and, finally, what are its methods. For these probably would lead to that point where a rest from the way and an end of his journeying awaits the traveller."

533    "Dear Glaucon," I said, "you will not yet be able to follow me—though not from any want of zeal on my part—but you would see no longer an image of that of which we are speaking, but the very truth—at least as

it appears to me. Whether it is actually so or not need not trouble us further now, but, that there is something of this sort to see, we must insist, must we not?"

"Yes."

"And also that the power of dialectic alone would reveal it, and only to one who has experience of the studies we have described, and that in no other way is this possible?"

"Yes," he said, "on that we may insist."

"In any case," I said, "no one will object to our saying that it is some further method which endeavours in every case systematically to apprehend concerning each reality that which it is. But all the other arts are concerned with beliefs and desires of men, or are directed towards becomings and compositions, or towards the care of growing or composite things. And as for the exceptions which we declared to partake in a measure of being, the art of geometry and those which follow it, we see that these dream about being. They cannot behold it with waking eyes so long as they use hypotheses and leave them uncriticized, without being able to give an account of them. For if a man's first principle is one he does not know, and his final conclusion and the intermediate stages are compounded out of that which he does not know, what possibility is there of such an agreement ever becoming knowledge?"

"None," he said.

"Then the dialectical method alone," I said, "proceeds in this way, destroying its hypotheses to get to the first principle of all and make itself secure. It finds the eye of the soul embedded in what is really a swamp of barbarism and gently draws and raises it upwards, using the arts which we have enumerated as handmaids in the work of conversion. These we have often from force of habit called knowledge, but they need another name, implying more brightness than belief, and more obscurity than knowledge. I think we previously called this understanding—but we are not, I think, disputing about a name. The subjects which we are considering are too important for that."

"No, we are not," he said.

"But will words which manifest somehow the quality of clear speaking in the soul be enough?"

"Yes."

"Then it will suffice," I said, "if as formerly we call 534 the first division knowledge, the second understanding, the third faith, and the fourth conjecture, the last two together belief and the first two intelligence; and say that belief deals with becoming as intelligence with being; also that as being is to becoming, so is intelligence to belief; and as intelligence is to belief, so is knowledge to faith and understanding to conjecture. The proportion of the objects to which these apply, and the division of the spheres of the believed and the intelligible, we may leave alone, Glaucon, to avoid arguments many times as long as those we have had already."

"Well, as far as I can follow you, I certainly agree on those points," he said.

"Then do you call a dialectician him who always takes account of the reality? And will you not say that he who cannot do this, in so far as he cannot give account to himself or to another, has no intelligence on that subject?"

"Certainly I should," he said.

"Then it is the same in regard to the good. Unless a man can abstract the Form of the good from all else and distinguish it by analysis, unless he makes it run the gauntlet of every proof, and is eager to try it by the test not of seeming but of reality, and finally, unless he emerges from it all with his principle not overthrown, then will you not say that he does not know the real good or any other good, and if by any chance he grasps any image of it, he does so in belief but not by knowledge: he dreams and drowses through his present life, and, before ever awaking here, goes to his final slumber in Hades?"

"Yes, assuredly," he said, "I shall stoutly maintain all those statements."

"Then certainly if you ever had the actual rearing of those children of yours whose training and education you are now discussing, you would not allow them, I imagine, to be mere irrational quantities, if they are to rule in the city and control affairs of state?"

"Certainly not," he said.

"Then will you ordain that they must pay special attention to this branch of education which will teach them to ask questions and give answers most scientifically?"

"With your help," he said, "I shall."

"Now, do you not think," I said, "that we have placed dialectic like a coping-stone on the top of our studies, and that there is no other study which deserves to be put above it, and that the series is at last complete?"

535

"I do," he said.

"You are left, then," I said, "with a question of distribution, the question, namely, as to the persons to whom, and the manner in which, we shall assign these studies?"

"Obviously," he said.

"Do you remember the sort of men we chose in our former selection of the magistrates?"

"Of course I do," he said.

"Then thus far," I said, "consider that such natures are the ones to be selected. We must give preference to the steadiest, the bravest, and, as far as possible, the best looking. But, further, we have not only to look out for men of noble and sturdy morals, they must also have natural gifts suitable for our scheme of education."

"Then what do you determine these to be?"

"They must have keenness for their studies, my excellent friend," I said, "and find no difficulty in learning; for the soul plays the coward far more readily in severe study than in gymnastics. The exertion comes more home to it, being peculiar to itself, and not shared by the body."

"True," he said.

"The man of our search must also have a good memory, an unchangeable purpose, and an unflagging love of work. How else do you imagine that a man will consent to crown his bodily labours by all this study and practice?"

"No one but a man of exceptional natural abilities would do it," he answered.

"Yes," I said, "the reason for men's mistaken view, and for the disgrace under which philosophy now suffers, is, as we said before, that men apply themselves to it without considering their unworthiness. But it should be the privilege only of the genuine sons of philosophy, not of bastards."

"What do you mean?" he said.

"In the first place," I said, "he that is to study philosophy must not be lame in his love of work—zealous in the one half of it, and lazy in the other. And that is the description of a man who is fond of gymnastics and of hunting, and loves all bodily labours, but does not love study, is not fond of listening to others or of inquiring for himself, but hates any labour of that kind. And he whose love of work has taken the opposite direction is also halt."

"That is most true," he said.

"Similarly," I said, "in reference to truth, shall we not class as deformed a soul which, though it hates the lie told on purpose, and cannot endure it in itself, and is very angry when other people are deceitful, nevertheless is quite complacent to involuntary falsehood, and is not angry when it is found in a state of ignorance, but wallows in it like a bestial hog?"

"Most certainly," he said.                                    b36

"Then by reference to temperance," I said, "and courage, and high-mindedness, and all the elements of virtue we must most carefully distinguish between the true-born and the bastard. For if an individual or a city does not know how to observe carefully all these matters, they unwittingly employ cripples and bastards as friends or rulers in any of these services for which they have occasion."

"Yes," he said, "that is certainly the case."

"Then we must take all these precautions most carefully," I said. "Because if to this weighty study and severe discipline we bring men sound of limb and of sound mind, and train them therein, justice herself will find no fault with us, and we shall preserve the city and the constitution; but if we bring men of another stamp, the event will be in all respects the opposite, and we shall swamp philosophy in another flood of ridicule."

"That would be disgraceful," he said.

"Certainly," I said. "But probably I made myself ridiculous just now?"

"In what way?" he asked.

"I forgot," I said, "that we are playing, and I spoke too earnestly. For as I spoke I glanced at philosophy, and seeing her so undeservedly spurned and contemned, I think I got angry, and said what I said too severely, as though I had lost my temper with those who are responsible for it."

"No, by heaven," he said, "that did not strike me as I listened to you."

"But it did me as I spoke," I replied. "But do not let

us forget this point, that though in our former selection we chose old men, that will not now be possible. For we cannot agree with Solon that any one can learn much when he is old. An old man can sooner run than learn. All severe and frequent toil belongs to youth."

"Inevitably," he said.

"Calculation, then, and geometry, and all those preliminary studies which must pave the way for dialectic, should be set before our guardians when they are boys, and in such a fashion as will not seem compulsory."

"Why so?"

"Because," I said, "the free man should learn no study under bondage. And while enforced bodily labours do no harm to the body, study forced on the mind will not abide there."

"True," he said.

"Then, my excellent friend, train your children in their studies not by compulsion but by games, and you will be better able to see the natural abilities of each."

"What you say is reasonable," he said.

"Do you remember," I said, "that we declared that even in battles the children must be taken on horseback to look on, and must be taken near the fighting line if safety allowed, and have their taste of blood like puppies?"

"I remember," he said.

"Then he," I said, "who in all those toils and studies and alarms proves himself the readiest on every occasion will be put on a select list."

"At what age?" he asked.

"When they are released from the necessary gymnastics," I answered. "For in the two or three years occupied in those it will be impossible to do anything else. For weariness and sleep are foes to study. And at the same time the proficiency shown in gymnastics will be one of our tests, and that not the least important."

"Surely," he said.

"Then after this," I said, "from their twentieth year those who have been selected shall have special privileges, and the studies which they have come across at random in their education as children, they must now bring together so that they will have a general view of their kinship with one another and with the nature of Being."

"Yes," he said, "such knowledge alone is abiding in those who possess it."

"And it is also," I said, "the best test of a dialectical or non-dialectical nature. For the power of seeing things as a whole distinguishes the dialectician."

"I agree," he said.

"Then you will have to watch these tests," I said, "and see who best come up to our requirements, and are persevering in their studies, and persevering in battle and the other duties the law imposes upon them; and then when they are past thirty you must select those out of 'the selected,' and give them greater privileges, and by testing their power in dialectic examine which of them can do without his eyes and his other senses and approach in truth to real being. And this is a task requiring the greatest care, my friend."

"Why specially so?" he asked.

"Do you not see," I asked, "how serious is the evil from which dialectic is suffering at the present time?"

"What?" he asked.

"Surely," I said, "it is filled with lawlessness."

"Yes, certainly," he said.

"Then are you at all surprised that this should happen to its students; and can you not forgive them?" I said.

"Why particularly?" he said.

"Suppose," I said, "a child, brought up in wealthy surroundings as a member of a widely connected and <sub>533</sub>

distinguished family to which he thought he belonged, and surrounded by flatterers, and suppose that when he came to manhood he discovered that he was not the son of his self-styled parents, but could not find his real father and mother, can you divine the differences in his behaviour towards his flatterers and towards his spurious parents in the periods before and after his knowledge of his substitution? Or will you listen to my divination?"

"I will," he said.

"I divine then," I said, "that so long as he does not know the truth he will reverence his supposed father and mother and other relations more than his flatterers; he will devote his attention to the former rather than to the latter, will see that they lack nothing, and be careful not to trespass against them in word or deed, and not to disobey them on important questions."

"Probably," he said.

"But when he discovers the facts, I suspect that his reverence and respect will gradually be transferred from his supposed parents to his flatterers, that he will follow the suggestions of the latter more than he did before, will regulate his life by their standard, and openly associate with them, and, unless he has an exceptionally generous nature, will entirely neglect his former father and his other reputed relatives?"

"You describe just what would happen," he said. "But how does this simile apply to students of reasoning?"

"In this way. You know that from our childhood we have beliefs concerning things just and beautiful. We have been brought up in them; they have been like parents to us, and we obey and honour them."

"Yes."

"Now opposed to those are certain pleasurable pursuits which flatter our soul and strive to draw it after them, but can induce no man of any strength of character to follow them. Such men honour the beliefs of their fathers, and follow after them."

"That is so."

"Then," I said, "suppose that at this stage a question comes before the man as to what is the beautiful. He gives the answer he has heard from the lawgiver, and the argument proves him wrong. This happens again and again, and in all kinds of ways, till he is reduced to the opinion that what he has believed in is no more beautiful than ugly; and he comes to the same opinion about just and good, and the things he held in highest reverence. When this has happened, what kind of honour or obedience do you think he will pay these principles?"

"It is inevitable," he said, "that he will no longer honour or obey them in the same way."

"Then," I said, "when he does not think those principles so deserving of reverence, or so near to him as he did formerly, and cannot find the true principles, **539** can he naturally turn to any but the flattering life?"

"No," he said.

"Then I fancy he will seem to have given up lawfulness for lawlessness."

"Inevitably."

"Then," I said, "the fate of those who study dialectic is natural, and deserves, as I said, our full forgiveness?"

"Yes, and our pity," he said.

"Then if your thirty-year-olds are not to become objects of this pity, will you not have to take great precautions how you meddle with dialectic?"

"Most certainly," he replied.

"Then is not this one precaution we can always observe, we can prevent them from tasting dialectic while they are young? For I fancy that you must have seen young lads at their first taste of dialectic; how they treat it as a game, and use it only for purposes of contradiction? They imitate those who refute them, and refute others in their turn, delighting, like puppies, in dragging about and pulling to pieces with words whoever happens to be near them."

"Yes, they are wonderful," he said.

"Then when they have refuted many people, and been refuted by many, they quickly and decisively come to a rejection of all their previous opinions, and thus both they and the whole cause of philosophy are discredited in the eyes of the world."

"Most true," he said.

"But an older man," I said, "will not want to catch this madness. He will imitate him who wishes to converse and consider the truth, rather than the jester who employs it for amusement and contradiction. He will have greater discretion, and will make the pursuit more instead of less honourable."

"You are right," he said.

"And have not all our previous remarks been meant to ensure that those to whom arguments are to be allowed shall be of orderly and steady natures, and to prevent the approach of the casual and the unfit which prevails now?"

"Certainly," he said.

"Then for the acquisition of dialectic, is it sufficient if the student perseveres in constant and intense study to the exclusion of everything else, in the same way as he was disciplined in bodily exercises, but for twice the number of years?"

"Do you mean six or four?" he asked.

"It is of no consequence," I said. "Say five. And after that you will have to force them down into the cave again, and compel them to take command in war and in such offices as pertain to the young, in order that they may not come short of others in practical experience. And still in these pursuits also you must test

them and see whether they abide steadfastly every kind 540
of temptation, or whether they give way in anything."

"What time do you give for this?" he asked.

"Fifteen years," I said. "And when they are fifty,
those who have come safely through, and have always
triumphed throughout in word and deed, must at last
be taken to the goal; they must be compelled to look
upon that which gives light to all, and turn the gleam
of their soul upon it and see the real good; then using
that as the pattern for the rest of their life, they must
take their turn in ordering city and individuals and
their own lives; the most of their time they will spend
in philosophy, but when their turn comes, they will endure the toil of directing politics and being rulers for
the sake of their city, regarding such action not as anything noble but as a compulsion laid upon them; and
so each generation, having trained up others like to
themselves whom they can leave to be the city's guardians, will depart to the islands of the blest and dwell
there. The city shall establish monuments and sacrifices
to them, if the Pythian allows, honouring them as demigods, if not as happy and divine."

"You have finished off your ruling men most beautifully, Socrates, like a sculptor," he said.

"And the ruling women also, Glaucon," I replied;
"for don't imagine that anything I have said applies
any more to men than to women, so long as we have
women of adequate natural gifts."

"You are right," he said, "since they will share alike
with the men in all things, as we described."

"Well, then," I said, "do you agree that our words
concerning city and constitution are not mere pious
prayers; that our proposals are difficult, but are somehow practicable, and that in no other way than we have
described; when those who are truly philosophers, either
one or more of them, become rulers in a state and de-

spise the present objects of men's ambitions, thinking them worthless and mean; when holding precious the right and the prizes which it gives, and giving the chiefest and most essential place to justice, they serve and foster it, and so set their own city to rights?"

"How?" he asked.

"They must send into the country," I replied, "all in the city who are more than ten years old, and so get the children out of the moral influences of their parents, and train them in their own customs and laws, which are those we have enumerated. And will not a city and constitution, such as we have described, be thus most quickly and easily established, and enjoy happiness, and greatly benefit the nation in which it is found?"

"Surely," he said; "and I think, Socrates, that you have described well how, if ever, it would come into being."

"Then is not our discourse concerning this city, and the man who is like to it, now at last complete? For surely it is obvious what sort of nature we shall demand of him?"

"It is," he said; "and as for our subject, I think it is completed."

# BOOK VIII

"Good. We have agreed, then, Glaucon, that in the city whose constitution is to be perfect, wives and children and all education will be in common; so will warlike and peaceful occupation; and those who have shown themselves best in philosophy and war are to be their kings."

"We have," he said.

"We have also agreed to the proposal that when the rulers are established they shall assemble the soldiers, and settle them in dwellings such as we prescribed, dwellings common to all, and with nothing private for any one. And besides this we also, if you remember, came to an agreement about the manner of their holding property."

"Yes, I remember," he said, "that we thought that no one should possess any of those things which now constitute ordinary people's property; rather they were to be like warrior athletes and guardians, and to receive yearly sustenance for their needs from the other citizens as salary for their guardianship, and were to look after themselves and the rest of the city."

"Your account is correct," I said. "But come, we completed that subject, so let us go back to where we started this digression, and resume our old path."

"That is not difficult," he said. "You were practically at the point at which you are now. You were saying that we had completed our discussion of the city, and that you ranked as good the city so described and the man who was like it, even though you could apparently have told us of a still more beautiful city and man. But in any case, you said that since this city was right, all others were faulty. Of the other constitutions you said, I remember, that there were four forms worth considering, whose mistakes ought to be noticed; there were also men corresponding to them, all of whom we were to observe, in order that we might come to an agreement as to which was the best and which the worst man, and thus might consider whether the best was the happiest and the worst the most miserable or not. And while I was asking you which you meant by the four constitutions, Polemarchus and Adeimantus interrupted, and then you took up the discussion which has brought us to this point."

"Most accurately remembered," I said.

"But now, like a wrestler, get back to your original grip. Now that I am asking you the same question, try to tell us what you were then going to say."

"I will if I can," I answered.

"In any case," he said, "I am anxious to hear for myself which are the four forms of government you meant."

"There is no difficulty in your hearing," I said. "The forms of government, of which I speak, and which have distinct names, are these. There is the one which most people praise, the well-known Cretan and Lacedaemonian constitution; second in the list, and second in esteem, is a constitution fraught with many evils, called oligarchy. Set over against it and next in order, comes democracy; then tyranny the glorious, the chiefest of them all, is the fourth and final disease of a city. Do you know any other form of constitution which belongs to a distinct and manifest class? For the family governments and the sovereignties which are bought with money and other such constitutions are more or less intermediates to those four. They are found among barbarians and Hellenes alike."

"Yes," he said, "you hear of many extraordinary forms."

"But do you realize," I said, "that the specific types of men and of constitutions must be equal in number? Or do you imagine that constitutions grow at random 'from tree or stone,' and not from those characters of the men in the cities which preponderate and draw the rest of the city after them?"

"I certainly do not think they have any other source than that," he said.

"Then if the characters of cities are five, the dispositions of soul in individuals will be five also?"

"Of course."

"We have already described the man who is like aristocracy, and declared him to be just and good?"

"We have." 545

"Then must we not now go through the worse men— first, the contentious and ambitious man, who corresponds to the Laconian constitution, and after him the oligarchic and the democratic and the tyrannic man, that we may see the most unjust and set him over against the most just, and so may complete our inquiry of how pure justice stands to pure injustice in respect to the happiness and misery of him who possesses them, and so either be convinced by Thrasymachus and pursue injustice, or by the argument which is now coming into view and follow justice?"

"By all means let us do as you propose," he said.

"We began by examining characters in constitutions before we examined them in individuals, because that was the more luminous method. Should we now, therefore, first examine the ambitious constitution—I call it that because I know of no other name in use; we must call it either timocracy or timarchy; after that shall we consider the man corresponding to it; then oligarchy and the oligarchic man; and after that shall we first look at democracy, and then observe the democratic man; and, fourthly, go into the tyrannically governed city and see it, and in turn look into the tyrannic soul, and then endeavour to give a competent decision on the question we have proposed?"

"That would ensure reasonable observation and judgment," he said.

"Come, then," I said, "let us try to explain how timocracy will arise out of aristocracy. Is it not a universal fact, that a change in any constitution originates in those who hold office when dissension arises actually within the governing power; while so long as they are of one mind, however few they may be, the city cannot be changed?"

"That is so."

"How then, Glaucon, will our city be changed, and how will the auxiliaries and the rulers come to dissension with each other and among themselves? Or shall we, like Homer, pray the Muses to tell us how first dissension befell, and shall we say that treating us with jest and banter as though we were children they assume a lofty tragic style and an appearance of seriousness?"

"How?"

546 "In some such words as these: 'That a city so constituted should change is difficult; but since decay is the lot of everything that has come into being, even this constitution will not abide for ever, but will be dissolved. And its dissolution will be as follows: To all living things, not only to plants that grow in the earth, but also to animals that live upon its surface, come times of fertility or barrenness of soul and body as often as their revolutions complete for each species the circumferences of circles, which are short for the short-lived, and long for the long-lived. Now those whom you

have trained to be leaders of the city, in spite of their
wisdom will not be able by calculation and perception
to manage the production of offspring in your race so
that it shall either be good or not be at all, but it will
escape them, and they will some time or other beget
children wrongly. For a divine creature there is a period
comprehended by a perfect number; but for a human
creature the number is the first in which multiplications
of roots and squares (which contain three distances and
four limits of numbers that make like and unlike, wax
and wane) make all things consistent and rational with
one another. Of which numbers, three multiplied by
four and by five, and raised to the fourth power, produces two harmonies: the one is a square so many
times a hundred; the other a rectangle on the one side
of a hundred squares of rational diameters of five dimin-
ished by one or of irrational by two, on the other of
a hundred cubes of three. This complete geometrical
number is lord over better and worse births; and when
your guardians, through their ignorance of it, join
brides and bridegrooms at inopportune seasons, their
children will not have good natures or enjoy good fortune. The best of them will be appointed by their
predecessors, but when they come into their fathers'
powers, they will be unworthy, and, although guardians,
will begin to neglect us. First of all music will be esteemed too lightly by them and then gymnastic, and
so your young men will come to forget the Muses. Beginning in this way, they will show themselves indifferent guardians in the task of assaying your different
races, which are the same as Hesiod's gold and silver 547
and bronze and iron. So iron will be mixed with silver
and bronze with gold, and inequality and inharmonious
discrepancy will arise, results which always produce war
and strife wherever they occur. Such we must declare to
be the ancestry of sedition wherever she arises.' "

"And we must declare their answer to be correct," he said.

"Of course," I said, "the Muses' answer must be."

"Then what will the Muses say after that?" he asked.

"When sedition had arisen," I answered, "the two pairs of races began to pull different ways, the iron and bronze to money-making and possession of land and houses and gold and silver; the others, the gold and silver, since they were not in want but rich by nature, led their souls towards virtue and the old constitution. After violent conflict they came to a compromise, and distributed land and houses for private enjoyment. Those whom formerly they had protected as free men, friends and supporters, they then enslaved and treated as serfs and servants, reserving to themselves war and the duty of guarding the others."

"I think," he said, "that this is the origin of that revolution."

"Then," I asked, "will not this constitution be midway between an aristocracy and an oligarchy?"

"Certainly."

"Such, then, will be the revolution. But after revolution, how will it be governed? Is it not obvious that in some respects it will imitate the earlier constitution, and in others oligarchy, inasmuch as it lies between them, and that it will also have some features of its own?"

"Yes," he said.

"Then in reverence towards rulers, in the abstention of its warrior element from husbandry, handicrafts, and other forms of money-making, in the establishment of common meals, and in bestowing attention on gymnastic and the exercise of war, in all these matters will it not imitate the earlier constitution?"

"Yes."

"But will it not have many features of this kind

peculiar to itself? It will distrust the wise as rulers, for its wise men will now be of mixed character, not simple and sincere as before; it will prefer spirited and more straightforward men, made more for war than for peace, will have a great admiration for military tricks and stratagems, and will always be engaging in war?"

"Yes."

"Further," I said, "these men will be avaricious like the citizens in oligarchies, with a fierce secret passion for gold and silver. They will have storehouses and treasuries of their own where they will store their wealth in secret. They will be ringed round with dwellings, mere private nests where they may squander a lavish expenditure on their wives and whomsoever they please."

"Very true," he said.

"Further, they will be sparing of their money, reverencing it as men do whose money-getting is in secret, but their desires will make them enjoy spending other men's money. They will pluck the fruits of pleasure in secret, running away from the law, like boys running away from their father. Compulsion and not persuasion will have controlled their education, because they have neglected the true Muse, who is accompanied by reason and philosophy, and have honoured gymnastic above music."

"You describe," he said, "a constitution compounded throughout of good and evil."

"Yes, it is a compound," I said. "But one single feature is conspicuous in it, which arises from the prevalence of the spirited element, and that is rivalry and ambition."

"That is certainly the case," he said.

"Such, then," I said, "would be the origin and character of this constitution. We must merely sketch it in outline without giving an exhaustive and accurate description, because even a sketch will be enough to give us sight of the most just and the most unjust man. A description that included all constitutions and all types of character, and omitted no detail, would be impossibly long."

"You are right," he said.

"Then who is the man corresponding to this constitution? What will be his origin and character?"

"I fancy," said Adeimantus, "that in his emulous nature he will come somewhere near our friend Glaucon."

"Perhaps," I said. "But I think that his nature is unlike Glaucon's in these respects."

"In which?"

"He must be harder," I said, "and rather less musical, with an appreciation for music and for speeches, but no orator. He will be inclined to be cruel to slaves, not having the properly educated man's contempt for them. To free men he will be civil, to his rulers zealously obedient. Loving rule and honour, he will claim them not for speech or any such qualification, but for warlike deeds and warrior qualities. He will be a lover of gymnastic and of hunting."

"Yes," he said, "that is the character produced in that constitution."

"Again," I said, "will he not despise money when he is young, but as he gets older become more and more fond of it by reason of his participation in the character of the avaricious man, and because, since he has abandoned his best guardian, his virtue is not unalloyed?"

"Who is that guardian?" asked Adeimantus.

"Reason conjoined with music," I answered. "That alone, when it has entered into a man, abides with him through life, and is the saviour of his virtue."

"A fair speech," he said.

"Then such," I said, "is the character of the timo-cratic young man, and he is like the timocratic city."

"Certainly."

"He arises," I said, "in some such way as this. He is the son of a good father, who, as sometimes happens, lives in an ill-governed city, and avoids political hon-ours and office and litigation and all those things in which the active politician delights, and who is content to be got the better of if only he is not bothered."

"Then how does the son become what he is?" he said.

"Firstly," I said, "he hears his mother complaining that her husband is not one of the rulers, and that in consequence other women are set above her. Then she sees that her husband does not trouble himself much about money, and does not fight and wrangle in law-suits or in the assembly but takes all these matters very calmly, and she perceives that he is always attending to himself, treating her neither with marked reverence nor marked disrespect. All these things make her angry, and she tells her son that his father is unmanly and utterly casual, and treats him to all the many varied complaints which women love to make on such mat-ters."

"Yes," said Adeimantus, "they are numerous enough and characteristic of women."

"Then you know," I said, "that even the servants of such men, who are supposed to be friends of the family, sometimes say the same sort of things to the children if they see the father refusing to proceed against a man who owes him money or has done him an injustice; they exhort the son to take vengeance on them all when he 550 is grown up, and to be more of a man than his father. And outside of his family he sees and hears the same sort of thing: those who mind their own business in the city are called simpletons and held of no account, while those who do not are praised and honoured. The young man sees these things and hears this talk, and yet also hears his father's words, and from an intimate position sees his father's ways of life, and contrasts them with the ways of other men, and so is pulled by the two forces this way and that. His father waters and makes grow the reasoning element in his soul, while the others nourish the desiring and the spirited elements. In the end, inasmuch as he is not naturally a bad man, but has known bad company, he arrives under the impulsion of these two forces at a middle position, and gives over the rule within him to the middle element, the contentious and spirited, and becomes a loftyminded and ambitious man.

"An excellent description of his origin," he said.

"There, then," I said, "we have the second city and the second man."

"We have," he said.

"Then shall we now talk like Aeschylus, of 'another man against another city set,' though perhaps in accordance with our plan we should take the city first?"

"Yes," he said.

"Then oligarchy, I suppose, will be the next constitution?"

"What kind of government do you mean by oligarchy?" he asked.

"The constitution," I said, "which rests on property valuation, where the rich rule, and a poor man is debarred from office."

"I understand," he said.

"Then must we first declare how the change from timocracy to oligarchy comes about?"

"Yes."

"Well, surely that is clear even to a blind man," I said.

"How?"

"That treasure house," I said, "where each man stores his gold is the ruin of timocracy. For they begin by discovering ways of spending their money, and stretch the laws till they and their wives flout them."

"That is probable," he said.

"Then I fancy they watch and try to outrival one 551 another till they make the whole population like themselves?"

"Probably."

"From that point," I said, "they make steady progress in money-making, and the more they honour money the less they honour virtue. Is there not this strife between wealth and virtue; they always incline in opposite ways in the scales of the balance?"

"Most certainly," he said.

"Then when in a city wealth and the wealthy are honoured, virtue and the good are slighted?"

"Obviously."

"But men devote themselves to anything that is honoured, and neglect anything that is slighted?"

"Yes."

"Then in process of time, from men who love victory and honour they become lovers of money-getting and of money; they give their praise and admiration to the rich man, and elect him to rule over them, but the poor man they slight?"

"Certainly."

"Then they lay down a law which is the distinguishing feature of an oligarchic constitution. They prescribe a sum of money varying in amount as the oligarchy is more or less extreme, and proclaim all disqualified for office whose means do not amount to the prescribed sum. Either the proposal is put through by force of arms, or by threats and terrorism they manage to get an oligarchic constitution established without actual conflict. Is not that so?"

"Yes."

"Then this is more or less the way in which it is established?"

"Yes," he said. "But what is the character of the constitution? and what are the defects which we declared it to have?"

"Well, the first is this," I said; "its distinguishing feature is bad. For, consider, if any one appointed captains of ships on the principle of property qualifications and refused a ship to a poor man were he ever so skilful a navigator—"

"They would make a poor kind of cruise," he said. "That's plain."

"And does not the same apply to the government of anything else?"

"I fancy so."

"Is a city an exception?" I asked, "or does it hold of a city as well?"

"Anything but an exception," he said, "inasmuch as, of all things, a city's government is the most difficult and most important."

"Then oligarchy will have this one great defect?"

"Apparently."

"But is this any less a defect?"

"Which?"

"Such a city must of necessity be not one but two— the city of the rich and the city of the poor—rich and poor dwelling within the same walls, and always conspiring against one another."

"No, by heavens, that is not less," he said.

"And this again is not very pleasing: in all probability they will be unable to carry on a war because they are forced either to arm the common people and use them—and then they will stand more in fear of them than of the enemy—or if they don't do this, to prove themselves even in their fighting to be truly a government of few. And to add to their difficulties their love of money will make them unwilling to pay war taxes."

"No, that is not pleasing."

"Further, do you think it right (we attacked the practice before) that in this constitution the same men will play many parts, be farmers and money-makers and warriors?"

"No, certainly not."

"But now consider whether of all those evils this is not the greatest—and it is an evil which becomes possible for the first time in this city."

"What is that?"

"It is possible for a man to part with all that he has and for another to get possession of his goods; and then when his property is gone for him to live in the city, playing no part therein, being neither money-maker, craftsman, knight, nor hoplite, but dubbed pauper and penniless."

"Yes, this is the first city where that is possible," he said.

"In oligarchic states such things are not forbidden. If they were, there would not be plutocrats or paupers."

"That is true."

"Then consider this. All the time that this man was rich and was spending his money, did the city benefit thereby in any of those departments we have mentioned? Or while he had the appearance of a ruler, was he in reality neither ruler nor servant of the city—only a spender of what he had?"

"Yes," he said. "He seemed to be a ruler, but was nothing but a spender."

"May we say this of him—that as a drone is produced in a cell to plague the hive, so is he produced in a household, a drone to plague the city?"

"Certainly, Socrates," he said.

"Further, Adeimantus, has not God created the

drones that fly without stings, but the drones that walk he has created, some stingless, but some with terrible stings; to the stingless drones belong those who die paupers in their old age, to those with stings all who are called criminals?"

"Very true," he said.

"Then it is obvious that in a city where you see paupers there are also concealed somewhere about thieves and cut-purses, and temple-robbers, and contrivers of all such evils."

"It is obvious," he said.

"Then do you not see paupers in oligarchic cities?"

"Except for the rulers you see almost no one else," he said.

"Then we do not imagine, do we," I said, "that there are also many criminals in these cities, armed with stings, whom the government deliberately keeps in check by force?"

"Yes, but we do," he said.

"Then shall we say that such men are produced in that city through want of education, and bad nurture, and bad government?"

"We shall."

"Then this will be the character of the oligarchic city, and these, and possibly more than these, the evils it possesses?"

"Yes, more or less," he said.

553    "Then let that," I said, "complete for us this constitution which we call an oligarchy which elects its rulers on a property qualification. Next, let us examine the man that resembles it, how he is produced, and what, when produced, he is like."

"Certainly," he said.

"Then does this truly describe the change from that timocratic to an oligarchical man?"

"What?"

"He has a son who at first is zealous for his father and follows in his footsteps, but then he sees him suddenly broken upon the city as a ship is broken on a reef, so that he and all his possessions go to the bottom— he as been a general or held some other high office, sycophants get up a prosecution against him, and he is put to death or banished or disgraced, and all his fortune confiscated."

"That is likely enough," he said.

"Then seeing and suffering such things, my friend, and having lost his possessions, he suddenly, I fancy, becomes afraid; he drives ambition and the spirited element headlong from its throne in his soul; poverty makes him humble, and he turns greedily to money-making, and by hard work and careful saving he accumulates a fortune. Do you not conceive that such a man then seats the desiring and money-making element upon that throne, and makes it a mighty king within him, setting crowns upon its head and adorning it with chains of office and swords of state?"

"I do," he said.

"But the reasoning and the spirited elements, I imagine, he makes squat upon the ground beneath it, one here and the other there, and enslaves them. So that the first is allowed to reason of or consider nothing but how money may breed more money, while the second may admire or honour nothing but wealth and the wealthy, and be zealous for nothing but the acquisition of money and anything that may lead thereto."

"There is no other way," he said, "in which a young man who loves honour can become so swiftly and thoroughly a lover of money."

"Then is this man," I asked, "oligarchic?"

"In any case the man who preceded him was like the constitution which preceded oligarchy."

"Well, let us consider if he would be like oligarchy."

"Yes, let us."

"In the first place, then, will he not be so in the very high place he gives to money?"

"Certainly."

"And, further, surely in that he is niggardly and a hard worker, satisfying only his necessary desires, and refraining from any other expenditure. His other desires he regards as frivolous, and keeps in subjection."

"Yes."

"He is somewhat squalid in appearance," I said, "and there is nothing which he does not turn to his profit; he is a man to make a fortune and get the praise of the multitude for it. Would not he be like the constitution we have described?"

"I certainly think so," he said. "In any case, both he and the city give high honour to money."

"Yes," I said, "for I fancy that he has not spent much thought on education?"

"I think not," he answered, "for if he had, he would not have made a blind god the ruler of his chorus, and given him highest honour."

"Good," I answered. "Now consider this point. Shall we not say that owing to his lack of culture drone-like desires grow up within him, some pauper and some criminal, and only his care for other things holds them forcibly in check?"

"Certainly," he said.

"Then," I said, "do you know where to look if you want to see these men's evil deeds?"

"Where?" he said.

"Look to their guardianship of orphans, or any occasion that may come to them of securing a large impunity for injustice."

"That is true."

"And does not this show that in his other transactions, where his reputation depends on his preserving an appearance of justice, he controls other evil desires within him by a self-constraint that is virtuous after a fashion? He does not persuade them that this is the better course, nor does he assuage them by reason but by necessity and fear, because he is afraid to lose what he has already."

"Certainly," he said.

"Then, in good truth, my friend," I said, "in most of these men, when they have to spend other people's money, you will discover desires which are of kin to the drone."

"That you certainly will," he answered.

"Then such a man would not be without discord in himself; he would not be one man but two. Yet on the whole his better desires would control the worse."

"That is so."

"And for this reason, I fancy, he would be more respectable than many men, but the true virtue of a simple and harmonious soul would be far beyond him."

"I think so."

"And surely when matched with his fellow-citizens in any contest for victory or other honourable rivalry the niggardly man is a poor antagonist. He won't spend 555 money to win glory in such contests, because he is afraid of arousing his spendthrift desires and summoning them to fight and strive for victory along with him. So like a true oligarch he makes war with a small part of his forces, and is usually beaten and keeps his money."

"Certainly," he said.

"Then can we any longer disbelieve," I said, "that the niggardly and money-making man is set over against the oligarchic city, being like to it?"

"Certainly not," he said.

"We have next to consider, apparently, how democracy arises, and what is its nature when it has arisen, in order that we may then come to know the character of the democratic man, and set him up for judgment."

"That is our most consistent course," he said.

"Then does not the change from oligarchy to democracy," I asked, "come about in some such way as this, as the result of the uncontrolled pursuit of that which oligarchy has made its good, namely, the necessity of becoming as rich as possible?"

"How?"

"I imagine that since the position of the rulers in that city depends upon their great wealth, they will not be prepared to pass laws forbidding their dissolute young men to spend and waste their substance; for they hope by buying up their possessions and by lending them money on them to become richer and more esteemed than ever."

"That is certainly the case."

"Then is it not now obvious that it is impossible in this city to honour wealth, and at the same time to preserve proper discipline among the citizens? One or the other must be neglected."

"Yes," he said, "that is fairly obvious."

"In oligarchies, therefore, by their negligence and tolerance of evil living the citizens have sometimes driven men of no common stamp to poverty?"

"Certainly."

"And then, I imagine, these men settle in the city with their stings and their weapons, some of them debtors, some disenfranchised, some both, and hate and plot against the men who have got possession of their goods, and long for revolution?"

"That is so."

"Meanwhile the money-makers fix their eyes on the ground and pretend not to see them, and go on stabbing with their money any one of the other citizens who fails in the struggle, levying their interest till it exceeds by many times the parent sum, and so make the drone ⁵⁵⁶ and the beggar common in the city?"

"Yes, they certainly will be common," he said.

"And when this evil in the city is beginning to break into a flame," I said, "they are not prepared to extinguish it either in the way we mentioned, by laying down restrictions as to how a man may dispose of his money, or in this way, by using another law which will solve such difficulties."

"What is that?"

"It follows the one we have described, and compels the citizens to give heed to virtue. For if any one would ordain that the greater number of voluntary contracts should not be enforceable, the money-making in the city would be less shameless, and there would be a scantier crop of those evils we have just described."

"Yes, much scantier," he said.

"These, then," I said, "are the reasons which inspire this treatment of the ruled by the rulers in this city; while as for themselves and their families, are not their young men luxurious and idle in body and in mind, lazy, and able to offer but weak resistance to pleasures and pains?"

"What else?"

"And they themselves, with no thought but for the making of money, and as little concerned about virtue as are the poor?"

"Yes."

"Then these things being so, when rulers and ruled meet one another—it may be in the public highways or other places of meeting, at festivals or on a campaign; they may be fellow-sailors or fellow-soldiers, and see one another in the face of danger—in these circumstances will the poor be despised by the rich? Will it not rather often happen that the poor man, sturdy and bronzed with the sun, will be set in battle next a rich man who has lived an indoor life, and has more fat about him than ought to be; he will see him puffing and despairing, and come to the conclusion, will he not, that these men are rich, because they, the poor, are cowards, and so when they meet together by themselves one man will say to another, 'The men are in our hands, for they are good for nothing'?"

"I am quite sure," he said, "that they will do so."

"Then just as a sickly body needs to receive only a small shock from without to make it actually ill, and sometimes is at strife with itself even without external impulse, even so does the city, which is like it in condition, fall ill and make war on itself on the slightest excuse, when assistance is called in from without by one or the other party from an oligarchical or a democratic city: or does it not sometimes break into civil strife even without external assistance?"

557 "That is certainly the case."

"Then a democracy, I fancy, comes into being when the poor have gained the day; some of the opposite party they kill, some they banish, with the rest they share citizenship and office on equal terms; and, as a general rule, office in the city is given by lot."

"Yes," he said, "that is the establishment of the democracy, whether it is effected by actual force of arms, or by the other party yielding from fear."

"Then in what fashion will they live?" I asked; "and what will be the nature of such a constitution? For, obviously, a man of similar character will turn out to be democratic."

"Obviously," he said.

"Then, first and foremost, they are free, the city is crammed with liberty and freedom of speech, and there is permission to do there whatever any one desires?"

"So they say," he said.

"Then clearly where the permissive principle rules, each man will arrange his own life to suit himself?"

"Clearly."

"Then this constitution, I fancy, will be distinguished by the wonderful variety of men in it?"

"Surely."

"It will turn out to be the fairest of constitutions," I said. "Like a garment of many colours of every shade and variety, this constitution will be variegated with every character, and be most fair to look upon; and possibly, just as children and women admire many-coloured things, so many people will judge this city to be fairest of all."

"Most certainly they will," he said.

"And," I said, "it certainly is, my wonderful friend, a handy place to look for a constitution."

"What do you mean?"

"The permissive principle allows it all kinds of constitutions, and it seems as if the man who wanted to found a city, as we have just been doing, ought to step into the democratic city and choose the style that suited him. You may go to this universal provider of constitutions, make your choice, and found your city."

"Well, he will certainly find no lack of patterns," he said.

"In this city," I said, "there is no necessity to rule even if you are capable of ruling, or to be ruled if you don't want, or to be at war because the rest of the city is, or where the rest of the city is at peace, to observe peace if you don't wish to; if there is a law forbidding you to be a magistrate or a judge, that is no reason why you should not be both magistrate and judge if you have a 558 mind to. Is that not a life of heavenly pleasure for the time?"

"Perhaps," he said, "for the time."

"And is not the placid good temper of some of their

condemned criminals beautiful? Under this constitution, when they have been sentenced to death or exile, they let it make no difference, but stay on and stroll about the streets; and have you never noticed how the culprit saunters round, and no one pays any attention or sees him, just as though he were a spirit from the departed?"

"Yes, and such a number of them too," he said.

"Then think of the considerateness of the city, its entire superiority to trifles, its disregard of all those things we spoke of so proudly when we were founding our city: we said that, except from altogether extraordinary natures, no one could turn out a good man unless his earliest years were given to noble games, and he gave himself wholly to noble pursuits. Is it not sublime how this city tramples all such things under foot, and is supremely indifferent as to what life a man has led before he enters politics? If only he asserts his zeal for the multitude, it is ready to honour him."

"Yes," he said, "it is perfectly splendid."

"Then these and others of a like kind will be the marks of a democracy," I said. "It will be, apparently, a pleasant constitution, with no rulers and plenty of variety, distributing its peculiar kind of equality to equals and unequals impartially."

"Yes," he said, "what you say is notorious."

"Consider now," I said, "who is the individual resembling it; or, as in the case of the constitution, shall we first consider how he originates?"

"Yes," he said.

"Is it not in this manner? I fancy he would be the son of that thrifty and oligarchic man, and be brought up under his father's eye and in his father's way of life, would he not?"

"Surely."

"Like his father, holding down by force those desires

within him which are prodigal and not money-making? They are called the unnecessary desires?"

"Obviously," he said.

"Then," I said, "in order to avoid any obscurity in our argument, shall we first distinguish the necessary and the unnecessary desires?"

"Please," he answered.

"Then should we not rightly call necessary those which cannot be denied and those whose gratification does us good? Our nature must seek after both those kinds. Is not that so?"

"Yes, certainly."

"Then we may justly give these the title of necessary?" 559

"We may."

"Further, those of which we may get rid by dint of youthful training, and whose presence, moreover, does no good, and those which actually do harm, should we do well to call unnecessary?"

"We should."

"Shall we select an example of each class as they exist, in order that we may have a general idea of them?"

"Yes, we had better."

"Then would not the desire for eating within the limits of health and good condition, that is, the desire merely of bread and meat, be necessary?"

"I think so."

"The desire for bread, I fancy, is necessary for both reasons it does good, and it can't be done without while life lasts?"

"Yes."

"And the desire for meat is necessary in so far as it contributes to a good condition of body?"

"Certainly."

"What of desire that goes beyond those limits, desire for other foods than those we have mentioned? Most men, by dint of early discipline and training, can get rid of it. It is bad for the body, and bad for the insight and temperance of the soul. Would it not rightly be called unnecessary?"

"Yes, most rightly."

"Then may we not say that such desires are spendthrift, while those we mentioned before are profit- making, inasmuch as they are profitable for work?"

"Yes."

"And shall we say the same of sexual and other desires?"

"Yes."

"And by that epithet of 'drone' we used a moment ago, did we not mean the man who is full of such pleasures and desires, and who is ruled by the unnecessary desires, while he who is ruled by the necessary is the niggardly and oligarchic man?"

"Surely."

"Let us now return," I said, "to the change from the oligarchic to the democratic man. This seems to me its usual course."

"What?"

"When a young man who has been brought up as we described a moment ago, in an uncultured and niggardly atmosphere, has once tasted the drones' honey, and keeps company with fierce and terrible beasts of prey, men who can fashion pleasures of all kinds and tones and varieties, then you may picture the beginning of the revolution within him, the oligarchy in his soul turning into a democracy."

"That must be so," he said.

"As revolution broke out in the city when one of its factions was helped by an alliance of kindred spirits from without, does not the revolution begin similarly in the young man when one faction of the desires with-

in him gets help from a kindred and similar class of
desires without?"

"Most assuredly."

"And I fancy there will be a counter alliance to support the oligarchic element within him; possibly it may
come from his father, possibly from the advice and scold- 560
ings of the rest of his family; and then arise sedition
and counter sedition, and strife within and against himself?"

"Surely."

"It has sometimes happened, I fancy, that the democratic element yields to the oligarchic; some of the desires
are either destroyed or banished, a semblance of reverence is established in the young man's soul, and order is
restored?"

"Yes, that sometimes happens," he said.

"But in time other desires kindred to those that had
been banished were nourished in secret, because his
father did not know how to bring him up, and they
became many and strong?"

"Yes," he said, "it often happens so."

"These turned to the same bad company as before,
and their secret intercourse bred a swarm of children?"

"Certainly."

"Then in the end, I imagine, they seized the acropolis
of the young man's soul, finding it empty of learning or
fair practices or true thoughts, the best guardians and
protectors in the hearts of men whom the gods love?"

"Yes, that they are," he said.

"Since these were wanting, false and braggart thoughts
and beliefs, I fancy, ran up and seized upon that place
within him?"

"Most certainly," he said.

"Then does he not turn again to the land of those
Lotus-eaters and openly take up his abode there? And if

his relations offer any help to the niggardly principle in his soul, these braggart thoughts shut the gates of the palace wall within him, and will not allow the allies entry, nor admit in embassy wise words of wise seniors. They fight that principle and master it; reverence they name simple folly, and drive it out, a dishonoured fugitive; temperance they call cowardice, and expel with insult and contempt; moderation and an orderly expenditure they pretend to be boorishness and meanness, and calling a crowd of useless desires to help them, drive them over the frontier?"

"That is very true."

"Having made this clearance they purify the soul of which they are in possession with solemn rites of initiation, and when that is done they bring back insolence and lawlessness and profligacy and shamelessness, crowned with garlands and in bright array, accompanied by a thronging chorus singing their praises and heaping flatteries upon them; calling insolence good 561 breeding, lawlessness liberty, profligacy magnificence, and shamelessness bravery. Is it not in some such way as this," I asked, "that the young man deserts an upbringing in necessary desires for the freedom and licence of those that are unnecessary and useless?"

"That is very clearly the case," he answered.

"Then in his life henceforth I fancy he divides his expenditure of money, trouble, and time equally between necessary and unnecessary pleasures. He may be fortunate, and not have been driven past all bounds in that divine rage; perhaps, also, when he is older, and the worst of the tumult is over, he may receive back again some of the exiles, and not give himself over wholly to the invaders. Then he will establish a fashion of equality between pleasure and pleasure in this life. Each as it comes has the authority of the lot behind it, and, until he is satisfied, he surrenders to it the rule over himself and then passes it on to another. He dishonours none, and encourages all alike."

"Certainly."

"But," I said, "he will not receive nor suffer within the ramparts the true reasoning of any one who asserts that some pleasures spring from the desires that are good and noble, but others from those that are evil, and that the former should be fostered and honoured, and the latter disciplined and enslaved. To all such remarks he shakes his head, and says that all are alike and deserving of equal honour."

"Yes," he said, "that is exactly how that sort of man behaves."

"And this is his life," I said. "Day after day he gratifies the pleasures as they come—now fluting down the primrose path of wine, now given over to teetotalism and banting; one day in hard training, the next slacking and idling, and the third playing the philosopher. Often he will take to politics, leap to his feet and do or say whatever comes into his head; or he conceives an admiration for a general, and his interests are in war; or for a man of business, and straightway that is his line. He knows no order or necessity in life; but he calls life as he conceives it pleasant and free and divinely blessed, and is ever faithful to it."

"That is a perfect description," he said, "of the life of a man to whom all laws are equal."

"Yes," I said, "I fancy that this man has within him all sorts and conditions of men; he is the fair man of many colours, like the democratic city. His is the life that many men and many women envy; almost all constitutions and ways of behaviour are contained within it."

"Yes," he said, "that is he."

"Then may we put this man over against the demo- 562 cratic city and justly call him democratic?"

"We may."

"Then there still remain to us," I said, "the fairest constitution and the fairest man—tyranny and the tyrant?"

"Just so," he said.

"Come now, dear friend, what is the nature of tyranny? As to its origin, it is fairly obvious that it is a transformation of democracy."

"That is obvious."

"Does not democracy become tyranny in the same sort of way as oligarchy becomes democracy?"

"How?"

"The oligarchies set a good before themselves and made it the principle of oligarchy, that good being wealth. Is not that so?"

"Yes."

"But the excess of wealth, and the neglect of all else but money-making, destroyed oligarchy?"

"True," he said.

"And does not the excess of the good as conceived by democracy dissolve it in its turn?"

"What good is that?"

"Liberty," I said. "In a democratic city men will tell you that liberty is their fairest possession, and that therefore theirs is the only city where a man who has a free nature can rightly dwell."

"Yes," he said, "that is a sentiment you hear very often."

"Now," I asked, "does not the excess of this quality, as I was saying a moment ago, and the neglect of everything else for it, subvert this constitution, and make men ready to want a tyranny?"

"In what way?" he said.

"The democratic city is athirst for the wine of liberty, and they that are set over it to fill its cup with that wine may be evil; and so I fancy it takes more of unmixed liberty than is proper and gets drunk, and then if its rulers are not absolutely obliging in giving it liberty in plenty, it chastises them and accuses them of being wicked oligarchs."

"Yes, that it does," he said.

"Those that are obedient to the rulers," I said, "it reviles as willing slaves and nobodies, but bestows honour and praise in public and in private on rulers who are like their subjects, and subjects who are like their rulers. In such a state will not liberty inevitably go beyond all bounds?"

"Surely."

"And lawlessness, my friend," I said, "will make its way down into private homes, and end by implanting itself in the very animals."

"How does that show itself?" he asked.

"Well, the father, for example," I said, "accustoms himself to become like his child and to fear his sons, and the son in his desire for freedom becomes like his father 563 and has no fear or reverence for his parent. Metic[1] is like citizen, and citizen like metic, and stranger like both."

"Yes, that happens," he said.

"And there are other trifles of this kind," I said. "The schoolmaster fears and flatters his pupils, and the pupils despise both their schoolmasters and their tutors. And altogether, the young act like their seniors, and compete with them in speech and in action; while the old men condescend to the young and become triumphs of versatility and wit, imitating their juniors in order to avoid the appearance of being sour or despotic."

"Very true," he said.

"But my friend," I said, "the last stage of this wealth of liberty exhibited by such a city is reached when men and women, who have been sold as slaves, are every whit as free as those who bought them. And we almost forgot to mention the wonderful equality of law and the liberty

[1] Resident alien.

that prevails in the mutual relations of men and women."

"Well, in the words of Aeschylus," he said, " 'shall we utter what is on our lips?' "

"Certainly," I said, "and that is what I am doing. No one who has not seen it would believe how much freer is the life of the domestic animals in this state than elsewhere. Why, the very dogs take the proverb literally, and are like their mistresses; and there arise also horses and asses who have learnt a wonderfully free and glorious way of walking, and run into every one they meet in the streets unless he gets out of their way; and everything else in the state is equally full of liberty."

"No need to tell me that," he said. "I often suffer from such animals when I am going into the country."

"But do you observe," I said, "that the main result of all these things, taken together, is that it makes the souls of the citizens so sensitive that they take offence, and will not put up with the faintest suspicion of slavery that any one may introduce? For, finally, you know they set entirely at naught both unwritten and written laws, so afraid are they of any kind of master?"

"Yes, I know that," he said.

"Then this, my friend," I said, "with all its beauty and youthful insolence, is the government from which, in my opinion, springs tyranny."

"It is insolent enough," he said. "But what is the next stage in the process?"

"That disease that appeared in oligarchy and destroyed it," I said, "appears in this city likewise, gains in size and strength, profiting by the permission accorded to it, and enslaves democracy. In truth, any kind of excessive action is wont to lead to excessive reaction. This is true of the weather, of plants and of bodies, and not least of constitutions."

"That is likely enough," he said.

"Excessive liberty, then, is likely to give place to nothing else than excessive slavery, both in individual and state?"

'Probably."

"Then probably," I said, "tyranny arises from no other constitution than democracy, severest and most cruel slavery following, I fancy, the extreme of liberty."

"Yes, that is reasonable," he said.

"But I imagine," I said, "that was not what you wanted to know; you were asking, rather, what is the disease which is found both in oligarchy and democracy, and which enslaves the latter?"

"You are right," he said.

"I was referring," I said, "to that class of idle and dissolute men; some of them are desperately brave and leaders of the whole, the rest are more cowardly and follow. We compared them to drones, the first to stinged, the second to stingless?"

"Yes, and we were right," he said.

"Now those two classes," I said, "when they arise make a disturbance in the whole constitution, just as phlegm and bile disturb the body; and he who is a good doctor and lawgiver of a city must take as careful precautions against them as the wise bee-keeper does against drones. His first care must be not to let them get into the city; and his second, if he is frustrated in the first, to cut them out as quickly as possible, combs and all."

"Yes, by heaven," he said, "that he must assuredly do."

"Now shall we proceed in this way?" I asked. "It will give us a more discerning view of our problem."

"In what way?"

"Let us divide the democratic city in our argument into three parts, as it is divided in fact. The class we have described makes one, and that, you know, by reason of the permissive principle, flourishes as much here as in the oligarchic city."

"That is so."

"But it is much fiercer in the democracy."

"How?"

"In the oligarchy it is not held in honour, but is excluded from office; it has therefore nothing to exercise itself upon, and no opportunity of becoming strong. But in a democracy, you know, this class practically rules the state. The fiercest of them speak and act, and the rest crowd buzzing round the platform and won't hear of any opposition, so that almost everything in this constitution is managed by the drones."

"It is indeed," he answered.

"Another class of this nature may always be distinguished in the crowd."

"What is that?"

"Of all the men engaged in making money, those that are of a most orderly nature usually become the richest, do they not?"

"Probably."

"Then from them, I imagine, honey oozes for the drones in greatest profusion and readiness?"

"Well, no one could squeeze honey from the poor," he said.

"Then these rich men, I fancy, are called the drones' garden?"

"Something like that," he said.

565 "The people would form a third class including all who work with their hands and take no part in affairs, who have got but few possessions. And in a democracy this class, when it is assembled, is the most numerous and most powerful."

"It is," he said. "But it won't come to the assembly often unless it gets a share of the honey."

"And therefore it always gets a share," I answered, "so long as the leaders can manage to plunder the propertied classes, divide the spoil among the people, and yet keep the biggest share for themselves."

"Yes, those are the terms on which it shares," he answered.

"Those who are plundered, I fancy, are forced to defend themselves, in speeches before the people and in any other way they can contrive?"

"Surely."

"And then even if they have no thought of revolution, they are accused by their opponents of plotting against the public and of being oligarchs."

"Surely."

"And in the end, when they see the public doing their best to injure them, not from wanton malice but because it is ignorant and is led away by their detractors, then indeed, whether they like it or not, they become oligarchs in good earnest. Not that they do this deliberately. This evil also is engendered by the drone's sting."

"That it certainly is."

"Thereupon follow impeachments, and judgments, and contests between man and man?"

"Certainly."

"And is it not the invariable custom of the public to put one man in high presidency over them, and to foster and strengthen him till he becomes great?"

"It is."

"This then is clear," I said, "that when a tyrant is begotten he springs from this root of presidency, and from nowhere else."

"Yes, that is clear."

"Then what is the beginning of the change from president to tyrant? Is it not obviously when the president begins to follow the story which is told concerning the temples of Zeus Lycaeus in Arcadia?"

"What is that?" he asked.

"That he who tasted the human flesh which had been cut up with the other sacrifices must of necessity become a wolf. Have you heard the legend?"

"I have."

"And he who is president of the people finds a mob more than ready to obey him, and does not keep his hands from the blood of his kindred. He heaps unjust accusations on them—a favourite device—hales them before the courts, and murders them, with unholy tongue and mouth tasting his brothers' blood. He exiles and kills and throws out hints of cancelled debts and divided land. After this, is there not a fearful necessity upon him either to be slain by his enemies or to be a tyrant, and become a wolf instead of a man?"

"Yes, a powerful necessity," he said.

"This, then," I said, "is the man who makes war upon the propertied classes?"

"It is."

"Does he become a full-blown tyrant when he has been banished and has forced his return in the face of his enemies' opposition?"

"Clearly."

"But if these are unable to procure his banishment or death by accusing him to the city, they then conspire to murder him in secret?"

"That happens often enough," he answered.

"Thereupon all who have gone thus far hit upon the tyrant's special request of which we have heard so much—they ask the public for a guard for their person, that the people's champion may be preserved to them."

"That they do," he said.

"And the people, I fancy, give it; they fear for him, and are confident for themselves?"

"Yes, indeed."

"And when this comes to the notice of a man who

has money, and along with his money a name for being a hater of the people, then, my friend, to quote the words of the oracle given to Croesus:

> By Hermus' pebbled shore he flees,
> Stays not, and feels no shame to run in fear.

"If he did," he said, "he would not get another chance of feeling shame."

"No," I said, "I fancy that if he is caught, he is killed?"

"Inevitably."

"But as for our president himself he obviously does not fall 'a glorious victim,' but after casting down many rivals takes his stand upon the chariot of the state; he is no longer a president, but a finished and perfect tyrant."

"What else?" he said.

"Shall we now," I asked, "describe the happiness of this man and of the city in which such a mortal finds himself?"

"Certainly," he said; "let us do so."

"In the early days," I said, "has he not a smile and a welcome for every man he meets; he denies that he is a tyrant, and is full of promises to the individual and to the public; he grants release from debts, distributes lands to the public and to his party, and pretends to be gracious and good-natured to all?"

"That he must do," he said.

"But soon he disposes of his enemies without the city, coming to a compromise with some and killing others, and when he is no longer troubled by them, then, I fancy, he begins to stir up one war after another in order to keep the public in need of a general?"

"That is likely enough."

"He also hopes, does he not, that the taxes they have 567 to pay will impoverish them, so that they will be compelled to give their minds to getting their daily bread, and not to conspiring against him?"

"Obviously."

"And if there are, as I fancy there may be, some whom he suspects of harbouring free thoughts and of being prepared not to submit to his rule, does he not hope to find an excuse for surrendering them to the enemy, and so destroying them? Do not all these reasons compel the tyrant to be always stirring up war?"

"Inevitably."

"And compel him also, because of his actions, to be prepared to be more and more disliked by the citizens?"

"Surely."

"And is it not inevitable that of those who have helped to establish him in power, and who are in positions of influence, some, that is to say, the bravest of them, will speak freely both against him and against each other, and express their dissatisfaction with the course of events?"

"Probably."

"And the tyrant, if he hopes to rule, must weed out all such persons, until he has left no one of any account, whether friend or foe?"

"Clearly."

"He must have a sharp eye also for the man who is courageous or high-minded or wise or wealthy; and it is his great happiness to have to be the enemy of all such whether he likes it or not, and plot against them until he purges the city of their presence."

"Surely a noble purification," he said.

"Yes," I answered, "just the reverse of medical purgation. For doctors remove the worst and leave the best; he does the opposite."

"Apparently he must do it," he said, "if he is to rule."

"Yes," I said, "he is bound by a most blessed necessity, which ordains that he shall live with a crowd of worthless creatures, and be hated by them, or not live at all."

"That it does," he said.

"And as by these actions he becomes more and more unpopular with the citizens, will he not need a more numerous and loyal bodyguard?"

"Surely."

"But who will these loyal persons be? and where will he get them?"

"They will come flying in numbers without the asking," he said, "if he pays them."

"By the dog," I said, "you seem to be talking of a kind of drone imported from abroad, and most miscellaneous in character."

"You are right," he said.

"And whom will he get from the city itself? Or will he not go so far as that?"

"So far as what?"

"As to rob the citizens of their slaves, set them free, and enrol them in his bodyguard."

"Certainly he will," he said, "for they will be his most loyal adherents."

"What a glorious and blessed thing," I said, "is a tyrant as you describe him, if these are his friends and faithful followers when he has got his former associates out of the way." 568

"Yes," he said, "these are his friends."

"Then," I said, "he enjoys the admiration of those followers and the company of the new-made citizens, but decent men hate and avoid him."

"What else could they do?"

"It is not without reason," I said, "that tragedy in general is thought wise, and Euripides a master of tragedy."

"Why?"

"Because he made that remark which betrays a deep

understanding, that tyrants are wise by reason of the companionship of the wise, and by 'the wise' he obviously meant the tyrant's associates."

"He also praises tyranny as equal to godhead," he said, "and there are many other similar statements made by Euripides and other poets."

"And yet," I said, "those tragic poets, since they are wise, will excuse us and those who follow our constitution, though we intend to refuse them entrance into our city because they are praisers of tyrants."

"Yes, I think the best of them will excuse us," he said.

"They go round all the other cities, I fancy, get together great crowds, and hire men with beautiful, sonorous, and persuasive voices, and all that they may draw the constitutions to tyranny and democracy."

"That is very true."

"In return for these services, moreover, they get reward and honour, mostly, of course, from tyrants, but also from democracies. But as they climb higher up the hill of constitutions, their honour becomes less and less, until they have to stop for want of breath."

"Certainly."

"But we have digressed from our subject," I said. "Let us turn again to the tyrant's army, that beautiful, numerous, many-coloured, and ever-changing body, and consider how it will be supported."

"It is clear," he said, "that he will sell all the sacred property in the city's temples, and spend the whole of the money, and so be able to demand lighter taxes from the public."

"What will he do when this source of revenue is exhausted?"

"Clearly," he said, "he and his drink-mates, his comrades and his mistresses, will live on the paternal inheritance."

"I understand," I replied. "The public that begat the tyrant will support him and his companions?"

"It will be sternly compelled to do so," he said.

"But what do you say to this?" I said. "Suppose the public begin to grumble, and say that it is not just that a grown-up son should be supported by his father—the other way about is the right way—and that they did not give him birth and set him where he is in order that 569 when he grew to greatness they should become slaves of their own slaves and support him and their slaves and other rabble; they hoped under his presidency to be freed from the rich and the so-called gentlemanly party in the city; and they now therefore order him and his companions to leave the city, as a father might drive his son and his rabble of boon companions from the house."

"Then, by Zeus," he said, "the public will learn what a monster they have begotten, and welcomed, and made to grow, and what kind of match it is for them. They will find that they are weak, and those they are trying to drive out are strong."

"What do you mean?" I asked. "Will the tyrant dare to put compulsion on his parent, and to beat him if he resists?"

"Yes," he said, "after he has managed to disarm him."

"The tyrant as you describe him," I said, "is a parricide and a cruel guardian of the aged, and now at last, apparently, we have come to acknowledged tyranny; the public, as they say in the proverb, in trying to escape from the smoke of servitude to free men has fallen into the fire of the dominion of slaves: instead of the plentiful and unseasonable liberty which it once enjoyed, it has clothed itself with the hardest and bitterest servitude to slaves?"

"Yes," he said, "that is exactly the course of events."

"Well, then," I said, "shall we not be right in saying that we have given an adequate description of the change from democracy to tyranny, and of the nature of tyranny when that change is accomplished?"

"Yes, a perfectly adequate one," he said.

# BOOK IX

"Then now at last," I said, "the tyrannical man is left for us to consider, his change from the democratic man, his character after the change is accomplished, and his mode of life, whether miserable or blessed?"

"Yes," he said, "he is left."

"Do you know," I asked, "what I still feel to be missing?"

"What?"

"I don't think that we have adequately specified the number and nature of the desires. And till this defect is remedied, there will be more obscurity than there ought to be in our investigation."

"Well, it is not too late," he said.

"No certainly not. Will you consider what it is that I want to understand about the desires? It is this. Of the unnecessary pleasures and desires, some seem to me to be unlawful. They are probably innate in every one, but if disciplined by law and by the better desires, with the assistance of reason, they may in some men be entirely eradicated, or at least left few and weak, while in other men they are stronger and more numerous."

"And what are those desires?" he asked.

"Those that are active during sleep," I answered. "When the rest of the soul, the reasoning, gentle, and ruling part of it, is asleep, then the bestial and savage part, when it has had its fill of food or wine, begins to leap about, pushes sleep aside, and tries to go and gratify its instincts. You know how in such a state it will dare everything, as though it were freed and released from all shame or discernment. It does not shrink from attempting incestual intercourse, in its dream, with a mother or with any man or god or beast. It is ready for any deed of blood, and there is no unhallowed food it will not eat. In a word, it falls short of no extreme of folly or shamelessness.

"That is very true," he said.

"But I fancy that a man who is of healthy body and sound mind, before he goes to sleep, stirs up the reasoning part within him and feasts it on noble arguments and problems, and so comes to peace and understanding with himself. The desiring element he neither starves nor 572 surfeits in order that it may go to sleep and not trouble the best part with its joy or with its sorrow, but may leave it undisturbed, alone by itself, to inquire into and stretch out after the apprehension of what it does not know, whether of things past or present or future. In the same way also he soothes the spirited element, and will not go to sleep with his spirit stirred into activity in anger against any man. These two elements he sets at rest, and the third, in which thought abides, he arouses, and so takes his repose. In such case you know that he comes nearer to grasping truth than at any other time, and the visions of his dreams are never unlawful."

"I think it is absolutely as you say," he said.

"In what we were saying we have gone rather beyond the immediate point. What we want to be sure of is this, that a terrible, fierce, and lawless class of desires exists in every man, even in those of us who have every appearance of being decent people. Its existence is revealed in dreams. Consider whether you agree with me and think I am right."

"I agree."

"And remember how we described the man of the people. His origin, if you recollect, lay in an early training under a parsimonious father, one who honoured only the money-making desires, and slighted those that are unnecessary and that would not exist but for purposes of amusement and display. Is that right?"

"Yes."

"He associates with a smarter set of men, who are full of the desires we have just described, and plunges into all their insolent kind of conduct in disgust at his father's parsimony. But he has a better nature than his corrupters, and so is drawn both ways until he settles down to a compromise between the two modes of life. He takes his pleasure from either side in what he conceives as moderation, and leads a life which is neither mean nor lawless, having, from an oligarch, become a man of the people."

"That was and is," he said, "my opinion concerning such a man."

"Now suppose," I said, "this man in his turn grown old, with a young son who has been trained in his father's ways of life."

"Yes."

"Now suppose, further, that he is subjected to the same influences as his father was, and is drawn into entire unlawfulness, which his seducers call entire liberty; suppose, too, that his father and his other relatives come to the assistance of these middle desires, while his companions rally to the help of the other side. When these terrible magicians and tyrant-makers have given up hope of securing their hold on the young man in any other way, they contrive to implant within him a love that shall preside over the idle desires which consume whatever is given 573 them—some winged and mighty drone. Do you think love in such men could be anything else?"

"No," he answered, "nothing but that."

"Then the other desires buzz round it. They have their fill of incense and myrrh, and garlands and wine, and all the pleasures that run riot in these assemblies. Feeding and fattening the drone to the utmost of their power, they implant in him the sting of longing; when this is done, this president of the soul has madness as his bodyguard and runs amuck: if he finds within the man any beliefs or desires that make pretence of decency and have still some sense of shame, he kills them or drives them beyond his borders, until he has made a clearance of temperance, and introduced madness to fill its place."

"Your description of the origin of the tyrannical man is perfect," he said.

"Then," I said, "was it not because of this that Love has always been called a tyrant?"

"Probably," he said.

"Has not a drunken man also a tyrannical spirit, my friend?" I said.

"He has."

"He who is mad and deranged, moreover, aspires to rule both men and gods alike, and imagines that he is quite capable of doing it?"

"He does," he said.

"Then, my wonderful friend," I said, "whenever you find a man whom nature or an evil life, or both, have made drunken and lustful and mad, there you have a tyrannical man, in the strictest sense, come into being."

"Most certainly."

"This apparently is the origin of the tyrannical man. Now, how does he live?"

"As they say about riddles, I give it up. Tell me yourself," he answered.

"I will," I said. "The next stage, I fancy, with those in whose souls a tyrant love dwells ruling all therein, is a time of feasting and rioting and revelling and mistresses, and all such follies."

"Inevitably," he said.

"Then does not every day and night produce a thick crop of terrible desires whose wants are many?"

"Yes, thick it is."

"Then any revenue there may be is speedily consumed?"

"Surely."

"And the next step is borrowing and encroachment on his capital?"

"It is."

"When all resources are becoming exhausted, is it not inevitable that the crowded greedy nestful of desires will begin to clamour; and these men are driven by the goads of other desires; but above all by Love himself, whose spearsmen and bodyguard all the others are, and they run riot, looking for any one with money whom they can rob by cheating or by force?"

"Most certainly," he said.

"The man is compelled to plunder from every source or be racked by pains and aches?"

"He is."

"As the new pleasures that arose within him were set above the old and stole their share, will not the man likewise set himself above his father and mother, who are his elders, rob them, and divide his parents' goods when he has spent his own?"

"Yes, certainly," he said.

"But if they won't make their money over to him, will he not try to cheat and deceive his parents?"

"Yes."

"And if he fails in that, he will take to robbery and force?"

"I think so," he said.

"But, my wonderful friend, if the old man and woman resist and show fight, will he then desist and abstain from any tyrannical deed?"

"Well," he said, "I have not much hope for that man's parents."

"Good heavens, Adeimantus, when it is a choice between a mistress whom he has loved for a day, and who has no claim upon him, and his mother, whom he has loved all his life, and who has every claim upon him, or between a fair youth to whom he is bound by no ties, the friend of a day, and his aged father, whose youth is gone, who is bound to him by the closest ties and is the oldest of his friends, do you really think that he will beat his parents, and make them the slaves of persons such as those, if he brings such under his roof?"

"Yes, assuredly he will," he said.

"How divinely blessed it seems to be," I said, "to have a tyrannical son."

"It is indeed," he said.

"Well, when he is coming to an end of his father's and mother's goods and has now a great swarm of pleasures gathered within him, will he not first begin to busy himself with the walls of other people's houses, or with the cloaks of evening pedestrians, and after that take to cleaning out a temple or two? And all this time the old beliefs which he had as a boy about right and wrong, and accounted just, will be held in subjection by those which are but newly released from slavery, who form Love's bodyguard and rule with him. Once they were let loose in sleep when he dreamed, in the time when he was still under laws and a father and had a democratic government in his soul. But when Love established his tyranny over him, he became for always, and in waking reality, the man he used occasionally to be in his dreams. And now he will stick at no frightful murder, no unhal- 575 lowed food or dreadful deed, but Love dwells tyrannically within him in all lawlessness and anarchy. He is sole ruler, and will lead the man in whom he dwells as in a city, into any kind of daring, by which he will support himself and his rabble following, the immigrants whom the man's evil companions have introduced, and the native born whom evil ways of life have released and set free. Is not that the life of such a man?"

"It is," he answered.

"And if the number of such men in a city is small," I said, "and the rest of the population is law-abiding, they emigrate and become some other tyrant's bodyguard or serve as mercenaries, if war is going on anywhere. But if the times are times of peace and security, then they stay in the city and commit petty crimes."

"What kind of crimes do you mean?"

"Well, they are thieves, burglars, cutpurses, pick-pockets, temple robbers, kidnappers. Sometimes, if they have a ready tongue, they take to corrupt practices, and give false witness and take bribes."

"Well, these are small evils," he said, "if there are only a few of them."

"Yes," I said "because small is small in comparison with great, and all those crimes, in their effect on a city's wretchedness and misery, don't, as they say, come near a tyrant. For when a city comes to contain many such men, and others who will follow their lead, and they find out how numerous they are, it is then that, helped by the folly of the public, they produce a tyrant, him who of them all has the greatest and mightiest tyrant within himself."

"Naturally," he said, "for he will be the most tyrannical."

"All this if men yield without a struggle. But if the city will not submit to him, then as he once chastised his father and mother, so he will now, if he can, chastise his fatherland. He will import a new band of followers, and will have and hold enslaved his once loved fatherland, or motherland, as the Cretans call it. And this is where the desire of this man ends."

"Truly," he said, "it is."

"Then this," I said, "is the character revealed by these men in private life before they obtain power. Firstly, for their company they associate with men who flatter them and will do anything to please them; or if they want a

576 favour from any man, they will take to cringing themselves; to gain their end they will cut any figure that is
required, and be more than kin; once the favour is
granted, they are strangers again."

"That is very true."

"So they live their life long, no man's friend, but always one man's master or another's slave. True liberty
and friendship the tyrannic nature never tastes."

"True."

"May we not rightly call such men faithless?"

"Surely."

"And as unjust as men may be, if the definition of
justice we arrived at some time ago was correct?"

"It certainly was that," he answered.

"Then let us sum up the worst of men," I said. "He is
surely the man who expresses in waking reality the character we attributed to a man in his dreams?"

"Certainly."

"And this man is found in him who being in his own
nature most tyrannical wields solitary rule, and the
longer he leads a tyrant's life, the more surely does he
become the man we have described."

"That is inevitable," said Glaucon, taking his turn in
the conversation.

"Now, I asked, "will he who stands revealed the wicked-
est of men, be shown to be also the most miserable? And
will he who has borne tyrant rule longest and most triumphantly have been in truth the longest and most em-
phatically miserable? Though the multitude will always
have varying opinions about him."

"It is inevitable," he said, "that things should be as
you say."

"Then," I said, "will not the tyrannical man and the
city governed by a tyrant be set over against one another
as alike, a man of the people against a democratic city,
and so on with the others?"

"Surely."

"Then in respect to virtue and happiness, the same relations will hold between man and man as between city and city, will they not?"

"Certainly."

"How does the city governed by a tyrant compare in virtue with the kingly city as we originally described it?"

"They are exact opposites," he said. "The one is the best of cities, the other the worst."

"I shall not ask which is which," I said, "for that is obvious. Do you give the same decision regarding their happiness or misery, or not? Don't let us be dazzled by gazing at the individual tyrant or a few of his followers. We must enter the city and examine the whole of it. So let us creep in and take a look all round, and then give our opinion."

"Your claim is perfectly just," he said. "It is obvious to any man that there is no more wretched city than that governed by a tyrant, none happier than the royal city."

"Now if I make the same claim concerning the individual man," I said, "shall I not be right in demanding that he alone shall give his judgment on them whose thought can enter in and discern each man's heart, who is not like a child dazzled by what he sees from the outside—the circumstance and pomp of tyranny which is assumed for the benefit of the outside world—but who can look through right to the heart? May I not also claim that it is right for all of us to listen to the man who is able to judge, who has lived under the same roof with the tyrant, who has been by his side while he lived his ordinary family life at home and has observed his behaviour to the different members of his family (among whom, if anywhere, he may be seen stripped of his stage trappings), and who has seen him also in public dangers; and may we not summon him who has seen all this to declare to us how the tyrant compares with the others in respect of happiness and virtue?"

"That also is perfectly fair," he said.

"Shall we, then, pretend," I said, "that we are among those who are able to judge, or have met with such, in order that we may have someone to answer our questions?"

"Certainly."

"Come now," I said, "consider the question in this way. Keep in your mind the likeness of man and city, and so, examining them point by point, enumerate the characteristics of each in turn."

"To which do you refer?" he said.

"Well, to begin with a city," I said. "Do you call the tyrant-governed city free or a slave?"

"As much a slave as it could possibly be," he said.

"Then do you see therein masters and freemen?"

"Yes," he said, "a few. But almost all therein, and certainly all the best element, is in dishonourable and wretched servitude."

"Then if the man is like the city," I said, "must not the same disposition be found in him, and will not his soul be full of extreme slavery and lack of freedom, and all the most respectable elements in it be slaves, and a small part, and that the most wicked and the most mad, be master?"

"That is inevitable," he said.

"Well, will you call such a soul free or a slave?"

"I call it a slave, of course."

"But does not the slave city which is governed by a tyrant have least power of doing what it wants?"

"Much the least."

"Then the tyrant-governed soul will have least power of doing what it wants, or what the whole soul wants? It will ever be dragged about by a madness of desire, and and be full of confusion and remorse?"

"Surely."

"Must the tyrant-governed city be rich or poor?"

"Poor."

"Then the tyrannical soul also must be always poverty- [578] stricken and unsatisfied?"

"Yes," he said.

"Moreover, must not such a city and such a man be full of fear?"

"Yes, very much so."

"And in any other city, do you think that weepings and gnashings of teeth, lamentation and pain, will be more abundant?"

"No."

"Or more abundant in any individual than in this tyrannical man who is maddened by desires and lusts?"

"Certainly not."

"And it was your view of all those facts, and others like them, I imagine, that made you judge this city the most wretched of cities?"

"Was I not right?" he said.

"You certainly were," I answered. "But in view of these same facts, what have you to say of the tyrannical man?"

"That he is by far the most miserable of all men," he said.

"In making that remark you are no longer right."

"How is that?" he asked.

"In him we have not yet come to the most miserable."

"Then when shall we?"

"This man will seem to you perhaps even more miserable."

"What man?"

"He," I said, "who, being of tyrannical nature, does not lead his life in private, but is unfortunate, and is led by circumstances to be a tyrant."

"From what we have said before, I conjecture," he said, "that you are right."

"Yes," I said; "but it is not enough to fancy such things. You must examine them very carefully by the method we have agreed upon. For our inquiry is concerned with the greatest of questions—a good and an evil life."

"You are perfectly right," he said.

"Then consider whether there is anything in what I say. It seems to me that in our inquiry on this matter we must get light from the following sources."

"From which?"

"By examining each of those rich individuals in cities who own a great number of slaves; for they have this point of similarity with tyrants, that they are rulers of many. No doubt the tyrant has the best of it in point of numbers?"

"He has."

"You know, I suppose, that they live unconcernedly, and are not afraid of their servants?"

"Well, is there anything for them to fear?"

"Nothing," I said; "but do you see why that is?"

"Yes. The whole city gives assistance to each individual."

"Excellent," I said. "But supposing one of the gods were to take a man who possesses fifty slaves or even more, and were to lift him and his wife and children out of the city and put him down, with all his property and his slaves, in a desert place where there would be no free men to come to his assistance, do you not suppose that he would be in the most terrible fright in apprehension lest he and his children and his wife should be killed by their servants?"

"In the worst of frights," he answered.

579    "Would he not then be compelled to pay court to some of those his slaves, to make them many promises, and to set them free, quite against his desire, and so to stand revealed as his own servants' toady?"

"He would certainly have to do so or die," he said.

"And supposing the gods were to plant around him large colonies of neighbours who wouldn't tolerate any man claiming to be another's master, and who punished with the severest penalties any such person they might lay hands on?"

"In that case," he said, "I imagine that he would be in an even greater extremity of evil, ringed round by none but enemies."

"Is not this the prison-house in which the tyrant is bound? He has the nature we have described, full of thronging and diverse fears and lusts. He has a greedy soul, and yet he is the only man in the city who may not travel or go to see the things which all free men want to see. He lives hidden away in his house for all the world like a woman, thinking with envy of any of the other citizens who travel abroad and see things worth seeing."

"Assuredly," he said.

"Greater then by evils such as these is the harvest of the man, who having an evil constitution in his own soul, which tyrannical condition you have just judged to be most miserable of all, does not live as a private individual, but is compelled by some chance to be a tyrant, and when he cannot master himself, must try to rule others. You might as well compel a man with his body diseased and unable to control itself to have no private life, but to pass his days in public gymnastic contests and battles."

"Your comparison is exact and perfectly true, Socrates," he said.

"Then, my dear Glaucon," I said, "is not his condition altogether miserable, and does not the tyrant lead a life still harder than that which you pronounced hardest of all?"

"Certainly," he said.

"Then in good truth, and for all that any one may think, he who is really a tyrant is really a slave, the humblest cringer and servant, and a toady of the sorriest rascals. His desires he never satisfies, but to any man who can see his whole soul he appears in the barest want and truly poor. All his life long he is full of fear, a mass of convulsive movements and pains, if he is like the constitution of the city over which he rules. And he is, is he not?"

"Yes," he said.

580 "And besides all these things, shall we further assign to this man what we talked of before? It is inevitable that because of his rule he should be and should go on becoming more and more envious, faithless, unjust, friendless, impious, the welcomer and fosterer of every vice, and that with all these qualities he must be himself the most unfortunate of men, and must make his neighbours like him."

"No sensible man will dispute your assertion," he said.

"Well, now," I said, "the time has come, and, like the judge in the final contest, you must give your decision as to who in your opinion is first in happiness and who second, and give all the five their places in order, the royal man, the timocratic, oligarchic, democratic, and tyrannical."

"The decision is easy," he said. "For I place them as though I were judging tragic choruses, in the order in which they came upon the stage, with respect to virtue and vice, happiness and its opposite."

"Shall we hire a herald," I said, "or shall I announce myself that the son of Ariston has judged the best and justest man to be the happiest, and declared him to be the most kingly, bearing kingly rule over himself, while the worst and most unjust man he judges to be the most miserable, and declares him to be that man, whoever he is, who being in himself most tyrannical is also tyrant of his city."

"Yes, announce that," he said.

"May I add," I said, "that this holds whether their characters are known to or hidden from all gods and men?"

"Yes, do," he said.

"Good," I said. "We may take that as one demonstration. Now see whether you think there is anything in this second one."

"What is it?"

"Since the soul of each individual," I said, "is like the city, divided into three forms, it will admit, I think, of yet another demonstration."

"What is it?"

"It is this. Belonging to these three forms there appear to me to be three pleasures, one special pleasure attaching to each particular form, and so with desires and principles of rule."

"What do you mean?" he said.

"There is, first, that by which a man learns," I said; "secondly, that by which he is angry. The third contains such varied forms within it that we could find no one special name for it, but named it after the greatest and strongest thing in it. For we called it the desiring form because of the intensity of the desires concerned with food and drink and sex and so on; and we also called it money-loving, because such desires are usually satisfied with the help of money."

"And we were right," he said.                    581

"And if we were further to say that its pleasure and love is in gain, would not that be our best way of getting a satisfactory general expression to use in our argument, so that we should know what we were talking about when we referred to this part of the soul; and if we named it the money-loving or the gain-loving form, should we not be right?"

"I certainly think so," he said.

"Further, did we not say that the spirited element is ever wholly bent on mastery and victory and fame?"

"We did."

"Then should we be right in calling it the victory-loving and the honour-loving form?"

"Quite right."

"And, lastly, as to the part with which we learn, it is obvious to every one that it is for ever straining to know where the truth lies, and cares for money and reputation less than the others."

"Yes, much less."

"Will it be right if we call it learning-loving and philosophic?"

"Surely."

"And men's hearts," I said, "are ruled, are they not, some by this last element, others by one of the other two, as the case may be?"

"That is so," he said.

"Then it is for these reasons that we say that of men also there are three primary classes—the lovers of wisdom, the lovers of victory, and the lovers of gain?"

"Exactly so."

"Then there are also three kinds of pleasures, one for each of the three?"

"Yes."

"Now do you know," I said, "that if you were to ask three such men, each in turn, which of these lives is the most pleasant, each would extol his own life most highly? The money-maker will say, will he not, that, compared with the pleasures of gain, the pleasures of honour or of learning are worthless except in so far as they bring in money?"

"True," he said.

"And is not the lover of honour the same?" I said. "Does he not consider that the pleasures of money-making are rather vulgar, and those of learning, on the other hand, except in so far as learning brings honour, mere smoke and nonsense?"

"That is so," he said.

"Then how shall we imagine that the philosopher regards the other pleasures in comparison with the pleasure of knowing where the truth lies and of being always in a state akin to knowledge when he is learning? For him there can be no comparison, can there? He will call the others in good truth compulsory pleasures. He has no need for them, but they are forced upon him."

"Should we not make quite certain of that?" he said.

"Well," I said, "when the discussion concerns the pleasures, and in fact the whole life, of each type of man, and the question at issue is not their relative nobility or disgracefulness, their goodness or badness, but simply and solely which is most pleasant and least painful, how can 582 we know which of the three speaks most truly?"

"I can't say," he said.

"Well, look at the matter in this way. What is wanted for a judgment that is to turn out to be right? Is it not experience and insight and reason? Can you have any better test than these?"

"Of course not," he said.

"Now, consider. There are those three men. Which of them has had most experience of all these pleasures? Do you think that the gain-lover learns the nature of truth and acquires more experience of the pleasure of knowledge than the philosopher has the pleasure of gain?"

"The cases are very different," he said. "For the latter must of necessity start in childhood by testing both the other kinds; whereas there is no compulsion on the gain-lover to learn the nature of reality and taste the sweetness of this pleasure or to have any experience of it. Nay, if he had the best will in the world, he would find it no easy matter."

"Then the philosopher," I said, "far excels the gain-lover in his experience of both pleasures?"

"Yes."

"And the lover of honour also? Or has he less experience of the pleasures of honour than the other has of the pleasure derived from wisdom?"

"No," he said, "honour comes to them all if they accomplish their several aims. For the rich man is honoured by many. So is the brave man and the wise man. So that all have experience of the pleasure which comes from being honoured and know its nature; but it is impossible for any one but the philosopher to taste the pleasure contained in the vision of being."

"Then so far as experience is concerned," I said, "he will judge best of the three men?"

"Far the best."

"And his experience alone will involve insight?"

"Certainly."

"And, lastly, as to the necessary instrument of judgment, it is not the instrument of the gain-lover or of the honour-lover, but of the philosopher?"

"What is that instrument?"

"Surely we said that judgment must be made by means of reasoning?"

"Yes."

"But reasoning is this man's especial instrument?"

"Surely."

"Now, if what is being judged were best judged by means of wealth and profit, the praise and blame of the gain-lover would necessarily be the truest?"

"Necessarily."

"Or if by means of honour and victory and courage, the praise of the honour-and victory-lover would be truest?"

"Obviously."

"But since they are best judged by means of experience and insight and reason——?"

"It is inevitable," he said, "that the praise of the philosopher and lover of reason should be truest."

"Then of these three pleasures, will not that be the **583** pleasantest which belongs to the part of the soul wherewith we learn, and pleasantest also the life of him amongst us in whom this part rules?"

"How else?" he said. "The wise man's praise is decisive, and he praises his own life."

"What life and what pleasure does the judge declare to come second?"

"Obviously the pleasure of the warrior and the honour-lover, for that is nearer him than the pleasure of the money-maker."

"Then the gain-lover's apparently comes last?"

"Of course," he said.

"Then that makes twice running, and the just man has twice conquered the unjust. And now a third time in this Olympian conflict to Zeus the Saviour and Zeus the Olympian! Observe that the pleasure of the others beside that of the wise man is not altogether true or pure, but a sort of shadow picture, as I seem to have heard some wise man say. Now this will be the chiefest and most decisive of our falls."

"It will. But what do you mean?"

"If you will answer as I ask," I said, "I shall discover."

"Then ask," he said.

"Tell me then," I said. "Do we not say that pain is the opposite of pleasure?"

"Certainly."

"And do we say that there is such a thing as feeling neither pleasure nor pain?"

"We do."

"It is a mean between the two, and is a kind of rest

of the soul from these feelings. Is not that how you describe it?"

"It is," he answered.

"Now, do you remember," I asked, "how sick persons talk when they are ill?"

"How?"

"They say that there is nothing more pleasant than being well, but before they fell ill they never noticed how very pleasant it was."

"I remember," he said.

"Do you not also hear men who are in great pain saying that there is nothing pleasanter than respite from torment?"

"I do."

"But there are many other similar circumstances, I imagine, in which you find men who are suffering pain extolling as the greatest of pleasures not joy, but the absence of pain and relief from their condition."

"Well," he said, "perhaps in those circumstances this state of rest becomes pleasant and desirable."

"And when a man leaves off feeling pleasure, the respite from pleasure will be painful."

"Perhaps," he said.

"Then this state of rest which we asserted a moment ago to lie between the two, will be both pleasure and pain at times?"

"Apparently."

"But is it possible that what is neither one nor the other should become both?"

"I don't think so."

"Further, are not both pleasure and pain as they arise in the soul a kind of movement?"

"Yes."

"And has not that which is neither painful nor pleasant just been shown to be rest, and to lie between these two?"

584 "It has."

"Then is it possible to be right in thinking the absence of suffering pleasant, or the absence of joy terrible?"

"It is impossible."

"Then this state of rest," I said, "compared to suffering is not but appears to be pleasure, and compared to pleasure is not but appears to be suffering? In comparison with the reality of pleasure there is nothing solid in these visions; only a kind of magic?"

"That is certainly the result of the argument," he said.

"And consider pleasures," I said, "which do not come out of pains—for I don't want you to imagine in this instance that, in the nature of things, pleasure is cessation from pain, and pain cessation from pleasure."

"What instance," he said, "and what kind of pleasure do you mean?"

"There are many of them," I said; "but you will get the best example if you consider the pleasures of smell. For they arise in extraordinary intensity in a moment without any preceding pain, and on their cessation leave no pain behind them."

"That is perfectly true," he said.

"Then do not let us believe that the release from pain is pure pleasure, or from pleasure pure pain."

"No."

"Nevertheless," I said, "those so-called pleasures which make their way to the soul through the body, or at least the most and the greatest of them, are of this class, releases from pain."

"They are."

"And is it the same with anticipatory pleasures and pains which arise from expectation of pleasure and pain in the future?"

"It is."

"Do you know the nature of such feelings," I asked, "and what they are like?"

"What?" he said.

"Do you conceive," I said, "that the above, the below, and the middle exist in nature?"

"I do."

"And do you imagine that a man who was being lifted from the below to the middle would not think that he was being carried above? And if he stood in the middle, and looked down to the place he came from, could he think that he was anywhere but in the above, if he had not seen the real above?"

"Upon my word," he said, "I don't think that in those circumstances he could suppose anything else."

"If he were carried back again, would he not suppose that he was being carried below, and suppose truly?"

"Surely."

"And all this would be the result of his lack of experience of the true above and middle and below?"

"Obviously."

"And would it surprise you that those also who lack experience of truth have unsound doctrines on many subjects, and as regards pleasure, pain and the intermediary state are so situated that when they come in contact with pain their suppositions are true, and they do really feel pain; but when they change from pain to the intermediary state, then they have an intense conviction that they are experiencing satisfaction and pleasure? Like men who contrast black with grey, because they have not seen white, so they contrast pain with want of pain, because they have not experienced pleasure, and are deceived."

"No, by Zeus," he answered, "I should be much more surprised if that were not the case."

"Consider the question in this light," I said. "Are not hunger and thirst and so on what may be called emptinesses; they are empty conditions of the body?"

"Certainly."

"And is not ignorance and folly likewise an emptiness—an empty condition of the soul?"

"Assuredly."

"Then will not he who receives food and strengthens his mind be filled?"

"Surely."

"But which is the truer filling, to be filled with what is less or with what is more real?"

"Obviously with what is more real."

"And which class of things do you think has greater participation in pure being, the class containing bread and drink and meat and food generally, or the class containing true belief and knowledge and mind and, in short, all virtue? Decide in this way. Do you think that what is connected with the unchanging and immortal and with truth and which takes from these its character and its origin, is more real than what is connected with the ever-changing and the mortal, and which takes from these its character and its origin?"

"That which is connected with the unchanging far excels the other," he said.

"Does the being of the unchanging partake of being any more than of knowledge?"

"Certainly not."

"Or more than of truth?"

"Once again—no."

"Less participation in truth means less participation in being, does it not?"

"Inevitably."

"Then, speaking generally, do not those kinds of things which are concerned with the care of the body partake less of truth and being than those concerned with the care of the soul?"

"Very much less."

"And do you not think similarly of the relation of the body itself with the soul?"

"I do."

"Then that which is filled with things that more really

are, and which is itself more real, is more really filled than that which is filled with what less really is, and which is itself less real, is it not?"

"Surely."

"Now, if to be filled with what nature demands is pleasant, that which is more really filled with more real things will make a man rejoice more really and truly with true pleasure; while that which receives what is less real will be filled less really and certainly, and will receive more untrustworthy and less true pleasure."

"That is quite inevitable," he said.

**586** "Then they who have no experience of insight and virtue, but spend their whole time in revelling and such-like, are carried apparently from the middle to below and back again, and wander so all their life from one to the other; but never once have they gone beyond and seen or been carried to the true above, nor have they been really filled with what is real, nor tasted steadfast and pure pleasure. Like beasts of the field their eyes look ever downward, their heads are bent to the ground and to the table, and so like beasts they guzzle and satisfy their lusts, and in their greedy struggle for such pleasures they butt and kick with horns and hoofs of iron, and kill each other because they cannot be satisfied, inasmuch as what they are trying to fill is not the real and continent part of themselves, nor is what they are putting into it real."

"Truly perfect, Socrates," said Glaucon, "is your utterance regarding the life of the vulgar."

"Then must not the pleasures they live among be mixed with pains, images and shadow outlines of the true pleasure, and take their colour from the contrast of their setting? Thus both pleasures and pains have an appearance of intensity, and implant in the foolish mad desires for themselves, and are the objects of strife, like the image of Helen which Stesichorus says the men at Troy fought over in their ignorance of the truth?"

"It is quite inevitable," he said, "that their life should be more or less like that."

"Further, must not the same sort of thing," I asked, 'hold good of the spirited element if any man follow it with his whole heart, pursuing after a surfeit of honour and victory to the neglect of reason and understanding; satisfying his love of honour by envy, or his love of victory by violence, or his spirit by bad temper?"

"Yes, the same must hold of that also," he said.

"But may we not take heart," I asked, "and say even of those desires which are concerned with the love of gain and the love of victory, that if they follow after knowledge and reason, and pursuing pleasures in their company, accept those which insight points out, they will then, because they are following truth, receive the truest pleasures that they are capable of receiving, and those also that are their own, since that which is best for each thing is also most truly its own?"

"Yes," he said, "its very own."

"Then when the whole soul follows without dissension the philosophic part, not only may each part do its own work throughout and be just, but each may gather its own pleasures, the best and the truest of which it is capable?" 587

"Exactly so."

"But when one of the other two gets the upper hand, the result is that it does not contrive to gain its own pleasure, but even forces the others to pursue after a pleasure which is foreign to them and untrue?"

"Yes," he said.

"And will not this be especially the behaviour of the elements farthest removed from philosophy and reason?"

"It will."

"And is not that farthest removed from reason which is farthest removed from law and order?"

"Obviously."

"But have not the lustful and tyrannical desires been shown to be the farthest removed?"

"Very much the farthest."

"While the kingly and orderly desires are nearest?"

"Yes."

"In that case, I imagine, the tyrant will be farthest from true and intimate pleasure, and the king nearest?"

"Inevitably."

"And the tyrant," I said, "will lead the most unpleasant, the king the most pleasant of lives?"

"That is quite inevitable."

"Now do you know," I said, "how much more unpleasant the tyrant's life is than the king's?"

"Tell me," he said.

"There are apparently three pleasures, one genuine and two bastard, and the tyrant in his flight from law and reason goes to the very extremes of the bastard pleasures and beyond them, and lives with a bodyguard of slave-pleasures, and it is not very easy to say how great his inferiority is, but perhaps it may be expressed in this way."

"How?" he said.

"The tyrant is third removed from the oligarchic man, is he not? For the man of the people came between them."

"Yes."

"Then if what we have said is true, he will live with an image of pleasure the third removed in truthfulness from that of the oligarch."

"Yes."

"But taking the aristocratic and kingly man as one, the oligarchical is in his turn third from the kingly man."

"Yes, third."

"Then the tyrant," I said, "is removed from true pleasure three times three?"

"Apparently."

"The image of tyrannical pleasure," I said, "according to the number of the distance, will be in two dimensions, it seems?"

"Yes."

"But if we square and cube it is obvious how great the interval becomes."

"Obvious, no doubt, to an arithmetician," he said.

"Then if conversely any one wants to say how far the king is removed from the tyrant in truth of pleasure, he will find on completing the multiplication that he lives seven hundred and twenty-nine times more pleasantly, and the tyrant the same number of times more miserably."

"You have made a marvellous calculation," he said, "of the difference of the two men, the just and the unjust, 589 in respect of pleasure and pain."

"Yes, but it is true as well," I said, "and also a suitable number for men's lives, since days and nights and months and years are suitable."

"That they certainly are," he said.

"Now if the good and just man by so much surpasses the evil and unjust man in pleasure, is it not incalculable how greatly he will conquer him in grace of life and beauty and virtue?"

"Incalculable indeed," he said.

"Good," I said. "Now since we have come to this point in our argument, let us refer to the original statements which brought us here. It was stated, if you remember, that injustice is profitable to the perfectly unjust man, who is reputed to be just. Was not that the statement?"

"It was."

"Now," I said, "let us join argument with the author of this statement, since we have come to an agreement concerning the respective effects of unjust and just conduct."

"In what way?" he said.

"We shall mould in words an image of the soul, and he who said these things will realize what he has said."

"What kind of an image?" he asked.

"An image," I answered, "like one of those old-time natures we hear of in fable—Chimaera or Scylla or Cerberus, or the many others which are said to have combined several forms in one nature."

"Yes, there are these stories," he said.

"Fashion me, therefore, one form of a many-coloured and many-headed beast. There is a ring of heads both of tame and wild beasts, and it can change them and produce them out of itself at will."

"That is clever moulder's work," he said. "Still, words are easier to work in than wax and such materials, so you may suppose it done."

"Then give me two more forms, one of a lion and one of a man. But the first form of all is to be the largest, and the second, second largest."

"That," he said, "is easier, and is done."

"Now join these three into one so that somehow or other they have a common nature."

"They are joined," he said.

"Now outside mould round about them an individual image—that of a man—so that to him who cannot see within, but looks only at the outer shell, the whole appears one living creature, and that a man."

"That is done," he said.

"Now to him who says that injustice pays this man, and that just conduct is not to his advantage, let us declare that he is really saying that it pays him to feast and make strong the many-formed monster and the lion 588 and the lion's belongings, and to starve and weaken the man, so that he is dragged about wherever either of these takes him, and cannot teach them to become used to or

fond of one another, but must let them bite and fight
and devour one another."

"Yes," he said, "that is exactly what the praise of injustice comes to."

"On the other hand, would not he who declares that
justice pays say that we ought to do and say such things
as will make the man within have strongest control over
the whole man and look after the many-headed monster
like a gardener, fostering and nursing the tame heads,
and with the help of the lion nature preventing the wild
ones from sprouting; he will care for all in common, and
will help them by making them friendly to each other
and to himself?"

"Yes, that is just what the praiser of justice says."

"Then from every point of view, the praiser of justice
would speak truly, and the praiser of injustice falsely.
Whether we look to pleasure or good report or advantage,
he who praises justice speaks with truth, but as for him
who blames it, there is no soundness or knowledge in his
blame."

"I think not," he said; "none whatever."

"Well, let us be gently persuasive (for his mistake is
not of his own will), and ask him: 'My dear good sir, may
we not say that men's opinions on what is noble and disgraceful have the following origin: the noble actions
are those which put the wild-beast parts of the soul
under the control of the man, or perhaps we should
say of the divine element, while those which enslave the
human to the wild part are disgraceful?' Will he agree
or not?"

"He will, if he takes my advice," he said.

"Then will this argument allow that it can profit
any man to get gold unjustly; for the result is something
like this—he gets the money, but on condition of enslaving the best part of himself to the vilest? Now if he had
got the money by selling his son or his daugther as a slave,

and that into the hands of cruel and evil men, it would not have paid him to get mountains of gold on these terms: and if he enslaves the divinest part of himself to the most ungodly and the most abominable, and has no pity upon it, is he not then a miserable wretch, and 590 does he not buy his gold on terms of far more terrible death than Eriphyle, who got her necklace at the price of her husband's life?"

"Yes, far more terrible," said Glaucon. "I will answer you for him."

"And do you suppose that this is the reason why licentiousness has always been condemned, because it means that that dangerous, that great and many-formed monster is given more freedom than he ought to have?"

"Obviously," he said.

"And are not obstinacy and bad temper condemned because the lion and the serpent elements are increased and strengthened unfittingly?"

"Certainly."

"And are not luxury and softness condemned because of their relaxing and slackening effect on that same element when they implant cowardice in it?"

"Of course."

"And toadying and meanness, because the mean man subordinates this same spirited element to the mob-like beast, and accustoms it from early years to be flouted for the sake of money and the beast's insatiable greed, and to become a monkey and not a lion?"

"Yes," he said.

"And why do you think that mechanical work and work with one's hands are matters of reproach? Is it not because in some people the element of the best is naturally weak, unable to rule the monsters within them, and only capable of learning how to pamper them?"

"Apparently," he said.

"Well, then, is it not in order that even these men

may be ruled by something resembling the principle that rules in the best man, that we say they must be the slaves of that best man in whom the divine dwells; not that we agree with the opinion Thrasymachus had of the governed, and suppose that the slave ought to be ruled to his hurt, but we think that it is better for every man to be ruled by divinity and insight? It is best, of course, when he possesses that within him, but if he does not, it had better be put over him from without, and then all men, being guided by the same principle, will be equals and friends as far as may be."

"Yes, that is right," he said.

"And the law, by being an ally of all in the city," I said, "makes it quite plain that it approves something of this kind. So does the way in which children are ruled. We do not allow them to be free until we have set up a constitution in them, as you might in a city, and until by nourishing the best in them we have provided a guardian to bear 591 rule within them which is like and can take the place of our ruling principle, and then we give them their liberty."

"Yes," he said.

"Then under what conditions, Glaucon, or for what reasons can we say that there is profit in injustice, or licentiousness, or disgraceful conduct, when by them a man acquires more money or more power of any kind, and with it becomes a worse man?"

"Under no conditions," he answered.

"Then how will it profit him who acts unjustly to avoid discovery and punishment? If a man is not found out, does he not become still more wicked, while if he is discovered and punished the beast in him is laid to rest and tamed; the humane part is liberated, and the whole soul is set in the direction of the best nature, and so along with insight acquiring temperance and justice achieves a condition more precious than the condition of the body which with health acquires strength and beauty; in proportion as soul is more precious than body?"

"That is certainly the case," he said.

"Then will not the man of understanding live with all his power strained to this end? First of all, will he not reverence such studies as will fashion his soul after this pattern, and spurn all others?"

"Obviously," he said.

"And, secondly," I said, "as for the condition and nourishment of his body, he will not give that over to the pleasure of the beast and of unreason and turn his life in that direction; nor yet will health be his ideal; nor will he set great store in being strong or healthy or beautiful, unless with these he can also be temperate; but he will always make manifest that for him harmony of body has its purpose in unison of soul."

"Yes, that he will," he said, "if he is to be truly musical."

"And will he not for the same purpose," I said, "observe order and unison in the acquisition of wealth? He will not be dazzled by what the crowd calls blessedness, and heap up the mass of his wealth beyond all bounds, and so possess boundless evils?"

"I think not," he said.

"No," I said, "he will fix his eyes on the constitution within him, and keep watch that nothing therein is shaken by excess or poverty of bodily substance, and in adding to or spending that substance he will observe this guiding principle to the best of his power."

"Certainly he will," he said.

592    "And in regard to honours also, he will keep his eyes on the same end; some, which he thinks will make him a better man, he will gladly participate in and taste, but in public and in private he will fly from those which he thinks will disturb the condition of his soul."

"If that is his concern," he said, "he will not want to be a politician."

"Yes, by the dog, he will," I said; "at least in his own city; not perhaps in the country of his birth, unless some divine chance falls out."

"I understand," he said. "You speak of the city whose foundation we have been describing, which has its being in words; for there is no spot on earth, I imagine, where it exists."

"No," I said; "but perhaps it is laid up in heaven as a pattern for him who wills to see, and seeing, to found a city in himself. Whether it exists anywhere or ever will exist, is no matter. His conduct will be an expression of the laws of that city alone, and of no other."

"That is likely enough," he said.

# BOOK X

"THERE are a great many things about the city," I said. "which make me think in how extraordinarily sound a manner we have founded it; but I feel this most especially when I think about poetry."

"To what do you refer?" he said.

"To our refusal to admit all imitative poetry. Now that we have distinguished the different elements of the soul, it appears, I think, to be more obvious than ever that this refusal should be absolute."

"What do you mean?"

"Between ourselves—and don't denounce me to the tragic poets and all the other imitators—all such things seem to pollute the understanding of those who hear them, unless they possess a knowledge of their real nature; that is an antidote."

"What makes you say this?" he said.

"It must be uttered," I answered, "though a certain love and reverence for Homer which I have had from my childhood would forbid my speaking. For surely of all those noble tragic poets he is the master and the leader. Still I must not honour a man more than I honour truth, but must utter what I have to say."

"Yes, certainly," he said.

"Then listen, or rather answer."

"Ask your question."

"Could you tell me the general nature of imitation? For I don't myself quite understand what it sets out to be."

"Then it is likely, is it not, that I shall understand?" he said.

"There would be nothing out of the way if you did,"
I answered. "Dull eyes have often beaten sharp ones." **596**

"So they have," he said. "But if I had any opinion, I
should not be at all eager to express it in your presence.
So do you consider yourself."

"Shall we begin the inquiry according to our ordinary
method? We have been in the habit, if you remember,
of positing a Form, wherever we use the same name
in many instances, one Form for each 'many.' Do you
understand?"

"I do."

"And shall we take whatever 'many' you please. For
example, if this will do, there are many beds and
tables."

"Surely."

"But for these articles there are two Forms, one of a
bed and one of a table?"

"Yes."

"And have we not also been in the habit of saying,
that it is by looking at the Form that the manufacturer
of each article makes the beds or the tables which we
use, and so with other things? For no manufacturer
manufactures the actual Form, does he?"

"Certainly not."

"Now consider this manufacturer. What would you
call him?"

"Whom?"

"He who by himself makes all things which are made
by all the different craftsmen."

"A marvellous clever fellow!"

"Wait a little, and you will soon say that with more
reason. For this same craftsman is not only able to make
all manufactured articles, but he makes all things that
grow from the earth and fashions all living creatures,
himself with the rest of them, and, not content with

that, fashions earth and heaven, and gods and all things in heaven, or in Hades under the earth."

"What a perfectly marvellous genius!" he said.

"Do you not believe me?" I asked. "Tell me. Do you think there is no such manufacturer at all, or do you think that a man might be in a certain manner a maker of all these things and in another manner not? Don't you see that you yourself could make all these things in a certain manner?"

"And what is that manner?" he said.

"It is not hard," I answered, "but a frequent and easy mode of manufacture. It is most easily done perhaps if you take a mirror and turn it round to all sides. You will soon make a sun and stars, the earth, yourself, and other living creatures, manufactured articles and plants, and everything we have just described."

"Yes," he said, "make them in appearance, but surely not as they are in truth."

"Your remark is excellent," I answered, "and just what the argument wants. For the painter also, I imagine, is one of these manufacturers. Is he not?"

"Surely."

"But you will say, I fancy, that what he makes, he does not make truly. Though the painter also makes a bed in a manner, does he not?"

"Yes," he said, "he, like the other, makes a bed in appearance."

597 "What of the carpenter? But did you not say that he makes, not the Form which we asserted to be that which a bed is, but a particular bed?"

"Yes, I said so."

"Now, if he does not make what is, he will not make the real, but something which is of the same nature with but is not the real. And if any one were to say that the work of the carpenter or of any other craftsman was perfectly real, he would probably not be speaking the truth, would he?"

"No," he said, "at least not in the opinion of persons acquainted with this kind of reasoning."

"Then let us not be surprised if the manufactured article is also somewhat indistinct as compared with truth."

"No."

"Shall we then," I said, "take these as examples in our search after the nature of the imitator?"

"If you please," he said.

"Now there are these three beds, first the bed which exists in nature, which we should say, I fancy, was made by God. Should we not?"

"By God, I fancy."

"And one made by the carpenter?"

"Yes," he said.

"And one made by the painter?"

"Yes, let us suppose so."

"Painter, carpenter, and God, these three are set over the three classes of beds."

"Yes, these three."

"And God, whether because he so willed or because there was some necessity upon him not to make more than one bed in nature, made that one which is the reality of a bed and only that. But two or more such beds were never produced by God, and never will be."

"How is that?" he said.

"Because," I answered, "if God should make even no more than two, then yet another would be revealed whose Form the first two would express, and this, and not the two, would be the reality of a bed."

"You are right," he said.

"And God, I imagine, knew this, and wished to be really maker of a bed that really was and not only a particular manufacturer of a particular bed, and therefore produced this one natural bed."

"Probably."

"Then shall we call him the 'nature maker' of this thing, or something of that kind?"

"Yes, that is only just," he said, "when his making of this and all other things is nature's making of them."

"What of the carpenter? Do you call him a manufacturer of a bed?"

"Yes."

"And you call the painter also a manufacturer and maker of the same kind of thing?"

"Certainly not."

"Then what is he of a bed?"

"I think," he answered, "that he would be most fairly described as an imitator of what the other two manufacture."

"Good," I said. "You call him an imitator who is concerned with that which is begotten three removes from nature?"

"Certainly," he said.

"And the tragedian, since he is an imitator, will be then one whose nature is third from the king and from the truth, and all the other imitators will be like him?"

"That seems probable."

598    "Then we are agreed as to the imitator. But tell me this about the painter. Do you think that he tries to imitate each reality in nature, or the works of the manufacturers?"

"The works of the manufacturers," he said.

"To imitate them as they are, or as they appear? You must make this further distinction."

"What do you mean?" he said.

"This. Does a bed really differ from itself when you look at it from the side or from straight in front or from any other point of view, or does it remain the same but appear different? And so with other things."

"The second alternative is right," he said. "It appears, but is not different."

"Now consider this point. Which of these two governs the drawing of any subject? Is drawing an attempt to imitate the real as it is, or the appearance as it appears? Is it an imitation of an appearance or of a truth?"

"Of an appearance," he said.

"Imitation, then, is far from the truth, and apparently it manages to make all things just because it attacks only a small part of each, and that an image. The painter, for example, will paint us, we say, a shoemaker, a carpenter, and all other workmen, though he has no knowledge whatever of their crafts. But nevertheless, if he is a good painter, he may paint a carpenter and show the thing at some distance, and so cheat children and stupid men into thinking it is really a carpenter."

"Surely."

"Well, my friend, I imagine that we must come to this conclusion about all these matters. When any one announces to us that he has met a man who knows all handicrafts, and who of all the things known by each separate individual has a more exact knowledge than any of them, to such a person we must reply that he is more or less of a fool, and has apparently met with a wizard and imitator, and been cheated into thinking the man possessed of universal wisdom, all because he could not distinguish knowledge and lack of knowledge and imitation."

"Very true," he said.

"And after this," I said, "we must examine tragedy, and Homer its leader, since people tell us that tragedians know all arts and all things human that relate to virtue and vice and things divine. For a good poet, they say, if he is to make a beautiful poem on his subject, must do so with knowledge of that subject, or fail altogether. We must then inquire whether these persons have met with the imitators and been cheated, and, on seeing their productions, have failed to perceive that they are three removes from being, and can easily be made without knowledge of the truth— for their productions are appearances and not realities—or whether there is something in what they say, and good poets really have knowledge of those subjects of which their descriptions are approved by common opinion."

"Yes," he said, "this must certainly be investigated."

"Now, do you suppose that if any man could make both the object of imitation and the image, that he would trouble to set himself down to the manufacture of images, and would put this power in the forefront of his life as his best possession?"

"Not I."

"But, I imagine, if he had true knowledge of those things which he also imitates, he would be much more zealous in the doing than in the imitation of them, and would try to leave many beautiful deeds as memorials behind him. He would much rather be the hero whose praises are sung than the poet who sings them."

"I think so," he answered. "The honour and benefit are far greater."

"Well, on other questions we may give up the idea of calling Homer or any other poet to account, by asking whether any of them had medical knowledge, and was not merely an imitator of medical discourses; where are the people whom any poet, ancient or modern, is said to have restored to health, as Asclepius did; what students of medicine have they left behind them to match the descendants of Asclepius. And so with the other arts we may refrain from such questions, and let be. But when Homer tries to tell of the mightiest and most noble things, of wars and generalship and government of cities and the education of man, then it is only

fair we should question him, and inquire: "My dear
Homer, if, as you say, you are not thrice removed from
truth concerning virtue, a manufacturer of an image,
and what we have called an imitator; if you are but
twice removed, and can know what practices make men
better individuals and better citizens, can you not mention a city to which you gave a better government, such
as Lycurgus gave to Lacedaemon, and many other persons to many cities great and small? Does any city name
you a good lawgiver and its benefactor? So Italy and
Sicily named Charondas, and we Solon. Who so names
you?' Will he be able to mention one?"

"I think not," said Glaucon. "Why, even the devotees
of Homer don't say that."

"But is there an account of any war in that time
which was well waged under the command or advice of
Homer?"

"No."

"Well, is there mention of many inventions, contrivances of use in handicrafts or in any other branch of
action, which would show that he was a clever practical man, like Thales of Miletus, or Anarcharsis the
Scythian?"

"No, nothing of the kind."

"Well, if there is no mention of public services, do we
hear that Homer in his lifetime was guide and edu-
cator to certain individuals, who loved him for the
inspiration of his society, and who handed down to
those who came after them a Homeric way of life? Such
was Pythagoras. For that master was greatly loved for
such reasons, and his successors even up to the present
day talk of the Pythagorean manner of life, and seem
somehow to be quite distinct from other people."

"No," he said, "we do not hear of anything of that
kind. For if the stories about Homer are true, Socrates,
his companion Creophylus would as an example of edu-

cation be even funnier than his funny name. For they say that Homer was very much neglected in his lifetime, not to speak of what happened afterwards."

"Yes, so they say," I answered. "But consider, Glaucon, if Homer had really been able to educate men and make them better, if he had attained not merely to imitation but to knowledge of these subjects, would he not have made many disciples and been honoured and loved by them? Why, Protagoras of Abdera and Prodicus of Ceos and many others can by their private intercourse inspire their followers with the belief that they will be unable to rule either their households or their city unless these masters superintend their education, and for this wisdom of theirs they are so devotedly loved, that their disciples almost insist on carrying them about shoulder high. Now if Homer had been able to help men to be virtuous, would the men of the time have allowed him and Hesiod to wander about singing their songs; would they not have laid hold of them as more precious than gold, and compelled them to dwell at home with them; or if they had not succeeded in that, would they not have taken the direction of their education into their own hands and followed them wherever they went until they had got adequate instruction?"

"I think, Socrates," he said, "that what you say is most certainly true."

"Then may we lay down that, beginning with Homer, all the poets are imitators of images of virtue and of all the other subjects on which they write, and do not lay hold of truth; rather, as we said a moment ago, the painter will produce what seems to be a shoemaker, 601 though he himself has no understanding of shoemaking, and his spectators have none, but judge only by colour and form?"

"Certainly."

"And so, I imagine, we shall say that the poet also by means of words and sentences reproduces the colours, as it were, of the several arts, having only enough understanding to imitate; and he too has his spectators who judge by words and think if any one in metre and rhythm and musical mode describes shoemaking or generalship or any other subject, that what is said is good. Such is the great magical power which these things possess. For when the works of the poets are stripped of the colours that music gives them, and are spoken simply and by themselves, I fancy that you know what they look like. I dare say you have noticed?"

"I have," he said.

"Might we not compare them," I said, "to faces with the freshness of youth but without real beauty when they suffer change and have lost their early bloom?"

"Certainly," he replied.

"Come, then, consider this. The maker of the image, the imitator, we say, has no understanding of what is, but only of what appears; is it not so?"

"Yes."

"But let us not leave the question half stated, but consider it adequately."

"Speak on," he said.

"Will a painter, say, paint reins and bridle?"

"Yes."

"But a saddler and a smith will make them?"

"Certainly."

"Does the painter know what the reins and the bridle ought to be like? Or is it the case that not even the smith and the saddler, who made them, know that, but only the horseman, the man who knows how to use them?"

"Very true."

"And shall we not say the same about everything?"

"What?"

"That there are three arts concerned with each thing —one that uses, one that makes, and one that imitates?"

"Yes."

"Then are the virtue and beauty and correctness of every manufactured article and living creature and action determined by any other consideration than the use for which each is designed by art or nature?"

"No."

"Then it is quite inevitable that the user of each thing should have most experience of it, and should be the person to inform the maker what are the good and bad points of the instrument as he uses it. For example, the flute-player informs the flute-maker about the flutes which are to serve him in his fluting; he will prescribe how they ought to be made, and the maker will serve him."

"Surely."

"Then he who knows gives information about good and bad flutes, and the other will make them, relying on his statements?"

"Yes."

"Then the maker of any article will have a right belief concerning its beauty or badness, which he derives from his association with the knower, and from listening, as he is compelled to do, to what the knower says; but the user has knowledge?"

"Certainly."

"Now will the imitator have knowledge derived from use as to whether or not the subjects which he paints are beautiful and right, or will he have right belief derived from compulsory intercourse with the man who knows and from being told how he ought to depict them?"

"Neither."

"Then the imitator will neither know nor have right

belief concerning the beauty or the defects of the subjects of his imitation?"

"Apparently not."

"Then the poetic imitator will be charming in his wisdom on the subjects of his poetry?"

"Not so very charming."

"For all that he will imitate without knowing wherein each thing is bad or good; but he will probably imitate what appears to be beautiful to ordinary and ignorant people?"

"Certainly."

"Then apparently we have come to a thorough agreement on this, that the imitative man has no knowledge of any value on the subjects of his imitation; that imitation is a form of amusement and not a serious occupation; and that those who write tragic poetry in iambics and hexameters are all imitators in the highest degree?"

"Certainly."

"By Zeus," I said, "is not this imitation concerned with something that is third from the truth?"

"Yes."

"And what is it in man on which it exercises such effect as it has?"

"What kind of thing do you mean?"

"Something of this sort. You know that the same magnitude seen from a distance and from near at hand does not appear to us to be the same?"

"No."

"And the same thing appears bent when seen in water and straight when taken out of it, or both concave and convex, owing to a perversion of the vision by colours, and there is quite evidently a general confusion on this matter in our soul. It is this affection of our nature on which drawing in perspective relies to try all its magic arts upon us; and so it is in jugglery, and many other similar contrivances."

"True."

"And have not measurement and counting and weighing been shown to render most charming assistance in these difficulties? For the rule in our minds of the apparently larger or smaller or more or heavier, they substitute the rule of that which has counted or measured, or, if you like, weighed?"

"Surely."

"And this will be the work of the reasoning element in the soul?"

"It will."

"But when this element has made its measurements several times, and announces of any two things that one is greater or less than the other, or that they are equal, you have opposite conclusions about the same things appearing simultaneously."

"Yes."

"Now did we not say that it was impossible for the same element to come simultaneously to opposite conclusions about the same things?"

"We did, and rightly."

603  "Then that in the soul whose judgments disagree with the measurements, will not be the same as that whose judgments are in accordance with them?"

"No."

"But that which relies on calculation and measurement will be the best element in the soul?"

"Of course."

"Then that which opposes it will be one of the beggarly elements in us?"

"Inevitably."

"This was the point which I wanted to settle when I said that drawing and in fact all imitation produces its own work quite removed from truth, and also associates with that element in us which is removed from insight, and is its companion, and is friend to no healthy or true purpose."

"Certainly," he answered.

"Then imitation is a beggar wedded to a beggar and producing beggarly children?"

"Apparently."

"Does this apply only to visual imitation," I asked, "or also to imitation by sound, which we call poetry?"

"Naturally to that also," he said.

"Well," I said, "let us not rely on the natural analogy in painting but turn to that actual element of the understanding with which poetic imitation associates and see whether it is bad or good."

"Yes, we must."

"Let us put it in this way. Imitation, we say, imitates men acting compulsorily or voluntarily, thinking that in the event they have done well or ill, and throughout either feeling pain or rejoicing. Is there anything else besides that?"

"Nothing."

"Now in all this process, is a man in one and the same disposition of mind? Or just as in seeing he was in a state of dissension, and had in himself simultaneous and opposing beliefs about the same things, so likewise in conduct is he not also at dissension and war with himself? And I may remind you that there is no need for us now to come to an agreement on this; for in the previous discussion on all these points we came to an agreement that our soul is full of countless simultaneous oppositions of this kind."

"We were right," he said.

"We were," I answered. "But I think we must now discuss what we then omitted."

"What is that?" he said.

"We said at that time, if you remember," I answered,

"that a reasonable man, if he meets with a misfortune, like the loss of a son or anything else which he holds very dear, will bear it much more easily than other people."

"Certainly."

"Now let us consider this point. Will he feel no sorrow at all; or if that is an impossibility, will he show some sort of moderation in his grief?"

"The second alternative is nearer the truth," he said.

604  "Now tell me this about him. Do you fancy that he will fight and contend with his grief better when he is under the observation of his fellows, or when he is alone by himself in solitude?"

"Much better," he said, "when he is under observation."

"Yes. When he is alone I imagine he will utter many cries of which he would be ashamed if there were any one to hear him, and do many things which he would not allow any one to see him doing."

"That is so," he said.

"Now is not that which encourages him to resist reason and law, while that which draws him to his sufferings is the affliction itself?"

"True."

"And since there is in the man impulsion in contrary directions in regard to the same thing at the same time, we must say that the impulsions are two."

"Surely."

"And the one is ready to obey the law and follow its guidance?"

"Yes."

"Now the law says that it is best to take misfortunes as quietly as possible and not to grieve, because the good and evil in such matters are not certain, and to take them hardly makes things no better for the future; because no human affairs are worth taking very seriously;

and finally, because grief is a hinderance to that state of mind to which we should come in our troubles as quickly as possible."

"To what do you refer?" he asked.

"A man should take thought," I said, "on what has come to pass, and as we regulate our play by the fall of the dice, so he should regulate his affairs in the light of what has fallen out, as reason ordains will be best. We should not be like children who, when they have stumbled, go on holding the injured part and shrieking, but should always accustom the soul to turn as quickly as possible to the healing and restoring of that which is fallen and diseased, making lamentation to disappear before medicine."

"That certainly would be the most correct attitude to misfortune," he said.

"Now the best part in us, we say, wishes to follow this reasoning."

"Obviously."

"Then shall we not say that that element which impels us to recall our affliction and to lament, and which can never have enough of such things, is unreasoning and idle and a lover of cowardice?"

"Yes, we shall."

"Now the one, the complaining element, lends itself to much and diverse imitation, but the prudent and quiet character, which is always at one with itself, is not easily imitated, nor when imitated is it easily understood, especially in crowded audiences when men of every character flock to the theatre. For them it is the imitation of a disposition with which they are not familiar."

"Certainly."

"Then obviously it is not this character in the soul towards which the imitative poet is by nature set, or which his wisdom is bent on pleasing, since he is to win a great reputation with the common people, but rather the peevish and diverse character, because it is such a good object of imitation?"

"Obviously."

"Then we may now justly lay hold of the poet and set him over against the painter; for he resembles him in producing what has little value for truth, and also in associating with a similar part of the soul, which is not the best. And so we may now with justice refuse to allow him entrance to a city which is to be well governed, because he arouses and fosters and strengthens this part of the soul and destroys the reasoning part. Like one who gives a city over into the hands of villains, and destroys the better citizens, so we shall say that the imitative poet likewise implants an evil constitution in the soul of each individual; he gratifies the foolish element in it, that which cannot distinguish between great and small but thinks that the same things are sometimes great and sometimes small, and he manufactures images very far removed from the truth."

"Certainly."

"But we have not yet stated our mightiest accusation against imitation. For its power of corrupting even the good, all but a few, is surely most terrible of all."

"Surely, if it does actually do that."

"Listen and consider. Take the best of us listening to Homer or any other of the tragic poets, when he is imitating a hero in grief and spinning out a long melancholy lamentation or imitating men singing and disfiguring themselves in grief: you know that he gives us pleasure, and we give ourselves up to following him; we sympathize and are seriously impressed, and praise as a good poet whoever most affects us in this way."

"I know we do."

"But when an intimate sorrow comes to any of us,

you notice that we pride ourselves on the opposite kind
of behaviour, on being able to bear it with quiet and
endurance, as though this were playing a man's part,
and the other behaviour. which we then praised, were
playing a woman's."

"Yes," he said.

"Then is the praise rightly given?" I asked. "Is it
right to look at a man being what we ourselves should
not wish to be without shame, and so far from feeling
disgust, to enjoy and praise the performance?"

"No, by Zeus," he said, "it does not seem reasonable."

"That is right," I said, "if you look at it in that way." 606

"In what way?"

"If you consider that the element, which in our own
intimate misfortunes is held down by force and stinted
of its fill of weeping and lamentation, those things which
it is its nature to desire, is the very part which the poets
satisfy and please, while what by nature is best in us,
for want of being adequately trained either by reason
or by habit, relaxes its watch over the weeping element.
The sorrows which it beholds are not its own, and if
another man with pretensions to virtue grieves more
than he might, there is no disgrace for it in praising and
pitying him, but there is, it thinks, the actual profit of
the pleasure, and therefore it will not consent to lose
that pleasure by despising the whole poem. For it is
given to few, I fancy, to reflect that other men's sorrows
contribute to our own. For if we feed the element of pity
on others' misfortunes and make it strong, it is not easy
to control it in our own."

"Very true," he said.

"And does not the same argument apply to the humor-
ous? You may take an extraordinary pleasure in hearing
at a representation of comedy or in a circle of friends
jests which you would be ashamed to make yourself, and

will not hate them for their vileness; but are you not doing just what you did in tragic performances? It was by reason, again, that you held down that in you which wanted to jest, because you feared to be thought a buffoon, and now you let it free and pamper it at these performances, with the result that often you have quite unconsciously gone the length of being a comic poet in your own conduct?"

"Certainly," he said.

"And with regard to sexual desires, and anger, and all feelings of desire and pain and pleasure in the soul, which we say follow all our actions, you observe that poetic imitation produces all these effects in us. They should be withered, and it waters them and makes them grow. It makes them rule over us, when they ought to be subjects if we are to become better and happier, instead of worse and more miserable."

"I can't disagree with you," he said.

"Then, Glaucon," I said, "when you find Homer's admirers saying that this poet has educated Hellas, and that in questions of human conduct and culture a man ought to read and study Homer, and organize his whole life in accordance with the teaching of this poet, you must be friendly and kind to such people—they are as good as they know how to be—and agree that Homer is the most poetical and the first of the tragic poets, but be quite sure in your mind that only such specimens of poetry as are hymns to the gods or praises of good men are to be received into a city. If you receive the pleasure-seasoned Muse of song and epic, pleasure and pain will be kings in your city instead of law and the principle which at all times has been decided by the community to be best."

"Very true," he said.

"Let it, then," I said, "be our defence now that we have recurred to the subject of poetry, that it was only to be expected that we should expel poetry from the city, such being her nature. The argument compelled us. And let us tell her also, in case she should accuse us of brutality and boorishness, that there is an ancient quarrel between philosophy and poetry. Phrases like 'the bitch that at her master yelps,' 'the yelping hound that in assemblies of the fools exalts its head,' 'the conquering rabble of the overwise,' the statement that 'the men of subtle thought are beggars all,' and many others are signs of this ancient antagonism. Nevertheless, let us state that if the pleasure-producing poetry and imitation has any arguments to show that she is in her right place in a well-governed city, we shall be very glad to receive her back again. We are conscious of the charm she exercises upon us. Only to betray the truth as it appears to us is impious. Do not you, my friend, also feel her magic charm, especially when she speaks with Homer's lips?"

"Very much so."

"Then is it not just that she should return on those conditions, after she has published her defence in lyrical or any other metre?"

"Certainly."

"And we might also allow her champions, who are not poets, but lovers of poetry, to publish a prose defence on her behalf, showing that she is not only pleasant but also useful for political constitutions and for human life, and we shall listen with friendly feelings. For it will be to our profit if she is made out to be not only pleasant, but useful."

"Most certainly to our profit," he said.

"But if not, my dear comrade, then, as men who have loved but have come to the conclusion that their love is unprofitable, though it may cost a struggle, yet turn away; so likewise, though by reason of the love for such poetry that our nurture in beautiful constitutions has 608 bred in us we shall be glad of any manifestation of her goodness and truth, yet until she is able to defend herself, we will not listen to her without repeating to ourselves as a charm this argument of ours and this incantation, for fear of falling again into that childish love which is still shared by the many. We shall chant, therefore, that this poetry is not to be taken seriously, as though it were a solemn performance which had to do with truth, but that he who hears it is to keep watch on it, fearful for the city in his soul, and that we must lay down these laws concerning poetry which we have described."

"I entirely agree with you," he said.

"For much is at stake, my dear Glaucon," I said, "more than people think, in a man's becoming good or bad; and therefore he must not be seduced by honour or money or any office, or even by poetry, to dare to neglect justice and the rest of virtue."

"What we have said makes me agree with you," he said; "and I think every one else would do the same."

"And yet," I said, "we have not described the greatest prizes and rewards reserved for virtue."

"You must be speaking of some unexampled greatness," he said, "if there are others greater than those already enumerated."

"What could be great in a brief space of time?" I asked. "For surely the whole time from childhood to old age is compared to all time brief and short?"

"Yes," he said.

"Well, do you think that an immortal thing should take thought for a time no longer than the span of life and not for all time?"

"I agree with you," he said. "But why do you say this?"

"Have you not perceived," I asked, "that our soul is immortal, and never perishes?"

He looked at me, and said in amazement," By Zeus, not I. Can you say that?"

"Can!" I said. "I must. And I think you will go with me. It is not difficult."

"It is to me," he said. "But I should be very glad to hear this easy thing."

"Well, you may," I said.

"Then speak," he said.

"Do you talk of a good and an evil?" I asked.

"I do."

"Do you conceive them as I do?

"In what way?"

"That which destroys and corrupts everything is the evil; that which preserves and benefits, the good."

"Yes," he said.

"Further, do you talk of an evil and a good belonging to each thing? For example, there is ophthalmia for 602 eyes, disease for the whole body, mould for bread, rot for wood, rust for brass and iron; and, as I say, all things have each their natural evil and disease?"

"I agree," he said.

"When one of these evils comes upon anything, does it not cause defects in that on which it settles, and finally altogether dissolve and destroy it?"

"Surely."

"But each thing is destroyed by its own natural evil and badness, and if that does not destroy it there is nothing else that can harm it. For the good will certainly never destroy it, nor will that which is neither evil nor good."

"How could it?" he said.

"Then if we discover anything among existences which has its own evil which makes it worse, and find that this evil is unable to destroy and dissolve it, shall we not then know that of a thing so constituted there is no destruction?"

"Yes," he said, "that is probable."

"Now," I said, "has the soul that which makes it evil?"

"Of course," he said. "All the things we have described—injustice and licentiousness, and cowardice and ignorance."

"But does any one of these dissolve and destroy the soul? And see that we are not cheated into thinking that the unjust and foolish man when he is caught in his evil conduct is then destroyed by injustice, the proper badness of his soul. Consider the question in this way. Disease, which is the badness of the body, makes the body waste away and dissolve till it is no longer a body; and so all things which we mentioned a moment ago are brought to nothing by their own evil, which takes its seat within them, and so destroys them. Is it not so?"

"Yes."

"Come, now, and consider the soul in the same way. Does injustice and vice in general when it dwells in the soul destroy it by having its seat and abode there, and make it wither away until it brings it down to death and parts soul from body?"

"No, certainly not," he said.

"But it is unreasonable," I said, "that the badness of anything else should destroy it, when its own badness does not?"

"It is."

"Now consider, Glaucon," I said, "that we do not think that the body must be destroyed by the badness of articles of food, whatever that may be—age or rottenness of anything else. But if the badness of articles of food produces in the body an evil condition of body, then we say that the body has been destroyed by its own evil, which is disease resulting from the bad food. 610 But we shall never allow that body, which is one thing, is destroyed by the badness of food, which is another, unless the evil of the other produces the natural intimate evil of the first."

"What you say is perfectly right," he said.

"But according to the same argument," I said, "unless the badness of the body produces in the soul badness of the soul, we shall not allow that the soul is destroyed by the evil of another thing without the action of its own peculiar badness, so that one thing is destroyed by the evil of another."

"That is reasonable," he said.

"Then either let us prove that our argument is unsound, or, until that be done, let us say that the soul is never in the least destroyed by fever, or any disease, or by the edge of the sword, not if you cut the body into the smallest pieces, unless it is demonstrated that these sufferings of the body make the soul more unjust and more impious. Let us not allow any one to say that the soul, or anything else, can be destroyed by an alien evil occurring in something else while its own peculiar evil does not occur in it."

"But nobody will ever prove," he said, "that when men die, death makes their souls more unjust."

"And if any one," I said, "dares to face the argument, and to say that death makes a man worse and more unjust, simply so as not to be compelled to admit that our souls are immortal, then we may fairly claim, if what he says is true, that injustice is as mortal as disease to its possessor, and that because the power to kill is part of its nature, those who take it should die by it, the most unjust dying quicker, the less unjust more slowly; whereas, as it is, the unjust are killed by other people punishing them because of their injustice."

"By Zeus," he said, "injustice will not then appear so very terrible, if it is mortal to him that receives it: for that would be a respite from evil. But I fancy, rather, that we shall find just the opposite—that injustice kills other people to the best of its power, but makes its possessor even more alive than before, and not only alive, but always awake; so very far is it from being mortal, apparently."

"Well said," I answered. "For when the soul cannot be killed and destroyed by its own badness and its own evil, it will be a long time before the evil which is ordained for the destruction of something different will kill it or anything else than that ordained thing."

"A long time, naturally enough," he said.

"Then when there is no one evil, whether belonging to itself or another, which destroys the soul, it must obviously exist always, and if it exists always, be immortal."

"It must," he said.

"Well, we may suppose that that is the case," I said, "and if it is, you will notice that there will always be the same number of souls. For, of course, they could not become fewer by any being destroyed, nor, again, could they become more numerous. If anything immortal increased, that would involve, you know, the mortal becoming immortal, so that finally everything would be immortal."

"True."

"But," I said, "let us not believe this, which the argument will not allow, or that the soul in its truest nature is such as to be full of great diversity and inequality and difference from itself."

"What do you mean?" he said.

"Everlastingness," I answered, "cannot easily be a property of a thing which is compounded out of many, and that not with the fairest composition; and yet such the soul has appeared to us to be."

"No, it is not likely."

"Yet our recent argument and the other proofs com-

pel us to the conclusion that the soul is immortal. But
if we are to see it as it is in truth, we ought not to see it
as we do at present, polluted by the association of the
body and other evils; we ought to behold it properly
by the help of reason, as it is when it is purified, and
then we shall find it far more lovely, and shall discern more clearly justices and injustices and all that
we have described. But in the meantime we have declared the truth regarding it as it appears at present.
For we have looked upon the soul as men who saw the
sea god Glaucus. His original nature was no longer
easily visible. The old limbs were broken off or worn
away and all deformed by the force of the waves, while
he was overgrown with shell-fish and seaweed and
stones, so that to look at he might have been any kind
of beast instead of what he really was. So do we look
upon the soul reduced to this condition by countless
evils. But we must turn our eyes yonder, Glaucon."

"Whither?" he asked.

"To the soul's love of wisdom, and observe what she
apprehends, and after what company she strives, led
on by her kinship to the divine and immortal and that
which ever is; and what she would become if she followed this with her whole being, and by this impulsion
were rescued from the sea in which she lies now, and
could strike off the stones and shell-fish that cover her; 612
for now she feasts upon earth, and from those feastings
that men call happy there has grown upon her a cov-
ering of earth and stone, thick and rough. Then one
might see her true nature, whether it is manifold or
single, or how and in what manner she is constituted.
Meanwhile, I imagine, we have given a fair description
of the states and varieties which she manifests in human
life?"

"Certainly," he said.

"And now," I said, "have we not in our argument

cleared away all other objections? In especial we have not praised the rewards and reputation of justice as you said was done by Hesiod and Homer, but have found that justice itself is best for the soul itself—found, too, that the soul must act justly whether she have the ring of Gyges or not; yes, though she have with that ring the cap of darkness."

"What you say is very true," he said.

"Then, Glaucon," I said, "can there now be any harm in our going further and restoring to justice and the rest of virtue the rewards, in their proper number and kinds, which it renders to the soul at the hands of gods and men, both in a man's lifetime and after he is dead?"

"None whatever," he said.

"Then will you give me back what you borrowed from me in the discussion?"

"What do you mean in particular?"

"I allowed to you that the just man should appear unjust, and the unjust just. For you asked that even supposing those things could not be concealed from gods and men, we should yet grant, for the sake of argument, that they could, in order to judge between justice pure and simple and injustice pure and simple. Do you not remember?"

"It would be unjust of me did I not," he said.

"Well, now that judgment has been given," I said, "I demand back for justice that we too should agree to give her the reputation which she actually enjoys with gods and men, that she may get even those prizes of victory which she acquires from seeming and bestows on those who possess her. For we have found that she really gives the good things which come from being, and does not deceive those who really accept her."

"Your demand is just," he said.

"In that case," I said, "will you first of all allow that

the gods are not deceived as to the natures of the two men?"

"We will," he said.

"Then if they are not, the one man will be loved by the gods, the other hated, as we agreed originally?"

"Yes."

"And shall we not agree that to those whom the gods love, all things which come from the hands of the gods **618** are as good as they can be, except perhaps for some evil which has been necessitated by sin in a previous existence?"

"Certainly."

"Then must we not assume the same for the just man, that though he live in poverty, in disease, or any other seeming evil, these things will in the end work out well for him either in life or after death. For surely the gods do not neglect him who will bestir himself to become just, and by the practice of virtue to make himself as like God as man may."

"It is only natural," he said, "that God should not neglect him who is like himself."

"Then ought we not to suppose the opposite of the unjust?"

"Most certainly."

"Then at the hands of gods the just man will get some such prizes as these?"

"That is at any rate my opinion," he asked.

"And what at the hands of men?" I asked. "Does not the case stand thus if we must state the fact? Do not the clever unjust men act like those runners who run well from the top end of the course to the bottom, but not from the bottom to the top; at the start they leap off at a great pace, but at the finish are laughed off the course and go away, their ears sunk down to their shoulders, and no crown on their heads. But the true runners run to a finish, receive their prizes, and are crowned. Is it not usually the same with the just? At the end of every action and partnership, and at the end of life, they win a good report and carry off prizes at men's hands."

"Certainly."

"Then will you suffer me to say of them what you yourself said of the unjust? For I shall say that the just, when they advance in years, will hold office in their city if they desire office, will take a wife from what family they please and give in marriage to whom they will; and all the things you said of the unjust I now say of the just. And I shall say also of the unjust that most of them, though they may not be found out while they are young, are caught at the end of their course and are laughed to scorn. When they become old men they are miserably insulted by strangers and townsmen, they are scourged and suffer all those punishments—racking and burning—which you truly described as cruel. You may suppose me to enumerate them all. Will you suffer what I am saying?"

"Most certainly," he said, "for your words are just."

"Then such," I said, "will be the prizes and rewards and gifts which the just man has at the hands of gods and men during his life, besides those advantages given by justice itself."

"Yes," he said, "and they are fair and steadfast."

"But these," I said, "are nothing in number or greatness compared with those which await each man after death. And these must be heard in order that each man may receive in full the words that the argument owes him.'

"Speak on," he said. "There are few things I should be more glad to hear."

"I shall tell you," I said, "a story, not of Alcinous, but of a valiant man, Er, son of Armenius, of the race of Pamphylia. Once upon a time he fell in battle. On the tenth day they took up the dead, who were now stinking, but his body was found fresh. They took him home, and were going to bury him when on the twelfth day he came to life as he was lying on the pyre. When he had revived, he told them what he had seen yonder. His soul, he said, departed from him, and journeyed along with a great company, until they arrived at a certain ghostly place where there were two openings in the earth side by side, and opposite them and above two openings in the heaven. In the middle sat judges. These, when they had given their judgment, ordered the just to take the road to the right, which led upward through heaven, first binding tablets on them in front signifying their judgments. The unjust they ordered to take the road to the left, which led downward. They also had tablets signifying all that they had done bound on their backs. When it came to his turn they told him that it was laid upon him to be a messenger to men concerning the things that were there, and they ordered him to listen to and look at everything in the place. Then he saw there souls departing, after judgment had been delivered upon them, by one of the openings of heaven and one of earth; by the other two souls were arriving, on the one side coming up out of the earth, travel-stained and dusty, on the other coming down from heaven, shining pure. They all seemed on their arrival to have come a long journey, and were glad to turn aside into the meadow. There they encamped as in an assembly, and those who were acquaintances recognized one another. They who had come out of the earth inquired of the others concerning the things above, and those from heaven inquired of the first in their turn concerning the things that had happened to them. So they discoursed with one another, some weeping and lamenting as they called to mind all that they 615 had suffered and seen, both much and terrible, in their journey below the earth, a journey of a thousand years, while the others, who had come from heaven, recounted the extraordinary beauty of their happiness and their vision. There were many things, Glaucon, which would take long to relate. But this, he said, was the sum of it. For all the unjust deeds that each man has ever done, and for all the men to whom he has done injustice, he pays penalty in due course, ten times for each (now this is once in every hundred years, for so long is the span of human life), in order that he may pay a ten-fold ransom for his wrong-doing. If there be any who have caused the deaths of many men, either by betray-ing cities or armies, or by casting men into slavery, or taking part in any other villainy, for all these crimes they suffer torments tenfold for each; and on the other hand, if they have done any deeds of kindness and have been just and holy, they get their reward on the same terms. Concerning infants who died as soon as they were born, or had lived but a short time, there were other things he said not worth remembering. For im-piety or piety to gods and to parents and for murder there were still greater requitals, which he described.

"For he said that he stood by while one man asked another where Ardiaeus the Great was. Now this Ardiaeus had been tyrant in a city of Pamphylia a thousand years before that time; he had killed his old father and his elder brother, and had wrought many other impious deeds, so it was related. And he said that he who was questioned replied: 'He has not come, nor will he come hither. For this was one of the terrible sights we saw. When we were near the mouth and were about to go up, and had endured all our sufferings but this, suddenly we saw Ardiaeus and others with him. Most of them were tyrants, but there were also some private persons of the number of those who were great sinners. They thought that they were at last going to ascend, but the mouth would not receive them, and whenever any of those who had sunk into incurable wickedness, or any one who had not paid his punishment in full, tried to ascend, the mouth bellowed. And then,' he said, 'fierce men, like coals of fire to look upon, who were standing by and had heard the sound, came forward, and some they took in their arms and dragged away, but Ardiaeus and others they bound hand and foot and head, threw them down, and flayed them. They dragged them out of the way to a place apart, and there carded them on thorns, saying to all that passed that they were being taken away to be plunged into Tartarus, and explaining why this was done to them. After that,' he said, 'though many and diverse fears had come upon us, this was above them all. Each man feared that the voice would sound for him as he ascended, and it was with great joy that each went up without the mouth breaking silence.' Now, of this kind, he said, were the punishments and penalties, and the rewards corresponded to them. Each company passed seven days in the meadow, and on the eighth they had to rise up and go on their way, and after four days they came to a place whence they could look down on a straight beam of light, extended like a pillar through heaven and earth, more like the rainbow than anything else, but brighter and purer. To this they came after a day's journey, and there from the middle of the light they saw extended from heaven the ends of the chains which compose it. For this light chains heaven, holding together the whole circumference as under-girders bind a trireme. And from those ends is hung the spindle of Necessity, by means of which all the circles revolve. Now the shaft and hook thereof are of adamant, but the whorl is partly of adamant, partly of other materials. And the whorl is of this fashion. In shape it is like an ordinary whorl, but from his description you must con-

616

ceive of it as one great whorl with the inside completely cut out, and another similar but smaller whorl fitted into it, and within that a third, and within that a fourth, and then four others, fitted into one another like puzzle boxes. For there are eight whorls in all, fitted into one another, their upper rims showing in circles, so that they make up the continuous surface of one whorl round the shaft, and the shaft pierces right through the middle of the eighth. The circle made by the rim of the first and outside whorl is the broadest, that of the sixth the second broadest, that of the fourth third, of the eighth fourth, of the seventh fifth, of the fifth sixth, of the third seventh, and that of the second eighth broadest. The circle of the greatest is of many colours, the circle of the seventh is the brightest, the eighth gets its colour from the seventh shining upon it, the second and the fifth are very like each other, being ruddier than the others; the third is the whitest, the fourth is fiery red, and the sixth is second in whiteness. The whole spindle turns round with one circling motion, but as the whole revolves the seven inside circles spin round smoothly in an opposite direction to the whole. Of these the eighth turns fastest, and after it come the seventh, sixth, and fifth, all three at the same pace. Third in swiftness, so it seemed to them, circles the fourth, the third fourth, and the second fifth. The whole spindle is turned on the knees of Necessity. On the top of each circle sits a siren, who is carried round with the circle, uttering one note at one pitch, and the eight together make up a single harmony. Round about at equal distances others are seated, three in number, each on a throne. These are the Fates, daughters of Necessity, Lachesis and Clotho and Atropos. They are clothed in white and have garlands on their heads, and they sing to the accompaniment of the sirens' harmony, Lachesis of what has been, Clotho of what is, and

Atropos of what shall be. And Clotho from time to time lays her right hand on the outer circumference and helps to push it round, while Atropos does the same to the inner circles with her left hand; but Lachesis touches inner and outer with each hand in turn. Now the souls, when they came thither, had to go at once to Lachesis. Then a prophet first marshalled them in order, and then taking lots and patterns of lives from the lap of Lachesis, mounted upon a high pulpit and spoke: 'The word of the daughter of Necessity, maid Lachesis. Souls of a day, here beginneth another circle that bears the mortal race to death. The angel will not cast lots for you, but you shall choose your angel. Let him whose lot falls first have first choice of a life to which he shall be bound by Necessity. But virtue has no master, and as a man honours or despises her, so will he have more of her or less. The responsibility is on him that chooseth. There is none on God.'

"So saying, the prophet cast the lots to all, and each man took up the lot that fell beside him, except Er. Him the prophet forbade. And as each took it up he knew what order in the lot he had obtained. And after this the prophet laid on the ground before them the patterns of lives, many more patterns than there were persons present. Now there were patterns of all kinds. There were lives of all living creatures, and with them all human lives. Among them were tyrannies, some lasting, others destroyed in mid course and ending in poverty and exile and beggary. There were lives of famous men also, some famed for their comeliness and beauty, or for their strength and prowess, others for their lineage and the virtues of their ancestors; similarly there were lives of unknown men; and also the lives of women. But there was no determination of soul, because of necessity the soul becomes different according as she chooses a different life. All other things were mixed with each other, and with wealth and poverty; some with disease and some with health, and there were also mean conditions of these things. And it is here, it seems, my dear Glaucon, that man's greatest danger lies; and for those reasons we must give all heed that each of us, putting aside all other learning, may search after and study this alone, if in any way he may be able to learn and discover who will give him capacity and knowledge to discern the good and the evil in life, and always and everywhere to choose the better according to his ability. He will reckon up all the things we have just mentioned, taking them both together and separately, and estimate their contribution to virtue of life; and so he will know what of good or evil is worked by beauty, whether mixed with poverty or riches, and with what disposition of soul these are good and with what bad; and what of good or evil is worked by noble birth or ignoble birth, by private or public station, by strength or weakness of body, by learning or ignorance, and by all such properties as concern the soul, both natural and acquired, in their combinations with one another, so that he may be able to put all these considerations together, and looking to the nature of the soul may choose the worse or the better life, calling that worse which will lead the soul into greater injustice, and that better which will lead it into greater justice. But all other considerations he will leave alone. For we have seen that this is the greatest choice both for life and beyond it. And a man when he goes to the other world must have this belief 619 like adamant within him, in order that there also he may be unmoved by riches and evils of that sort, and may not by falling into tyranny or some such course of action, both commit and himself suffer in greater degree evils many and incurable, but may have knowledge to choose always the life that lies in the middle and avoid the extremes on both sides, both in this life, so

far as he may, and in the life to come. For so man wins
his greatest happiness.

"Now the messenger from yonder went on with his
tale, and told how the prophet spoke thus: 'Even for
him that comes last, if he choose with understanding,
and take heed in his life, there is laid up a life that is
not evil, with which he may be content. Let not him
who hath first choice be careless, or him who hath last
downhearted.'"

"He said that when the prophet had thus spoken, he
who had drawn first came forward and chose the mightiest of tyrannies, and from folly and greed he chose
without making a thorough examination, and so did
not notice that in his choice it was fated that he should
devour his own children and suffer other evil things.
So when he came to examine it at his leisure he began
to gash his breast and bewail his choice, not abiding by
the warnings of the prophet. For he did not blame himself for his evils, but chance and the angels and everything rather than himself. Now he was of those who
had come from heaven, and had lived in his former life
in a well-ordered city and had participated in virtue by
habit and not by philosophy. Generally speaking, not
the least part of those who were caught in this way had
come from heaven, for they had not been disciplined by
labours; while of those from earth, the most, because
they had themselves endured labours, and had seen the
labours of others, were in no hurry to make their choice.
For these reasons, and because of the fortune of the lot,
most souls had a change of evil and good. For if any
man always steadfastly pursues philosophy whenever he
comes to life in this world, and if the lot of choice falls
to him not among the last, it appears, from what we
are told from yonder, not only that he will be happy in
this life, but that his journey from here to the world
beyond and back again to this world will not be along

the rough and underground track, but along the smooth and heavenly way.

"And he said that it was a sight worth seeing to behold the several souls choose their lives. And a piteous and a laughable and amazing sight it was also. The choice was mostly governed by what they had been accustomed to in their former life. He said that he saw the soul which had once been Orpheus' choosing the life of a swan; his death at the hands of women had so made him hate the whole race, that he would not consent to be born of woman. The soul of Thamyras he saw choosing the life of a nightingale. He also saw a swan turning to choose a human life, and other musical creatures doing the same. The soul that had the twentieth choice took a lion's life. It was the soul of Ajax, the son of Telamon, who refused to become a man because he remembered the judgment concerning the armour. After him came the soul of Agamemnon. He also hated the human race by reason of his sufferings, and took in exchange the life of an eagle. The soul of Atalanta obtained her choice somewhere in the middle, and catching sight of the great honours of a man who was an athlete could not pass them by, but made that her choice. After her he saw the soul of Epeus, son of Panopeus, passing into the nature of a working woman. Quite among the last he saw the soul of the ridiculous Thersites becoming a monkey. It so happened that the soul of Odysseus came forward to choose the very last of all. He remembered his former labours and had ceased from his ambition and so he spent a long time going round looking for the life of a private and obscure man. At last he found it lying about, ignored by every one else; and when he saw it he took it gladly, and said that he would have made the same choice if the lot had fallen to him first. Similarly all the other animals changed into men and into each other, the unjust into fierce, and the just into tame animals, and there were all possible combinations.

"And when all the souls had chosen their lives they went unto Lachesis in the order of their choosing. And she gave each the angel he had chosen to be a guard throughout his life and to accomplish his choice. The angel first led the soul towards Clotho, passing it under her hand and under the sweep of the whirling spindle, so ratifying the fate which the man had chosen in his turn. He touched the spindle, and then led the soul on to where Atropos was spinning, so that the threads might be made unalterable. Thence the man went with- out turning under the throne of Necessity, and after coming out on the other side he first waited for the others to pass through, and then all proceeded through terrible burning heat to the plain of Lethe where grew no plants nor any trees. At last they encamped at eve- ning by the river of Forgetfulness, whose water no pitcher may hold. All had to drink a certain measure of this water, but those who were not preserved by wisdom drank more than the measure. Each as he drank it for- got everything. Then they went to sleep, and it was mid- night; there was thunder and an earthquake, and at once they were carried up from thence along different ways to their birth, shooting like stars. But he himself had been forbidden to drink of the water. When or how he returned to the body he did not know, but he suddenly opened his eyes and saw it was morning and he was lying on the pyre.

"And so, Glaucon, the tale was preserved and did not perish, and it will preserve us if we take heed to it, and cross the river of Lethe safely, and keep our souls un- defiled. But if you will listen to me, and believe that the soul is immortal and able to endure all evil and all good, we shall always hold to the upper road, and in every way follow justice and wisdom. So we shall be friends to ourselves and to the gods, both while we remain here and when, like victorious athletes who go about adding to their prizes, we receive the rewards of our justice; and here, and in the journey of a thousand years which I have described to you, we shall fare well."

## DUTTON PAPERBACKS

# DUTTON PAPERBACKS